THREADS *of* TRANSCENDENCE

Decoding Shiva Sutras and Mastering the Science of Being Free

Adi Suyash

AMARYLLIS

AMARYLLIS
An imprint of Manjul Publishing House Pvt. Ltd.
• C-16, Sector 3, Noida, Uttar Pradesh 201 301, India
Website: www.manjulindia.com
Registered Office:
• 10, Nishat Colony, Bhopal 462 003 – India
Distribution Centres
Ahmedabad, Bengaluru, Bhopal, Chennai, Hyderabad,
Kolkata, Mumbai, Noida, Pune

Threads of Transcendence by *Adi Suyash*

This paperback edition first published in India in 2024

ISBN 978-93-5543-689-4

Printed and bound in India by Repro India Limited

श्रीशिवार्पणमस्तु ॥

Let this be an offering to Lord Śiva

In the waltz of cosmic design, this body emerged,
Born of Mīnu, a fish in the boundless sea of consciousness,
And Manoja, whose existence—His mind's projection.
Their union birthed this earthly form, a vessel for possession.
May it now become the sacred abode, for the divine
lovers to possess
Let my essence, ecstatic, free and pure, shine forth its radiance.

To my beloved parents, whose boundless love and sacrifices I can never repay, I find myself humbly kneeling at your feet, offering my deepest gratitude and reverence.

Sanskrit Pronunciation Guide:

Vowels should be pronounced as in Italian; a lengthening sign, such as ā, indicates a long vowel, similar to the *a* in *art*; *e* is pronounced as the *a* in *day*; *ṛ* in Sanskrit is considered a vowel and should be pronounced similarly to *ri*, as in *rip*; *c* should be pronounced as *ch*, as in *chair*, or like *c* in the Italian *cicerone* ; *j* as in *joy*; *ś* and *ṣ* are similar to *sh* in *ash*; *h* after a consonant should be pronounced distinctly, like the *t-h* in *sweet-heart*; *jñ* is pronounced as *gnya.*

Contents

Introduction	9
Chapter 1	27
Chapter 2	49
Chapter 3	73
Chapter 4	107
Chapter 5	120
Chapter 6	145
Chapter 7	168
Chapter 8	185
Chapter 9	193
Chapter 10	204
Chapter 11	220
Chapter 12	242
Chapter 13	259
Chapter 14	273
Chapter 15	287
Chapter 16	307
The Twenty Two Sūtras	317

Introduction

दुःखान्यपि सुखायन्ते विषमप्यमृतायते । मोक्षायते च संसारो
यत्र मार्गः स शाङ्करः ॥

duḥkhāny api sukhāyante viṣam apy amṛtāyate | mokṣāyate ca saṁsāro yatra mārgaḥ sa śāṅkaraḥ ||

Where even suffering is transformed into joy, where even poison becomes nectar, where the world itself is a way of liberation: there is the way of Śiva

— Utpaladeva

Approximately eleven centuries ago, in the verdant embrace of Kashmir's valley, cradled in the bosom of the Himalayas—the sanctuary of sages and mystics, of siddhas and yoginīs, where esoteric scriptures whispered their secrets and revelations—numerous mountains stood sentinel. Among them dwelled Vasugupta, a spiritual luminary whose devotion to Śiva was like the river's love for the ocean or the compass needle's adoration for the North. This devotion sculpted him into the revered master he was soon to become.

In Kashmir's spiritual landscape, Buddhism, corrupted by the passage of time, then exerted its influence. Yet, Vasugupta, driven by an insatiable yearning for a truth beyond, remained unsatisfied. His heart sought a higher understanding, and he traversed the valleys of devotion in relentless pursuit. Amidst the prevailing beliefs, he felt an uncharted depth calling him.

One fateful night, within the realm of dreams, the divine answered his fervent plea. Śiva, the harbinger of the highest truth, spoke to Vasugupta, "Yonder, upon the sacred mountain, beneath a mighty stone, lies the esoteric doctrine—the pinnacle of truth. Seek it out, drink deep from its wellspring, and share its wisdom with those deserving of grace."

As dawn painted the sky with hues of awakening, Vasugupta embarked on a fervent search for the prophesied stone. With every step, guided by an unseen force, Vasugupta's anticipation heightened, and as he finally beheld a rock resembling the one described by Śiva, his heart quickened. Upon touching it, the stone responded to his devotion, turning around to reveal a sacred scripture engraved on its underside. This very scripture is now held in your hands.

As Vasugupta committed the divine Sūtras to memory, the stone turned once more, returning to its silent vigil on the mountain. There it remains to this day.

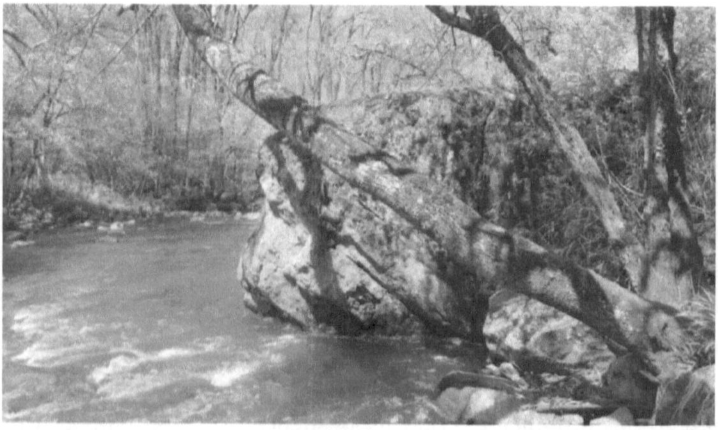

Śaṁkarpāl—the stone on the underside on which *Śiva Sūtras* were engraved.

For centuries, the invaluable knowledge of this elixir-like wisdom was passed down and safeguarded by Kashmiri Pandits, who held it dearer than life itself. By the fourteenth century, Islam had risen as the dominant religion in Kashmir, resulting in a devastating wave of temple destruction, the rape of Kashmiri women, and their ruthless sale as slaves, and the merciless slaughter of Kashmiri

Pandits. In 1389, Sultan Sikandar ascended to power, instituting oppressive measures against non-Muslims, including heavy taxation, forced conversions, and ruthless religious persecution. His reign earned him the title *But-Shikan*—the destroyer of idols, as he razed countless temples to the ground.

The *Rājtarangini*, a historical account of Kashmir, mentions that there was no place in Kashmir, even as small as a sesame seed, where there wasn't a sacred pilgrimage site. Numerous temples once stood there, now reduced to ruins.

Throughout millennia, Kashmiri Pandits endured forced exoduses from their homeland. They abandoned their land, houses, and all possessions to avoid being robbed of their religion and culture. The sole possessions they clung to were these scriptures, meticulously copied and recopied by hand for generation after generation.

Attempting to encapsulate the atrocities inflicted upon them in a single page would be an injustice; such matters warrant detailed discussion elsewhere. I share this to give you some context, to help you understand the preciousness of these Sūtras, and the fact that we can read them today—its mere existence in any language, with or without commentary—is nothing short of a miracle in itself.

What are Sūtras? The term Sūtra literally translates to a thread or string. Similar to a piece of fabric, the type of fabric—whether silk, cotton, linen, or georgette—can be identified by studying just one thread. Understanding that single thread reveals the essence of the entire fabric, woven and formed by it. Similarly, a Sūtra embodies the essence of an entire philosophy or perspective. In Eastern Philosophy, every perspective is initially expressed in the form of Sūtras. Whether it's Vedānta in the form of *Brahma Sūtras*, or yoga through *Yoga Sūtras*, and likewise, *Nārada Bhakti Sūtras*, *Maheśvara Sūtras*, and so on. I must emphasise that these Sūtras were only expressions of the truth that always existed. They are simply a means to transmit; neither did Patañjali create the principles of yoga, nor did Vedavyāsa originate Vedānta. These principles have always existed, much like gravity, which was not discovered by Newton but was mathematically expressed by him.

The seer who realised the truth in their heart usually remained silent, for the truth cannot be expressed in words. Lao Tzu writes, 'Those who know the truth don't talk. Those who talk don't know.' This sentiment is echoed in the Upaniṣads and Tantra as well. Words, especially English words, are inadequate to convey the truth because they are created by humans of a certain culture and religious belief to refer to worldly things or their cultural ideas of otherworldly things. Anything beyond the worldly realm and their culture cannot be accurately referred to by these words. Any attempt to do so would result in misinterpretation.

For example, the word God; this term was created by the English to refer to the Biblical deity worshipped in the church. When I use God, I do not refer to the Biblical God; I refer to something completely different. Therefore, I have mostly refrained from using the word God in this book; I have used Śiva instead. The same goes for words like consciousness and soul.

Secondly, there are aspects in the dimension of supreme truth for which there are no adequate words. To refer to them, I would have to resort to approximation. When knowledge is imparted about an unfamiliar system, one that the reader or listener is not acquainted with, they are likely to misinterpret it due to an unfamiliar use of a certain expression. If the topic is familiar, the reader is aided by their memory in understanding the particular sense in which the linguistic expression is being used by the communicator. However, when the topic is entirely unfamiliar, it becomes challenging for them to understand.

Because the truth, for which no words—specifically English words—have been crafted yet to refer to, will require approximation, as a reader, you would interpret these approximations in various ways. None of them would fit perfectly, leading to potential misinterpretation or blame on me, the author, for being illogical or incomprehensible.

This is why those who are enlightened choose to remain silent, keeping the truth within their hearts. In Eastern traditions, such individuals are referred to as munis, meaning those who do not speak, or the silent ones. This is because, on one hand, the truth cannot be expressed, and on the other hand, any attempt to express it would lead to misinterpretation.

And the third point is, why would one feel the need to express that truth? When I experienced the ultimate truth through intense *Śaktipāta* from Śiva, I wanted to leave the physical body because the attachment to the body had dissolved. It was like when an orange ripens; it naturally starts detaching from its peel. I felt the same way. My body felt like a loose, flowing piece of cloth that could fall off at any moment. At that time, I had no desire to preach this truth because why bother? Someone's life won't change by hearing it; they will continue to live as they are. They might listen, find temporary peace and happiness, only to return to the same cycle of crying, anger, greed, and jealousy. Out of millions, perhaps one person might find this knowledge helpful, while the rest will continue their usual way. Even preaching to that one person would be futile because if they can understand me, they are already close to enlightenment and don't need my help; they will find their way on their own, sooner or later. That's why I wanted to leave the body.

However, every time I tried to do so, I felt as if something were holding me back, preventing me from leaving. I would hear voices screaming and crying at me, as if numerous souls were clinging to me, relying on me with expectations. Maybe that's why I occasionally make an effort now. Therefore, sometimes, I describe myself as a creator of lies—lies that can reveal the truth to you. Because the truth cannot be expressed in words, whatever I say about the truth is a lie, an illusion. However, these illusions might uncover the truth for you, much like someone throwing water on you in a dream. It's a dream, a lie, but it can wake you up to the truth.

Therefore, those who have experienced the truth for these reasons often keep their realisations unexpressed. However, when they are filled with great compassion, they express their heart in very concise sentences, speaking as little as possible, with brevity, only as much as necessary.

That's why these threads are very short sentences, crafted from carefully chosen words. Every single word that could be omitted is omitted by the *sūtrakāra*. Yet within them, so much is contained, so much is compressed, that each Sūtra contains atomic energy.

Alternatively, a better analogy might be GPS coordinates, as I have explained in Chapter two:

"Sūtras resemble GPS coordinates or *what3words*, pinpointing locations within the terrain of your inner world—the geography of your consciousness. It is for you to embark and explore.

Contemplation will take you there. Contemplation is the hike to that specific location within your valley of consciousness. Upon arrival, you can embrace and understand the Sūtra firsthand. Through this commentary, I endeavour to verbalise what I see in those locations of the valley of my consciousness. Not the entirety, but rather the significant elements. Just as with geographic landscapes, even if the scenery remains one, each individual depicts it uniquely, highlighting what they find important and skipping the rest."

The *Śiva Sūtras* comprise seventy-seven Sūtras divided into three books. The first book contains twenty-two Sūtras, centred on *śāmbhavopāya,* the direct method of realising truth. The second section comprises ten Sūtras, addressing *śaktopāya,* which lies between direct and indirect. The third book, focusing on *āṇavopāya,* the indirect method, consists of forty-five Sūtras.

Let me quote a brief explanation of these three *upāyas* or methods, that I have discussed in the fifth chapter. There, instead of 'method,' I used the word 'effort.'

"Efforts are of two types: active and passive, direct and indirect; And, there exists a third type that falls somewhere in between. For instance, reciting a mantra, performing noble and selfless actions, practising breathing exercises, or engaging in worship—these are indirect efforts toward attaining truth. These falls under the category of *āṇavopāya*—the path to attaining the divine, where distinctions exist between me and the deity I am meditating on, or between me and the mantra I am chanting, etc. This path is considered the lowest, as it is indirect. Worshipping an idol and chanting mantras are methods employed to purify the mind. We undertake these practices to free our minds from thoughts that create differences, to clear such thoughts that I am separate from the rest of the world. Through idol worship or selfless actions, we strive to purify our minds of such divisive thoughts. Both the devotee and the object of devotion experience a sense of oneness through worship. Chanting mantras eradicates thoughts that create differences. With selfless actions, we feel one with all living beings, finding joy in their happiness and feeling their sorrows. We rise above thoughts that create differences. This is also achieved through breathing exercises. Once the mind is purified, we progress to *śaktopāya,* where both duality and non-duality coexist. Here, we meditate on ourselves, contemplating 'Who am I?'—Here also there is a difference between the unknown entity we connect with using terms like 'who' and 'what,' and our own Self. Although both are referring to the same entity, therefore, both duality and non-duality coexist here. Pure thoughts are crucial for this technique—thoughts that do not create differences.

However, *śaktopāya* does not fall under the category of active effort either; it lies between the direct and indirect, between active and passive effort."

"*Śāmbhavopāya* is the effort that directly unites us with Bhairava, happening instantaneously. It is an active and direct means that aligns you immediately with Bhairava. This is the pathless path."

This volume specifically deals with *śāmbhavopāya,* which immediately transcends us from our body, mind, name, form, limitations, desires, sorrows, etc. Transcendence doesn't imply that one is no longer their body, mind, name, or form, nor does it imply that one has become incapable of doing something or feeling a certain emotion. There is a common misunderstanding that spiritual inclination or enlightenment entails the eradication of anger and desires, etc., or an inability to engage in worldly pursuits such as earning money or living a materialistic life. Some hold the opinion that enlightened beings are disconnected from contemporary life, unable to drive, use gadgets, or wear modern attire, etc. It is because their idea of a spiritual being is very ancient, when none of these existed, and secondly because they mistake transcendence as renunciation. These ideas are utterly erroneous. Transcendence isn't about losing aspects of life or becoming disabled in any way; rather, it is about becoming complete, totally free, and capable of engaging in all aspects of life. Enlightened beings still identify with their body, but unlike others, they identify not only with their own body but with all bodies in the world. Transcendence entails becoming unlimited. Currently, our body and mind serve as our limitations because of our identification with them. When we transcend the body-mind, we still retain our identification with them, but we also recognize ourselves as more expansive than mere physical and mental constructs, thereby transcending their limitations. Then the body and mind no longer limit us. When I say 'you are not your body,' I mean that your identity transcends your physical form; you are more than just your corporeal existence. This is the meaning of transcendence. If this concept is still unclear, don't worry; as you continue reading, it will become clearer. Hence, the title of this book—*Threads of Transcendence.*

So, when numerous editions, translations and commentaries have already been published on the *Śiva Sūtras*, what is the necessity for yet another commentary? I may answer in the words of the great commentator Kṣemarāja, "Having noticed confusion in the various commentaries and interpretations of *Śiva Sūtras* owing to inconsistency with the sacred tradition of the teachers, I am expounding the *Śiva Sūtras* according to their real meaning, in order to dispel the wrong notion caused by the other commentaries." *(āsamañjasyamālocya vṛttīnāmiha tattvataḥ, śivasūtraṁ vyākaromi gurvāmnāyavigānataḥ.)*

It is true that there are numerous translations, editions, and commentaries of this scripture. Among them, those authored by famous spiritual leaders are the most popular, and unfortunately, they are responsible for most of the misconceptions. Many of these contain inaccuracies in their interpretations, and in some instances, the Sūtras have been altogether wrongly translated from Sanskrit to English. Certain interpretations by these leaders are so inaccurate that they deviate even from the basic principles of Śiva's philosophy. While I won't single out any specific commentary, let's consider a common example. In this philosophy, the term *śakti-cakra* refers to a collective whole of energies and their continuous cycle. These energies are, simply put, the energy of consciousness, cognition, senses, and the external world—four distinct yet interconnected energies. The term *cakra* in Sanskrit carries dual meanings: a collective whole and a continuous cycle. The energies flow out from one another (emergence of the world) and merge back into each other (dissolution of the world), constituting a cyclic process, hence the name *śakti-cakra*

However, most commentators, lacking technical understanding of this tradition, superimposed their own philosophy onto these principles. They used these Sūtras as a canvas for their ideologies, painting scriptural evidence to validate their interpretations. For instance, in the sixth Sūtra, the term *śakti-cakra* is directly used, and most of these commentators associated it with *kuṇḍalini śakti* and the concept of seven *cakras*. One of them, as far as I have read, interpreted it as total involvement, suggesting that *śakti-cakra-saṃdhān* means to put all of one's energy into any task, to become fully involved and so on. This is just one example among many, and collectively this renders the scripture useless. No matter how many editions and translations there are—if they are interpreted or translated wrongly, they will do more harm than good. The purpose of this commentary is to clear all confusions and dispel all doubts. In fact, I will suggest that you read various popular commentaries alongside my commentary that will reveal the necessity behind my commentary on this text.

The translation of Jaideva Singh with the commentary of Kṣemarāja is my favourite thus far, but one thing I feel it lacks is ease of understanding. That edition leans heavily towards scholars and lacks practical, in-depth explanations that would resonate with more simple-hearted readers. Before me lay two options: to write an erudite commentary or to craft a simple and in-depth practical commentary. The former would be meaningful and accessible only to experts, while the latter would cater to those who lack extensive knowledge of this tradition but are curious about it. I chose the latter to ensure that this intricate tradition and philosophy could reach as many people as possible with utmost simplicity, allowing everyone to experience the marvel, the wonder of consciousness. Writing a commentary for the experts serves no purpose. They are unlikely to practically implement these teachings anyway; their false sense of knowledge won't allow them to do so. However, the common devotee, who yearns for the nectar-like wisdom of Śiva, who genuinely wants to transform their lives, they are the ones deserving of grace, and it is to them that Śiva intended these teachings to reach.

So then arises the question: who qualifies me to commentate on this scripture? What right do I have to deem others wrong? Who gives me the authority to authentically represent this tradition, especially when I am not even part of the *guru-śiṣya-krama* of this tradition? It's true that I don't have any living guru from whom I received physical initiation—but that doesn't mean I don't have the right to represent this tradition or that I don't belong to it or that I am inferior in any way, simply because I don't have a living guru. The path of Śiva is about experience. Here, only experience is considered supreme. Two individuals stand distinct: one initiated by a living guru, and the other, self-realised without such guidance. Should hierarchy exist, Śiva would consider the latter superior. Though everyone is the same, no one is superior or inferior, yet I feel the need to write this for the sake of clarifying my authority. I see my knowledge as my authority, thus I entrust you, the reader, to decide whether I hold any authority to commentate on this text. But still, out of respect for the tradition, let me briefly discuss my authority within its framework.

My guru is Śiva. I don't have any living, physically embodied human guru—my own *saṃvid* is my master—my consciousness. Śiva himself has performed my *abhiṣekam* (initiation) into this tradition. Enlightened masters fall into one of two categories: those in whom the awakening of knowledge, transcendental discernment, occurs without the need for any guru—and others who require a living guru to attain this knowledge. The former type of masters are called *akalpit*, which literally translates to not artificial or manufactured; natural, genuine. They are those who have become enlightened through their own energy, without the support of anyone else. *Abhinavagupta* writes about them as *"gurutaḥ śāstrataḥ svataḥ"*, meaning they become gurus through their own power, and the knowledge of scriptures, the knowledge of this tradition, has naturally arisen within them. I belong to this category. The other category of enlightened masters are called *kalpit*—meaning those who follow the normal *guru-śiṣya* tradition. Although both types of masters have become Śiva, both have the knowledge of their true selves, there is no difference between them—in dualistic Tantra, a hierarchy has been given; those who have become enlightened without a physical guru have been considered superior. In some places in tantra, it has even been said as far as that such individuals have the right to initiate the whole world, and where they are available, in their presence, the *kalpit* master has no right to initiate anyone.

सच सांसिद्धिकः शास्त्रे प्रोक्तः स्वप्रत्ययात्मकः। किरणायां यदप्युक्तं गुरुतः शास्त्रतः स्वतः ॥
तत्रोत्तरोत्तरं मुख्यं पूर्वपूर्व उपायकः। यस्य स्वतोऽयं सत्तर्कः सर्वत्रैवाधिकारवान् ॥
अभिषिक्तः स्वसंवित्तिदेवीभिर्दीक्षितश्च सः। स एव सर्वाचार्याणां मध्ये मुख्यः प्रकीर्तितः ॥
तत्संनिधाने नान्येषु कल्पितेष्वधिकारिता। स समस्तं च शास्त्रार्थं सत्तर्कादिव मन्यते ॥

sac sāṁsiddhikaḥ śāstre proktaḥ svapratyayātmakaḥ | kiraṇāyāṁ yadapyuktaṁ gurutaḥ śāstrataḥ svataḥ ||
tatrottarottaraṁ mukhyaṁ pūrvapūrva upāyakaḥ | yasya svato'yaṁ sattarkaḥ sarvatraivādhikāravān ||
abhiṣiktaḥ svasaṁvittidevībhirdīkṣitaśca saḥ | sa eva sarvācāryāṇāṁ madhye mukhyaḥ prakīrtitaḥ ||
tatsannidhāne nānyeṣu kalpiteṣvadhikāritā | sa samastaṁ ca śāstrārthaṁ sattarkādeva manyate ||

Such a person has been characterised in the scripture as *sāmsiddhika* and *svapratyayātmaka*, perfectly accomplished and self-awakened. In the *Kiṛaṇa Śastra* it has been laid down that enlightenment can come via anyone of the sources, namely, the teacher, the scripture and from within oneself. From amongst these three sources, the later the source is put here, the more important it is while the earlier ones are just a means to it. (In other words, enlightenment from within oneself is more important than enlightenment through scriptures, which is more important than enlightenment through a guru. The other two are only means through which one can attain enlightenment from within.)

The aspirant, in whom the transcendental discernment has sprouted automatically, deserves to be authorised in all respects. His own consciousness has performed his *abhiṣekam* (initiation), and thus, being crowned by deities of self-consciousness as initiated, he occupies the main position among all the teachers. No one else deserves to be authorised in his presence. In such a teacher emerges the knowledge of all the *Śāstras,* as he is established in transcendental discernment.

(*Tantrāloka* IV.41-44)

However, I respectfully disagree with this perspective. In my view, every master who has attained the realisation of self, who holds the correct knowledge of Śiva's philosophy, whether initiated by a physical master or not, is equally great and worthy of respect.

There are even subcategories of the *akalpit*—those who have become enlightened without the support of any practice, scripture, or guru, who have spontaneously attained enlightenment without a trace of doubt in their realisation, who possess clarity about everything, and this clarity, this godly characteristic, is expressed well in their conduct and life—they are *sāmsiddhikas*, they are considered at the pinnacle of this superficial hierarchy. However, this is an extremely rare case, like one in eight billion people, or perhaps not even one. Such individuals have always been enlightened—those divine beings typically referred to as incarnations—they are the ones, like Lord Kṛṣṇa. Yes, there will be millions of imitators because it is very easy to deceive those who are ignorant. You will encounter many who claim, "I went to a mountain, sat on a rock, and became enlightened!"—such people are usually liars.

Descending in this hierarchy are *akalpit kalpakas*, the *akalpit* masters who have achieved enlightenment through their practices, through their own efforts, without any physical initiation. They could have attained realisation through practices like meditation, chanting, *yoginīmelaka*, and so on. They might have also sought support from scriptures. I belong to this subcategory. Both these subcategories of *akalpit* masters are considered superior to the *kalpit* master in the hierarchy.

This sums up the authority part in the context of this tradition. Another point is that I have given myself this authority; it was my heartfelt desire to expound on this scripture. In a way, it is an expression of my deep gratitude. This philosophy has given me a new life—Śiva has given me a new life, this knowledge, and freedom, and all the enlightening experiences, through which I have been fortunate enough to help people and received their blessings—thus, giving me everything that I have today. Otherwise, I would have been no one, nothing, just a miserable being on the face of earth. When my grandfather passed away, I also went to the banks of Holy Ganges to cremate him, at Sultānganj Ghāt, from where Kanwariyas fetch the water of the Ganges and embark on a 111 kilometre journey on foot to the Bābā Baidyanāth temple for the offering of water (*abhiṣekam*). Hence, that place is sacred. My grandfather's name was Dāmodar Jhā, and we belong to the Maithil Brahmin lineage, descendants of Śiva devotees. I was deeply attached to my grandfather. His departure left a vacuum, a void in my heart, sucking away my life force. His influence on me has been immense; even today, the Rudrākṣa necklace he gave me hangs around my neck. He suffered a cardiac arrest on the sacred night of *Mahā Śivaratri,* hospitalised, and a month later, he passed away. It was after his death that my spiritual journey began, much like Abhinavgupta's journey after losing his parents.

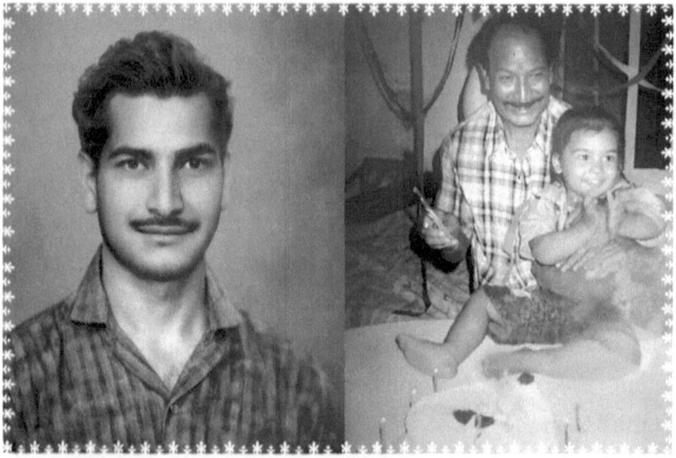

My grandfather during his college years; Celebrating my second birthday with him.

On that evening, as his body was engulfed in flames, I sat nearby, watching him alone. A part of his face was visible. I witnessed how that body, that face to which I was so attached, slowly burned away, melting until eventually, after a while, only charred bones—the skull—remained, and then, after some time, even that disappeared, turning to ashes in the flames. I sat there watching him for some hours until he turned completely into ashes. I couldn't quite process what was happening. And then, that vision, the sight of that burning corpse, became permanently etched in my mind; whenever I closed my eyes, all I could see was a body burning. At home, in school, on the playground; eventually I began to see myself lying down in place of that body, as if I were the one burning. I would lie down, close my eyes, and continue watching. Watching myself burning, turning into ashes, in the classroom, at home, on the bed while sleeping at night, whenever I found the time, it would happen spontaneously. Surprisingly, it was quite a blissful experience. Alongside this, I began to delve into the study of death, what happens after death, where does the departed soul go—and this study led me towards yogic and Tantric scriptures. During that time, I came across a scripture—the *Vijñāna Bhairava Tantra*, which belonged to the Kashmir Śaiva tradition, the same tradition as the *Śiva Sūtras*. And within it, I found a method—

कालग्निना कालपदादुत्थितेन स्वकं पुरम् । प्लुष्टं विचिन्तयेदन्ते
शान्ताभासस्तदा भवेत् ॥

kālaghinā kālapadādutthitena svakaṁ puram | pluṣṭaṁ
vicintayedante śāntābhāsastadā bhavet ||

One should meditate on one's own body as if it were engulfed by a fierce fire, rising from the foot. At the end of this meditation, the peaceful state will manifest.

एवमेव जगत्सर्वं दग्धं ध्यात्वा विकल्पतः । अनन्यचेतसः पुंसः पुंभावः
परमो भवेत् ॥

evameva jagatsarvaṁ dagdhaṁ dhyātvā vikalpataḥ |
ananyacetasaḥ puṁsaḥ puṁbhāvaḥ paramo bhavet ||

Meditating in this way by imagining that the entire world has been burnt, a person whose mind is undisturbed will attain the highest human condition.

(*Vijñāna Bhairava Tantra* 52, 53)

I had been unknowingly practising it all along. Since then, I have considered Śiva, the author of that scripture, as my Master, diligently practising his teachings. Then, I delved even more deeply into the Tantric texts; I dropped out of school, and for years, spent the entirety of my days practising various methods mentioned in that scripture—and here I am today. So, I am simply grateful for the scriptures, for this philosophy, for Śiva—and this present commentary and all other commentaries that I will write on the Tantric texts in the future are just an expression of this gratitude for me. And nothing more. I want everyone to experience the intoxication that I have experienced. Everyone should be able to savour the nectar of this philosophy—that's all I want.

Thus, I am writing this commentary. It is not, strictly speaking, a commentary. Yes, I have used the term commentary, for the lack of better words, but this is not a commentary. Commentaries stem from the pens of scholars, intellectuals, holders of PhDs, or university professors. I, on the other hand, am merely a high school dropout—barely educated. I don't know much to be able to commentate. I've never undergone training in English writing either. What I am writing is just a response. When I ponder upon these Sūtras, when I contemplate on these teachings, I hear an echo within me, a world unfolds before me, and I simply express that in words. I am not attempting to explain what Śiva is saying. Who am I to do so? Rather, I aim to express the echoes they stir within me. I'm merely articulating the inner response these Sūtras evoke. There's nothing more to it.

Therefore, refrain from approaching them as conventional commentaries or textbooks. Instead, view them as pathways leading towards a wordless silence, from which these words originate. Strive to attain the heart of these teachings. Throughout this work, I've reiterated key concepts multiple times to ensure clarity and resonance within your heart. Śiva Himself has reiterated these points across various contexts to prevent misinterpretation and ensure they resonate within you, becoming an integral part of your life and compelling you to tread the paths He has revealed throughout this scripture.

With this humble prayer, I offer this gift to all of you.

Oṁ Namaḥ Śivāyaḥ

CHAPTER ONE

कोऽहं कथमिदं किं वा कथं मरणजन्मनी ।
विचारयान्तरे वेत्थं महत्तत्फलमेष्यसि ॥

ko'haṁ kathamidaṁ kiṁ vā kathaṁ maraṇajanmanī |
vicārayāntare vetthaṁ mahattatphalameṣyasi ||

Who am I? How came this world? What is it? How came death and birth? Thus inquire within yourself; Great will be the benefit you will derive from such inquiry.

(*Annapūrṇā Upaniṣad* I.40)

Knowing who you are is the fundamental prerequisite before delving into any other knowledge. The spiritual journey begins with the Self, the 'I'. From the earliest stages of life, our attention is directed outward, away from ourselves. Who we are was never taught to us. Immediately after birth, the instinctual search for sustenance is directed outside toward the mother's breast. And soon after, we are initiated into an education that acquaints us with the information of the external world. No one guides us to understand who we truly are. When asked, 'Who are you?', we were trained, like a parrot, to mimic a name as an answer, 'I am Suyash,' 'I am Simran,' 'Salman,' or 'Stephen,' perhaps adding our parents' names if pressed further. Yet, beyond these superficial identifiers, nothing is revealed about our true selves. Yes, we are shown images of our physical bodies and told that this is who we are, yet these images change year after year, because those entrusted with our education remain in the dark about their own identity; no one enlightened them. So how can they guide us?

The curiosity to explore the Self never arises either. It remains dormant, suppressed, because since childhood we are taught that everything worth having exists outside of ourselves.

When we used to cry, when we experienced incompleteness, we were comforted with toys, a bottle of milk, and cartoons on the television, all intended to divert our attention from that sense of incompleteness and keep our minds occupied. Gradually, however, these diversions lost their effectiveness. As we matured, the awareness and intensity of this unfulfillment deepened, and we were led to believe that fulfilment would accompany academic success and good marks in school, yet, despite achieving those marks, the promised fulfilment remained elusive. Instead, the narrative shifted to clearing the entrance exam of a prestigious college as the key to a settled life, where fulfilment would be attained, and suffering would dissipate. However, that didn't happen. On the contrary, it only became more stressful.

We then heard various ideas about fulfilment—that securing a job equated to fulfilment and happiness. So, we pursued education relentlessly, endured days and nights of sorrow, lived in stress, and when we finally got a job, it dawned on us that the stress and suffering we endured in obtaining employment were just a glimpse of what lies ahead. It was there to prepare us for the life ahead, which would be much more challenging, urging us to adapt to this suffering, learn to endure, and work in the office without shedding tears. The requirement was the ability to work under stressful conditions, and that's what we were being prepared for, because the future life will be filled with suffering and stress.

We then heard from someone that happiness and completeness can only be found through marriage. Only then are you complete when your better half enters your life. And we held onto the belief that a partner would bring us joy and completeness. However, when this expectation fell short, blame was placed on the partner for not being an ideal companion, for not treating us right. Then, some of us, unconsciously seeking a supposed 'better partner' or *twin flame*, found ourselves entangled in extramarital affairs.

Others sought completeness through having children, burdening these innocent beings with the weight of their expectations. The definition of fulfilment became synonymous with ensuring that these children became 'well-settled' in life.

It is an undeniable fact that more than ninety per-cent of parents are only living for their children. Their own lives have come to an end, and their hopes are now invested in their children. Children become a reflection of their parents' youth. Then the same cycle starts with the children: educating them, getting them employed, arranging marriages, and asking for grandchildren. However, this time, they want their child to study in a good school, the kind they couldn't attend, and get good grades, better than them, because they still believe it's the solution.

They also arrange the child's marriage according to their own preferences, as they still believe that marriage is the solution, and they just happened to get trapped with the wrong partner. Humans don't seem to learn from their mistakes, much like the camel that loves eating cactus despite getting hurt. The cactus spines prick its mouth, tongue, and teeth, causing pain and bleeding, yet it continues to eat the same cactus. It doesn't learn from its mistakes, and the vicious cycle continues. Even after death, humans don't seem to understand. That's why they keep reincarnating.

It happened. There once was a sage who attained enlightenment through his spiritual practices. One day, he was passing through a village, and the road seemed endless. Exhausted and thirsty from hours of walking, he noticed a grocery store and decided to stop. Approaching the shopkeeper, he requested some water. The merchant warmly welcomed the sage, quenching his thirst and offering him a meal. The shopkeeper even arranged a comfortable bed for the tired sage.

While the sage slept, the shopkeeper observed that the sage's garment was torn in several places. Taking a needle and thread, the shopkeeper meticulously repaired it. When the sage awoke, he was pleasantly surprised and expressed gratitude for the kind gesture. The sage said, "I am grateful for your hospitality. I have the power to take you to *Śivaloka,* the eternal abode of Lord Śiva. There, you will be free from any desire or suffering, experiencing eternal joy. Come, let's go."

Hearing this, the shopkeeper replied, "Swāmi, I am deeply moved by your generous offer. I am willing to accompany you, but not now. My children are still young, and I need to save some money for their well-being. Let me stay here for seven years, and I will be ready to go."

The sage agreed, and they parted ways with the promise that the sage would return in seven years.

Seven years passed. True to his word, the sage returned to take the shopkeeper to *Śivaloka.* Upon seeing him, the shopkeeper said, "Swāmi, I am grateful beyond words for your kindness. However, I am still not ready to leave. My youngest son is very ill, and there are other matters to attend to. Please give me seven more years."

The sage, understanding the shopkeeper's situation, agreed and departed. After another seven years, when the sage returned, he discovered that the shopkeeper had passed away. Using his meditative insight, the sage realised that the shopkeeper had been reborn as a bull, now attached to the plough and diligently ploughing his son's fields. The death of the previous bull had deeply worried the shopkeeper. Therefore, in his next life, he took birth as a bull to continue ploughing the fields.

The sage found the bull-former shopkeeper and said, "Let's go. Why do you still want to stay on Earth?" The humble bull replied, "I cannot leave now, Lord. Please grant me seven more years to ensure my son's happiness and prosperity. After that, I will undoubtedly accompany you."

With a sense of disappointment, the sage bowed his head and departed. Seven more years passed, and when the sage returned, he could not find the bull-former shopkeeper. Upon meditation, the sage realised that the shopkeeper had reincarnated as a dog, faithfully guarding his son's fields.

Approaching the dog-former shopkeeper, the sage questioned, "Have you not learned from your experiences? How much longer do you wish to endure this suffering? Do you intend to remain ensnared forever in illusion?" The dog, with tears welling up in its eyes, replied, "Swāmi, I don't want to refuse you once more. But, what can I do? If I leave now, no one will safeguard my son's crops. Kindly grant me a few more years."

Disheartened, the sage departed. Another seven years lapsed, and upon his return, he discovered that the man had reincarnated as a snake. In this form, the shopkeeper guarded a buried treasure, thinking of ways for his youngest son to discover it. The sage, now angered and resolute, decided that enough was enough.

Calling the shopkeeper's youngest son, the sage disclosed the location of the buried treasure. After unearthing the riches, the son followed the sage's instructions to kill the snake. As the soul left the snake and was about to seize another form, the sage quickly caught it and ascended to *Śivaloka,* before he could inhabit another body.

The saying goes that history repeats itself, but I contend otherwise: history doesn't repeat itself; rather, it's people who fail to learn from history that repeat mistakes. After numerous cycles of birth and death, some fortunate souls, through divine grace, come to the realisation that their pursuits will not yield the desired outcomes if they continue on their current path. They recognize that something is amiss, as the happiness and fulfilment they tirelessly seek seems to slip away from them. In childhood, they recall experiencing greater joy, completeness, robust health, and unwavering focus. Somewhere along the line, their efforts have gone awry; their approach has been misguided. The expectation was that life should have become increasingly joyous, healthier, more focused, and fulfilling since childhood, not the opposite.

These fortunate souls begin to turn inward, questioning who they really are and their purpose. Having tasted what society deems as success, they find it similar to a chewing gum that offers only transient sweetness followed by a bland, sometimes bitter aftertaste. Now, they have come to understand that what they truly seek cannot be found outside, in worldly achievements. This marks the recommencement of their journey, starting anew with the fundamental question, *Who am I?*

And here begins *Śiva Sūtras*. Be mindful that if you still believe that a little more wealth would bring completeness and joy to your life, or that finding a slightly better life partner would make your life whole, or if marrying that particular boy or girl would fulfil everything, or if getting admission to a slightly better university, perhaps Oxford, would solve all your problems—if you still think this way, then please return this book—it is not meant for you. May you marry your crush, earn abundant wealth, and may all your aspirations be realised—that is my heartfelt wish for you.

...However, if you are still reading, I understand that you have realised that what you have done so far was not the solution, because the solution doesn't exist outside, and you have taken the first step towards the inner dimension by asking yourself, *Who am I?*
Śiva *Sūtras* begins with the answer to this question.

चैतन्यमात्मा ॥१॥

|| CAITANYAMĀTMĀ || 1 ||

Consciousness is the Self, the reality (of all that is).

This Sūtra is formed by the combination of two Sanskrit words—*Caitanya* and *ātmā. Ātmā* or *ātman* means who I truly Am. The direct translation of *ātmā* is Self, as in self-dependent (*ātma-nirbhar*) or self-respect (*ātma-sammān*). However, over time, the term *ātmā* has become associated with the soul in Abrahamic religions, and the concept of the soul in these religions differs significantly from the Eastern concept of *ātmā*.

In Abrahamic beliefs, the soul is described as a separate entity, possessing a form resembling the physical body it inhabits, albeit slightly transparent, resembling mist. In Eastern philosophy, we do not dismiss the existence of this soul, but it is not the true Self either; it is also a body like the physical body, just subtler. The *ātmā* is even more subtle than that. *Ātmā,* in its simplest definition, is who I am. It is not a body. It is not a separate entity. It is your innermost Self, your unchanging essence, your very existence.

When I say something exists, it means that the thing will never be non-existent. If something can be non-existent, then it never truly existed. It just seems to exist.

So everything that changes is illusory. They don't really exist. Because changes are only on the surface. What is within, the innermost reality, the root, never changes. It is, and it is in the present. You can never say it was; you can never say it will be. Whenever it is, it just is.

Therefore, the term *ātmā* does not refer to a ghost or spirit. Unfortunately, in contemporary times, the Hindi dubbing of Hollywood productions has led to an erroneous association of the term *ātmā* with ghosts. When the scriptures convey that the *ātmā* cannot be seen, it is not because it is translucent or mist-like. Instead, the impossibility arises because the *ātmā* itself is the perceiver. Just as eyes cannot see themselves, the *ātmā*, being the perceiver, cannot perceive itself.

In this verse from *Dṛg Dṛśya Viveka*, the idea is artfully articulated:

रूपं दृश्यं लोचनं दृक् तद्दृश्यं दृक्तु मानसम्।
दृश्या धीवृत्तयस्साक्षी दृगेव न तु दृश्यते॥

rūpaṁ dṛśyaṁ locanaṁ dṛk tadṛśyaṁ dṛk-tu mānasam I
dṛśyā dhī-vṛttayas sākṣī dṛg-eva na tu dṛśyate II

The eye is the seer, the form is the seen. That eye is the seen and the mind is the seer. The witness alone is the Seer of mind and never the seen.

It cannot be seen because it is the one that sees, beyond which there is no other. Moving forward in this book, I will use the term Self for *ātmā*.

We will discuss more about the Self. First, let's understand the meaning of the second word *Caitanyam*. *Caitanyam* translates to the state of consciousness, a state, not a being. *Cetana* translates to a conscious being, one who conscires, or one who cognizes, and *Caitanyam* (with the *taddhita* affix *ṣyañ*) means the state of that conscious being. This Sūtra is asserting that this state is your true Self. When Śiva speaks of the Self, he is not referring to the Self of a particular individual. His response is all-encompassing—everything is consciousness. He is providing the answer for all. Whether or not you have acknowledged your identity as consciousness, Śiva is giving the answer for you as well. In his answer, everyone is included; there are no exceptions.

Therefore, if we all share the same innermost Self, it implies that we all are one. Do not assume that you are separate from me, or that you are distinct from other beings, or even from that stone. This aphorism does not acknowledge any distinction between your Self and mine. And even if there is a difference, but the innermost Self is the same, then what is the difference? The difference is superficial. A clay pot and a clay elephant, both are made of the same clay. The difference between them is the same as it is in you and everything else. Yes, there is a difference in quantity.

Often, the argument is presented that even if a drop of water and the ocean are the same, their innermost selves are the same; they are both made up of the same hydrogen and oxygen molecules. Still, there is a vast difference between a drop and the ocean. There is a difference in quantity. This argument is flawed because it takes an analogy literally. We are talking about an ocean that is timeless, infinite. Other than it, there exists nothing else. It is everywhere, so where is the drop separate from it? The drop is within the ocean itself. There is nothing that is separating that drop from the ocean because there is nothing else. Everything is that water. The innermost Self of everything is that water. Yes, if you can separate that drop from the water, the difference becomes clear, but where will you separate it, how will you separate it, where will you take it? Everywhere is that water.

Rumi said, "You are not a drop in the ocean, you are the ocean in a drop." There is no difference between the drop and the ocean. This understanding can also be approached differently. Consciousness exists beyond the limitations of time and space. Śiva says, in the *Vijñāna Bhairava Tantra*:

दिक्कालकलनोन्मुक्ता देशोद्देशाविशेषिणी ।
व्यपदेष्टमशक्यासावकथ्या परमार्थतः ॥

dik-kāla-kalanonmuktā deśoddēśāviśēṣiṇī |
vyapadēṣṭumaśakyāsāv-akathyā paramārthataḥ ||

This state of Bhairava is free from the limitations of space, time, and form. It is not particularised by a specific place or designation. In reality, it is inexpressible because it cannot be described.

(*Vijñāna Bhairava Tantra* 14)

As I mentioned earlier, If something exists, it means that the thing will never be non-existent. It is, and it is in the present. You can never say it was; you can never say it will be. That's why it transcends time, it is beyond time—YOU are beyond time, unaffected by the changes of time, or space. You are everywhere simultaneously. You are neither in space nor in time; you pass through them, but you are not them. You can be in them, but you are not them. You move through them, you go beyond them; you enter, you exit. Space and time are your temporary abode; they are not you.

One of the names of Śiva is *Digaṃbara*, meaning He who is clothed in or covered by space. Space and time are like His garments. Just as clothing doesn't define a person, space doesn't define consciousness. This vast emptiness, with its ten directions, exists separately from consciousness. Consciousness is at its centre, free from space and time.

If something transcends space and time, then it cannot have divisions. Imagine dividing it: where would the separation occur, since there is no space? And how would you divide it in the first place? Suppose you have an object that is *x* metres long. You can only divide it if *x* is a quantifiable number. If *x* is 4 metres, then you can divide it. But here, there is no space, and since the metre is a unit of space or distance, then *x* will be 0 metres. If you divide 0 by 2, it will still be 0. You could divide it by a million and it would still be 0. And it would take time to do this division, even if you did it at the speed of light. There would still be a duration between before and after. But time is also absent.

Consciousness is free of time and space. This is why consciousness is one. It can only exist in singularity, not in plurality. And this singularity, this oneness underlies everything. Our perception of difference and multiplicity stems from ignorance, which will be explored in the next chapter.

Therefore, in this Sūtra, Śiva includes everything that exists. The innermost Self of everything, the essence of all existence is consciousness. Śiva is consciousness, you are consciousness, I am consciousness, that person is consciousness, this book is consciousness—everything is one.

Śiva confirms this in the *Vijñāna Bhairava Tantra*,

चिद्धर्मा सर्वदेहेषु विशेषो नास्ति कुत्रचित् ।
अतश्च तन्मयं सर्वं भावयन्भवजिज्जनः ॥

cid-dharmā sarva-deheṣu viśeṣo nāsti kutracit |
ataśca tanmayaṁ sarvaṁ bhāvayan-bhavajij-janaḥ ||

The One which is characterised as Consciousness is residing in all the bodies; there is no differentiation in anything. Therefore, if a person realises that everything is full of that (very Consciousness), he conquers the world of becoming.

(*Vijñāna Bhairava Tantra* 100)

And *Netra Tantra*,

परमात्मस्वरूपं तु सर्वोपाधिविवर्जितम् ।
चैतन्यमात्मनो रूपं सर्वशास्त्रेषु पठयते ॥

parāmātmasvarūpaṁ tu sarvopādhivivarjitam |
caitanyamātmano rūpaṁ sarvaśāstreṣu paṭhayate ||

Consciousness is the nature of Self which verily is the Śiva freed of all limiting conditions. This is what has been described in all the *Śāstras*.

(*Netra Tantra* VIII.28)

Well, it is still understandable that the reality, the innermost Self of every sentient being, is consciousness. However, when applied to an insentient object, like a stone, for example, it becomes difficult to comprehend. How can we attribute consciousness to something inanimate? How can we assert that even a toilet seat is consciousness?

There are two ways we can approach this question. Firstly, we can answer it from the perspective of the macrocosm. Today, thanks to Albert Einstein, it has become common knowledge that matter and energy are essentially the same—matter being the subtle form of energy, and energy being the gross form of matter. Just as water and ice are related, so are energy and matter. Although this analogy is not entirely accurate, it suffices for understanding. This has been mathematically proven and is a universally accepted truth within the scientific community. However, a lesser-known truth is that even energy is not entirely in its subtlest state; in its most subtle form, it exists as consciousness. Consciousness is the subtlest, with a slightly grosser form as energy, and the grossest manifestation as matter. Just as vapour is subtler than water, and water is subtler than ice.

Just as dry ice, in its solid form, is carbon dioxide gas, if we were to say that its real nature is as a formless, invisible gas, it might seem counterintuitive for a moment, but it is the truth.

Similarly, the true nature of every sentient and insentient being, their innermost Self, is consciousness. Just as the solid form is condensed gas, in the same way, the condensed form of consciousness is this physical world. A prayer eloquently expresses this idea:

आश्यानं चिद्रसस्यौघं साकारत्वमुपागतम् ।
जगद्रूपतया वन्दे प्रत्यक्षं भैरवं वपुः ।।

āśyānaṁ cidrasasyaughaṁ sākāratvam upāgatam |
jagad rūpatayā vande pratyakṣaṁ bhairavaṁ vapuḥ ||

I worship Bhairava in the form of the world
who has assumed form as a condensation
of the essence of Consciousness.

(Quoted in *Tantrāloka Viveka* by Jayaratha on VIII.2)

In the hymns of Utpaldeva, it is exquisitely expressed how a devotee can perceive consciousness, Śiva in everything:

In a state of union with You
let me perceive every object
as pervaded by You.
Filled with great joy
let me then wander about
free from any desire.

Let me experience the whole world
as filled by you, Oh Lord!
Then I will be completely satisfied
and will not trouble you with my prayers!

With my eyes closed
relishing the wonder of inner devotion,
May I worship even the blades of grass thus:
Homage to Śiva, my very own Self!

(Śiva *Stotrāvali* VI.5-6, V.15)

Often, confusion arises here as we tend to conflate cognition and feelings with consciousness. We believe that being conscious implies mentally recognizing things, feeling sensations, and it is obvious that an inanimate object like a stone or a toilet seat in the bathroom cannot cognize or feel, hence it cannot be consciousness. However, this confusion arises due to a language barrier. The Sanskrit term I've translated as 'consciousness' differs significantly from the typical English usage of the word. Due to a lack of words, I find myself resorting to the word consciousness. The consciousness I am referring to transcends the mind and feelings. In the deep sleep state where there is neither mind nor feelings, consciousness still exists. That's why there is such profound joy and fulfilment upon waking up in the morning. Consciousness is the backdrop for cognition, feelings, and objectivity. It is the canvas upon which the cosmic picture is painted.

I am speaking of the consciousness that Nobel Prize laureate Max Planck referred to, when he said, "I regard consciousness as fundamental. I regard matter as derivative from consciousness. We cannot get behind consciousness. Everything that we talk about, everything that we regard as existing, postulates consciousness."[Interview in *The Observer* (25 January 1931), p.17, column 3]

Alternatively, we can address this question from the microcosmic or subjective perspective. You must question that these external existents, things outside you, which you consider non-living and hesitate to attribute consciousness to, do they truly exist? Is that piece of stone or that toilet seat real? They are merely form, taste, smell, touch, and sound. Beyond these five, what is the existence of that stone? You perceive the stone because it has a particular shape, a colour, or let's say, a unique blend of colours. It has a taste, perhaps one you have never tasted, and a certain distinct smell. It has a texture—if it's marble, it's soft, if it's sandstone, it's rough. Lastly, it has a sound. This composite of five attributes constitutes the entire existence of that thing.

However, these five don't reside outside consciousness. We will explore this in the upcoming chapters. Consider sound. Sound has no existence of its own unless there is an observer to hear it. As in the philosophical question, 'if a tree falls in a forest, or on a deserted island, and there's no one around to hear it, does it make a sound?' The answer is no; it only produces vibrations in the air. Those vibrations aren't considered sound until there is an observer to hear them. Similarly, colours like blue, green, red, yellow—they don't have any existence. Colours don't exist. Galileo Galilei, the father of modern science, wrote in 1623 that colours are "no more than mere names so far as the object in which we place them is concerned … they reside only in consciousness. Hence if the living creature were removed, all these qualities would be wiped away and annihilated"

Galileo also believed that just as colour has no existence outside of consciousness, similarly, scent, taste, and form have no existence outside of consciousness. All these elements reside within consciousness itself. If we were to eliminate consciousness, which is not possible, then reality would be formless, tasteless, odourless, silence. This much is universally accepted in the scientific community.

However, Śiva takes a step further than modern science here, asserting that the objective existents, such as all living beings, stones, even toilet seats, are not outside of consciousness either. They too cannot exist without consciousness.

Reality is like the projection of a film on a white backdrop. The only difference is that the projector is consciousness, projecting not only forms but also tastes, scents, touches, and sounds. It projects onto not just colourless fabric but onto a shapeless, odourless, tasteless, silence, or one might say, nothingness.

And in such a scenario, whether it be me, a stone, a toilet seat, or any inanimate object, we all share the same innermost Self, consciousness. Continuing with the analogy of a projector, imagine scenes projected onto a screen by the projector, depicting trees, stones, soil, and more. In reality, no matter how counterintuitive it may sound, the stone, soil, trees—everything on the screen—is just light. This is because only light emanates from the projector. Therefore, I can assert that the innermost nature of the stone on that screen is light. Even if you argue that the stone does not produce light, I would explain that the stone itself is formed of light.

Similarly, as I am explaining to you now, the stone or toilet seat that you perceive as inanimate and unconscious is also created from, or is, in fact, consciousness. This is because we are conscious of that toilet seat, hence; it exists. Therefore, irrespective of how impure, foul, or dirty it may seem to you, that object is inherently pure—it is pure consciousness.

In the *Ucchuṣmabhairava Tantra*, Śiva explains this:

यावन्न वेदका एते तावद्वेद्याः कथं प्रिये ।
वेदकं वेद्यमेकं तु तत्त्वं नास्त्यशुचिस्ततः ॥

yāvanna vedakā ete tāvadvedyāḥ kathaṁ priye |
vedakaṁ vedyamekaṁ tu tattvaṁ nāstyaśucistataḥ |

Oh dear one, so long as there are no knowers, how can there be anything known. The knower and the known are really the same principle. Therefore, there is nothing which is inherently impure.

Without a knower, without a conscious being, nothing can exist, so everything is consciousness.

The same idea is expressed in the *Spanda-Kārikās*:

यस्मात्सर्वमयो जीवः सर्वभावसमुद्भवात् ।
तत्संवेदनरूपेण तादाम्यप्रतिपत्तितः ॥
तस्माच्छब्दार्थचिन्तासु न सावस्था न या शिवः ।
भोक्तैव भोग्यभावेन सदा सर्वत्र संस्थितः ॥

yasmātsarvamayo jīvaḥ sarvabhāvasamudbhavāt |
tatsaṁvedanarūpeṇa tādāmyapratipattitaḥ ||
tasmācchabdārthacintāsu na sāvasthā na yā śivaḥ |
bhoktaiva bhogyabhāvena sadā sarvatra saṁsthitāḥ ||

The Self is the whole of reality, because all existents derive their existence from the Self, and because in the process of knowing, the known gets identified with the Self. Hence whether in the world or object or mental apprehension of it, there is no state which is not Siva. It is only the experient who always and everywhere exists in the form of the experienced.

(*Spanda-Kārikās* II.3,4)

So, *Consciousness is the Self, the reality of all that is.* And therefore it is everything. Because it is everything, it is inherently free. Śiva or consciousness possesses numerous abilities and qualities—being omniscient, transcending time, causing the creation and destruction of the universe—yet, all these are superficial, mere byproducts. The fundamental quality of consciousness is freedom. One could say they are two sides of the same coin; where there is consciousness, there is freedom, and where there is freedom, there is consciousness.

The degree of consciousness determines the degree of freedom. The more conscious one is, the more free they are, while the more unconscious, the more bound. For instance, a toilet seat is not conscious; hence, it lacks the freedom to move on its own will. On the other hand, a human, to some extent, is conscious and therefore has a certain level of freedom. Be mindful that being conscious is a quality possessed by a being existing in a state of consciousness. Everything has consciousness, but not everything is a conscious being. For example, a toilet seat has consciousness, but it is not a conscious being. You, as a conscious being, should not limit yourself to the identification with that being; instead, become self-aware. Dive into the depths, unite with that source, realise that you are consciousness itself. Go beyond the being, understand that consciousness is not a quality attached to you; you are consciousness. And you are inherently free.

Who is limited? Who is bound? One who is identified with a specific entity. Suppose you identify yourself with a certain position in a company. The limitations of that company's position become your limitations—limitations mean bondage. Understand this: limitations are the opposite of freedom. If your actions are confined, if you can only do so much and nothing more, then you are in bondage. If your thoughts are limited, if identifying with something sets a boundary on your thinking, then that is bondage. For example, if you identify yourself as religious, there are numerous things you are prohibited from thinking and doing—you cannot question the existence of God, cannot have physical relationships beyond your spouse, are forbidden from harbouring negative thoughts about others or causing harm. In such a scenario, you are not truly free; you are bound. Therefore, being limited is synonymous with being bound.

And where do these limitations come from? They stem from a particular identification. Identification is always connected to limitations. If you are a boy, you cannot cry; if you are a girl, you cannot laugh your heart out. If you are a spiritual leader, you are not supposed to amass great wealth, and so on.

And where does freedom come from? It comes from letting go of all identifications. I am everything, and I can do anything and everything. I am entirely free in action and cognition. Consciousness is everything. And because you are consciousness, you are everything. Therefore, you are free.

I am using the two words, consciousness and freedom, only to simplify the understanding of this mystery for you. Otherwise, both mean the same. *Consciousness is freedom.*

In fact, in Tantras, consciousness is defined exactly like this: *sarva-jñāna-kriyāmayaṁ paripurnaṁ svātantrayam*, which translates to 'absolute freedom of cognizing and doing everything.' The entire philosophy of Śaivism is based on this freedom. As we continue reading this book, the concepts of freedom and consciousness will become clearer. For now, if you want to bring it into practice, you can start with either becoming more free or becoming more conscious, and the other will naturally follow.

Free yourself from all conditionings, all limitations, and you will see that you become fully conscious. And when you are completely conscious, you will realise that you have become entirely free. Then, there is no reason for your existence, and there is no purpose.

Yes, when we ask the question *who am I?* inevitably follows the question *why am I?*, Just as after inhalation, exhalation follows, or when one foot moves forward while walking, the other foot follows suit. In the same way, after the *who*, the *why* follows inevitably.

Skipping a discussion on this second question and moving on to the next Sūtra feels unjust. See, purpose exists only for things that have a beginning and will have an end—anything subject to the law of change. Change implies the constant death of each moment, followed by the birth of a new moment. Just like your body undergoes changes; every second it is dying and being reborn. Over two and half million cells are dying and being reborn per second. So, all these changes are for a purpose, there is something to be achieved. It exists for a purpose. The moment the purpose is fulfilled, they become nonexistent. Their end comes.

Because if there is no end, and the purpose is fulfilled, then existence becomes futile. Therefore, only temporary, transient things have a purpose. They exist for a reason. They are means to an end. They exist to fulfil something. The moment that is fulfilled, they cease to exist. But consciousness is eternal. It neither had a beginning nor will it have an end. Therefore, it has no purpose.

And because you are consciousness, you also have no purpose. This understanding can also be approached differently.

The question: why *am I?*, when elaborated becomes: *what is the cause of my existence?* In this material world that we experience, everything that happens has a cause, and each happening becomes the cause of some event or the other. It is the law of cause and effect that we are so used to. However, upon deeper reflection, we come to realise that cause cannot exist without time and space.

Suppose something happens. Suppose a king cobra bites me and I die. Between the bite and my death, a chain of cause and effect will form. The first link in the chain of causes will be the cause of my death. The most common causes in such incidents are asphyxia and heart attacks. What was the chain of events that led to a heart attack? The freezing and paralysis of cardiac muscles over time. And paralysis in the diaphragm muscle (the one responsible for breathing) will be the cause of suffocation. What caused this paralysis? The neurotoxic venom of the king cobra. A neurotoxin is a substance that alters the structure or function of the nervous system. King cobra venom is neurotoxic. This causes nerve processes to shut down at the synapse level. This in turn causes paralysis of all the muscles including the diaphragm muscle and the heart muscle. Because messages from the brain were unable to reach. And what has to be the cause, the mechanism through which this neurotoxic venom enters the body? Cobra fangs, right. It was all a matter of cause and effect.

Getting bitten by a cobra *causes* Venom to be injected *causes* Neurotoxin present in the venom to enter, and began altering with the nerve processes *causes* Nervous system to shut down, and the contact to be broken *causes* Paralysis in the entire body, including the heart and the diaphragm *causes* Asphyxia and Heart attack *causes* Death.

In this material world, everything follows the same pattern. One thing causes another thing to happen which in turn becomes the cause of a third thing, and so on *ad infinitum*. We all are swimming in the huge ocean of cause and effect. However, consciousness, our real Self, is untouched by this law. Because it stays always in the absolute plane of existence, beyond time and space. Something can cause another thing only because there is time flowing from present to future. For instance, once the cobra fang penetrates the skin, it takes about fifteen minutes for me to collapse. A cause leads to an effect only because something known as time is present. Cobra bite and death cannot happen at the same moment. So when we say that there is a cause behind something, say *x*, we are taking for granted that time existed before *x* happened. Getting it?

But here, *x* equals consciousness, and it exists outside time and space. Consciousness never happened; past tense doesn't apply to consciousness. It has no beginning, and it is endless because it is consciousness that creates time and space. Thus, there cannot be a cause of consciousness, as a necessary ingredient (time) is missing, without which cause and effect cannot work.

So, what is your purpose? Why do you exist? There is no reason for it. This existence is purposeless. It is just a play, a drama. That's why it is called a *līlā* (play). I am not making this up; in the ninth Sūtra of the third volume of *Śiva Sūtras*, Śiva has said, "The Self is like an actor on the world stage. He is unaffected by the parts he plays." And the sole purpose of a play, a drama, is enjoyment. If you do not find joy in the play, if you are not entertained by watching a drama, if you do not enjoy it, then it is futile.

When you do not enjoy it, that's when the question arises in your mind: why am I here, what is my purpose? Notice that. When you are unhappy, when you start taking life seriously, when you start fearing the situations of life... That's when this question comes to mind: why, after all, why is all this happening, why did God create me, why was I born? This question does not arise in moments of happiness. When you are extremely happy in life, enjoying this play, experiencing joy, being in harmony with everything. Then this question does not arise in the mind because the purpose is right there; hence, the question does not arise. The purpose is to be happy, to enjoy this life, to be joyful, to dance, sing, live fully.

Then, this question will never arise in your mind because that is the answer to this question.

आनन्दो ब्रह्मेति व्यजानात् ।
आनन्दाध्येव खल्विमानि भूतानि जायन्ते ।
आनन्देन जातानि जीवन्ति ।
आनन्दं प्रयन्त्यभिसंविशन्तीति ॥ १ ॥

ānando brahmeti vyajānāt |
ānandādhyeva khalvimāni bhūtāni jāyante |
ānandena jātāni jīvanti |
ānandaṃ prayantyabhisaṃviśantīti || १ ||

That Joy was Brahman, he realised.
From Joy, indeed, are these beings verily born;
By Joy, when born, do they live;
Into Joy do they, when departing, enter.

(*Taittirīya Upaniṣad* III.2.6.1)

This concludes our study of Sūtra One.

CHAPTER TWO

ज्ञानं बंधः ॥२॥

|| JÑĀNAṀ BANDHAḤ ||2||

Knowledge is bondage.

Śiva, the God of Gods, has ingeniously crafted this Sūtra. It has two Sanskrit words: *jñāna*, meaning knowledge, and *bandhu*, which translates to bondage or entanglement—a state of being restricted, tied, or bound. The Sūtra literally translates to 'knowledge is bondage,' 'knowledge is what binds us'. This perspective seems peculiar because the entirety of Eastern philosophy, tradition, and scriptures assert that knowledge is liberation and ignorance is bondage. Yet, Śiva says otherwise. Why?

Indeed, it is ignorance that binds us. And Śiva has repeatedly emphasised this in his teachings. In the *Pūrva Śāstra* (*Mālinivijaya Tantra*), Śiva says that *malas* or impurities are simply ignorance (*malamajñānamicchanti*), causing the seeds of the world to sprout (*saṁsārāṁgkurakāraṇam*). This world of differentiated perception sprouts due to *ajñāna* (ignorance). The *Sarvacāra Tantra* echoes the same sentiment, *ajñānādbadhyate lokastataḥ sṛṣṭiśca saṁhṛtiḥ*, that people are bound by *ajñāna* (ignorance), and it is this ignorance that perpetuates the cycle of birth and death. So, why does Śiva seemingly contradict himself by saying that knowledge is the cause of bondage?

It is Śiva's way, his style! This is a Sūtra, Sūtras are meant to be short. So Śiva has artfully concealed the vast knowledge of scriptures within these concise combinations of letters. He not only unveils ignorance as the root cause of bondage but also reveals what ignorance is in reality, its true nature. Allow me to elucidate.

In the tradition, we read these *Śiva Sūtras* together, much like singing a song. During my early days as a seeker, each morning, I would recite these Sūtras poetically, somewhat in this manner: "*chaitanyamaatmaa 'jnaanambandhah 'yonivargahkalashareeram...*" This is the correct way of reciting them. By adhering to this method, the final ā sound of *chaitanyamātmā*, pronounced like double *a* (*aa*) as the *a* in *art*, acts as a prefix to the word *jñānaṁ*. It joins with *jñānaṁ*, transforming the second Sūtra from *jñānaṁ bandhaḥ* to *ajñānaṁ bandhaḥ*.

In Sanskrit, the prefix *a-* changes the word's meaning to its opposite, much like the *un-* prefix in English. Thus, *jñānaṁ*, meaning knowledge, changes to *ajñānaṁ*, meaning ignorance.
This lays bare the correct understanding of this Sūtra—that ignorance is undeniably the shackle that binds us, as asserted in both *Mālinivijaya* and *Sarvacāra*. First, understand this entirely. What is liberation? What does freedom mean? Discard any preconceived belief you may have about liberation. It has naught to do with transcending to some heavenly realm like *Goloka* or *Jannat* after death. Liberation has a singular meaning, succinctly put by Abhinavagupta:

मोक्षो हि नाम नैवान्यः स्वरूपप्रथनं हि तत् ।

Mokṣo hi nāma naivānyaḥ svarūpaprathanam hi tat |

Mokṣa or liberation is nothing else but the knowledge, the awareness of one's true nature.

To know oneself is liberation, and to not know oneself is bondage. Self-awareness itself is liberation. In the preceding chapter, I clarified that consciousness is liberation. When you become conscious or recognize your true Self as consciousness, you lose all identifications; you become totally free. Conversely, if you remain unconscious and unaware of your true self, then you will identify yourself with a limited entity, resulting in bondage. Consciousness is knowledge, and unconsciousness is ignorance.

What follows the realisation of the self? An individual undergoes a complete transformation, and the entire world transforms along with him. *Yathā dṛṣṭi tathā śṛṣṭi*—The world appears to us as we perceive it. It does not change into something else, nor does the Self transform into Śiva. Instead, we start seeing the truth that was always before us, yet unnoticed.

I will share a childhood anecdote as an illustration. Once, when I started sleeping alone in my room, an incident occurred. Late at night, feeling thirsty in the pitch-dark room, I heard what seemed like footsteps or sandals scraping on the floor outside my locked door. Frightened, I thought someone was waiting for me to come out. The fear persisted until morning, when the sun's rays streamed through the window, revealing that the large paper I had painted on and stuck to the wall with tape had fallen and was being swayed by the fan's breeze, causing the scraping noise. This experience completely transformed me, dispelling all fear and ignorance within me.

Liberation is similar to this experience—it dawns when the rising sun of awareness illuminates our understanding. It is like realising that what you believed to be a snake was, but a rope. This understanding cannot be conveyed by others; it must be experienced firsthand.

Now, Śiva has cleverly revealed the nature of ignorance in this Sūtra. To a layman, the Sūtra reads, *jñānaṁ bandhaḥ*. It should be read together with *caitanyamātmā* so that the *a* sound is added at the beginning, transforming the second Sūtra from '*jñānaṁ bandhaḥ*' to '*ajñānaṁ bandhaḥ*.' However, Śiva has intentionally kept it unclear. Therefore, out of ignorance and under the influence of Śiva's veiling power, we separate it and create a distinction between the two Sūtras.

However, separating it from the previous Sūtra makes it incomplete. By separating *jñānaṁ* (knowledge) from the *a* sound of the previous Sūtra, *jñānaṁ* (knowledge) remains incorrect and incomplete. This incomplete *jñānam* (knowledge) consequently leads to bondage. Similar to our existence in the real world where we are inherently one with Śiva, our own veiling power causes us to forget this oneness and perceive ourselves as separate from Śiva. We find ourselves perceiving, feeling, and understanding that we are distinct from Śiva, resulting in a sense of incompleteness. This understanding is incorrect and incomplete, and thus bondage.

It is indeed true that knowledge is the cause of bondage, but only the knowledge which creates a feeling of incompleteness. Just as in this Sūtra, knowledge is incomplete, similarly, the knowledge that instills in us a sense of incompleteness becomes the source of bondage. The belief that something is lacking within us, that there exists something beyond us or separate from us that can fulfil us, is a fundamental delusion, and such knowledge causes the seeds of the world to sprout. *Āṇava-mala*, they name it—the seed of bondage, sprouting from the soil of misguided understanding that we are incomplete within ourselves.

What is *mala*? I will elaborate on this in the upcoming chapter. For now, understand this much—*mala* means impurity. The purpose of these impurities is to hinder you, the individual soul, from becoming one with Śiva and instead, they keep you bound. Imagine gazing into a mirror that has gathered layers of dust and dirt, obstructing a clear view of your true reflection. You might mistakenly perceive these dust and haze layers as your reality. These layers of impurity are *malas*.

The deepest layer is the *āṇava-mala*—the belief in one's own incompleteness, the understanding that I am not whole within myself. This kind of knowledge is the seed of bondage. From this kind of knowledge, originates the shackles that confine us within the cycle of birth and death.

Śiva has purposely left this Sūtra incomplete to convey that, behold, incomplete knowledge is the root cause of bondage. He is saying that what we term as *ajñāna* (ignorance) is nothing else but incomplete and misguided *jñāna* (knowledge).

Now, believing that I am incomplete, within us arises a sense of duality, that there is something separate from me, and if I attain it, it will make me complete. This sense of duality is *māyā* (*māyīya-mala*). It has also been explained in this aphorism... how?

The first two Sūtras are meant to be read together, as one—*chaitanyamaatmaajnaanambandhah.* This is the correct way to read these Sūtras. Both of them should become one. Similarly, the correct way to live in the world is to become one with it, with a sense of non-duality. Live by making yourself one with the world. This is liberation, this is true knowledge.

If you create divisions between yourself and the world, between me and you, between mine and yours, it will become a bondage. Śiva is saying that the knowledge that you and I are separate, that everything is separate, is the cause of bondage. Just as if we read those two Sūtras separately, we are creating duality, and then, that *jñānaṁ* (knowledge) which arises from this duality, creates duality, and is bondage.

This perception of duality is *māyīya-mala*, the next layer of bondage, just after *āṇava-mala* which I have explained in the next chapter.

This Sūtra illustrates so skillfully what bondage is. Indeed, knowledge itself is bondage, and knowledge itself is liberation. What we term as ignorance is also knowledge. It's not that ignorance means a complete absence of knowledge—absolutely empty, devoid of knowing anything. In reality, such a state doesn't exist, but for the time being, let's assume that a stone is in such a state of complete ignorance. Or that fragment of iron buried somewhere within the earth is in ignorance. There is absolutely no knowledge within the stone and that iron; yet both are free from the world. They never have to experience birth and death. In fact, they are worshipped by sculpting them into a *Śivalingam* or an idol. Gods manifest within them. If ignorance were indeed the cause of the cycle of birth and death, as stated in *Mālinivijaya* and *Sarvacāra*, then even inert objects would be entangled in the cycle. Even the soil you tread upon and the book you are reading would experience this cycle. But that's not the case. And if ignorance is the cause of entanglement and knowledge is liberation, then why are you bound? It's not like you're completely ignorant. In fact, you are reading this book, gaining knowledge from scriptures, but still, you are not liberated. Still, you are entangled in the cycle of birth and death. So, how can ignorance be the cause of worldliness? Despite being in ignorance, the stone is not entangled in the world, while you, possessing knowledge, are still entangled by the cycle of worldly existence.

In reality, knowledge itself is the cause of bondage. Ignorance is also knowledge, but incorrect knowledge.

The same idea echoes in the writings of Abhinavagupta:

अज्ञानमिति न ज्ञानाभावश्चातिप्रसङ्गतः ।
स हि लोष्टादिकेऽप्यस्ति न च तस्यास्ति संसृतिः ॥

ajñānamiti na jñānābhāvaścātiprasaṅgataḥ |
sa hi loṣṭādike'pyasti na ca tasyāsti saṃsṛtiḥ ||

Ignorance is not merely absence of knowledge, because if it were then even a lifeless rock would have to be considered knowledgeable as it too does not have to move in the circle of birth and death.

And then he writes,

अतो ज्ञेयस्य तत्त्वस्य सामस्त्येनाप्रथात्मकम् ।
ज्ञानमेव तदज्ञानं शिवसूत्रेषु भाषितम् ॥

ato jñeyasya tattvasya sāmastyenāprathātmakam |
jñānameva tadajñānaṃ śivasūtreṣu bhāṣitam ||

In the Śiva *Sūtras* it is said that *jñāna* (knowledge) means that state of understanding in which what is to be known, what is worthy to be known is understood in its entirety, leaving no scope for any extension or expansion in the range of it. *Jñana* other than this has been characterised as *ajñāna*, ignorance.

(*Tantrāloka* I.25, 26)

Abhinavagupta also interprets the same meaning of this Sūtra of Śiva, that, *jñeyasya tattvasya*—knowing that which is worth knowing, leads to liberation. This knowledge is what liberates. And the knowledge worthy of knowing is Śiva, it is consciousness, and it is the Self. Because Śiva is your true Self. Recognize the self, and you will become free. '*Brahma veda brahmaiva bhavati*', He who knows Brahman becomes Brahman. However, worldly knowledge enslaves. Knowledge that convinces you of your incompleteness should be relinquished; it is a shackle. Knowledge that generates a sense of duality within you is a bondage. Such knowledge is poison and should be discarded as soon as possible. In conclusion, knowledge itself is bondage, and knowledge itself is liberation.

परामृतरसापायस्तस्य यः प्रत्ययोद्भवः ।
तेनास्वतन्त्रतामेति स च तन्मात्रगोचरः ॥

parāmṛtarasāpāyastasya yaḥ pratyayodbhavaḥ |
tenāsvatantratāmeti sa ca tanmātragocaraḥ ||

The rise, in the bound soul, of all sorts of ideas marks the disappearance of the bliss of supreme immortality. On account of this, he loses his independence. The appearance of the ideas has its sphere in sense-objects.

(*Spanda-Kārikās* III.14)

विद्या सा या विमुक्तये ॥

vidyā sā yā vimuktaye ||

True knowledge is that which gives Freedom.

(*Kulārnava Tantra* I.112)

Alternative Viewpoint

In my musings upon these Sūtras of Śiva, I often speak of a different interpretation of this particular Sūtra—one that I believe is worthy of being told. Neither Kṣemrāja nor any traditional commentator has approached this Sūtra in such a manner. As I forge ahead with my commentary on forthcoming Sūtras, I intend to interlace my personal interpretations with the traditional interpretations. In my view, these Sūtras resemble GPS coordinates or *what3words*, pinpointing locations within the terrain of your inner world—the geography of your consciousness. It is for you to embark and explore.

Contemplation will take you there. Contemplation is the hike to that specific location within your valley of consciousness. Upon arrival, you can embrace and understand the Sūtra firsthand. Through this commentary, I endeavour to verbalise what I see in those locations of the valley of my consciousness. Not the entirety, but rather the significant elements. Just as with geographic landscapes, even if the scenery remains one, each individual depicts it uniquely, highlighting what they find important and skipping the rest.

Kṣemarāja too gazed upon the same panorama that presently unfolds before me as I pen down this commentary. However, he described only a fragment of the scenery—that which held importance from his vantage point. Alongside Kṣemarāja's chosen focal points, I shall, with due deference, expound upon additional focal points that, from my perspective, hold value. These interpretations are born of my lived experiences and the insights bestowed upon me by my master, *Svacchaṃda Śiva*. Naturally, I will connect my interpretations to the scriptural evidence stemming from Śiva's utterances. Furthermore, I will reinforce these interpretations with a solid foundation of logic.

So, I was writing about a different interpretation of this specific verse. *Jñānaṁ bandhaḥ*—knowledge is bondage;

Once, a scholarly individual approached a Tāntrik master with the intention of learning Kashmir Śaivāgama. This individual, seemingly a university professor, made references to holding a doctorate in philosophy and extensively studying various Eastern philosophies. The Tāntrik master invited him to sit and began filling his cup with tea.

Throughout their conversation, the professor proudly highlighted his academic achievements and shared his half-baked theories and ideas about Śaivism. Concurrently, the Tāntrik master, in a deliberate manner, continued to pour tea at a measured pace. Eventually, the tea overflowed, spilling onto the table and then onto the professor's thighs and robes. Startled, the professor exclaimed, "What are you doing? Can't you see the cup is full? It won't take any more!"

The Tāntrik master looked at him with a smile and said, "Much like this cup, you are brimming with your own theories and opinions. Until you empty your mind, I cannot teach Śaivism to you."

Hinduism is not based on a single book; rather, it draws its foundation from a vast library of scriptures—Smṛtis, Śāstras, Sūtras, Tantras, Purāṇas, Itihāsa, Stotras, Subhāṣitas, along with their countless interpretations. It is like an unfathomable ocean, and becoming entangled within it is a simple trap to fall into. Śiva says,

परमार्थं न जानन्ति पशुपाशनियन्त्रिताः ॥
वेदशास्त्रार्णवे घोरे ताड्यमाना इतस्ततः ।
कालोर्मिग्राहग्रस्ताश्च तिष्ठन्ति हि कुतार्किकाः ॥

paramārthaṁ na jānanti paśupāśaniyantritāḥ ||
vedaśāstrārṇave ghore tāḍyamānā itastataḥ |
kālormigrāhagrastāśca tiṣṭhanti hi kutārkikāḥ |

Those who have plunged into the deep well of the philosophies, yet remain ensnared by the shackles of animal bondage, are incapable of reaching the ultimate zenith—Śiva. As they struggle within the depths of the ocean of Vedas and scriptures, they become entangled in the fierce currents and lurking crocodiles of fallacious reasoning and philosophical arguments.

(*Kulārnava Tantra* I.87, 88)

Whenever I explained the meanings of words like *māyā* or liberation in this book, I consistently emphasised that you must discard any preconceived notions accumulated from your prior readings or hearsay, as such beliefs may hinder your understanding. It is important that you keep your cup empty. The philosophy of Śiva is very different from any other system of philosophy. Here, you must be very open-minded, and you must leave behind whatever you have read or learned so far about spirituality. Otherwise, you may not understand it, and you'll doubt the authenticity of these teachings based on your limited knowledge, and then disagree with me. Even if you don't, you may interpret them incorrectly. And incorrect knowledge is bondage. As Śiva says,

अन्यथा परमं तत्त्वं जनाः क्लिश्यन्ति चान्यथा अन्यथा शास्त्रसद्भावो व्याख्यां कुर्वन्ति चान्यथा ॥

anyathā paramaṁ tatvaṁ janāḥ kliśyanti cānyathā anyathā śāstrasadbhāvo vyākhyāṁ kurvanti cānyathā ||

The real truth is one and what they understand is quite other; one is the purport of the Scriptures and the other is what they interpret.

(*Kulārnava Tantra* I.62)

I observe many individuals for whom knowledge has become enslavement. Firstly, there are those who are deeply attached to their scriptures and doctrines, entangled in the web of their beliefs. This attachment is fueled by their ego, making it unlikely for them to ever explore Śiva's teachings or attempt to understand them. Consequently, due to a lack of true knowledge, they remain forever enslaved. Such individuals are often fanatical in their devotion to their religion, whether it be Islam or Christianity. Even within the broader framework of *Sanātana Dharma*, there are numerous sects whose followers are bound by their knowledge. The majority belongs to the Vaiṣṇava sect, who consider only one scripture to be true and superior, feeding their ego—because their tradition is superior, their scripture is superior, so they become superior. In Hinduism, the Vaiṣṇava sect tends to be the most fanatical. This sentiment is echoed by Śiva in the *Parameśvara Āgama:*

वैष्णवाद्याः समस्तास्ते विद्यारागेण रञ्जिताः ।
न विन्दन्ति परं तत्त्वं सर्वज्ञज्ञानवर्जिताः ॥

Vaiṣṇavādyāḥ samastāste vidyārāgeṇa rañjitāḥ |
Na vindanti paraṁ tattvaṁ sarvajñajñānavarjitāḥ ||

All the Vaiṣṇavas, etc., are restricted by their attachment to (limited) knowledge. They fail to understand the nature of the supreme reality only because they are devoid of knowledge emerging from omniscience.

Abhinavagupta elaborates further in his *Tantrasāra*:

अहम्, अतो विश्वोत्तीर्णो विश्वात्मा च अहम् इति । स च अयं मायान्धानां न उत्पद्यते सत्तर्कादीनाम् अभावात् वैष्णवाद्या हि तावन्मात्र एव आगमे रागतत्त्वेन नियमिता इति न ऊर्ध्वदर्शनेऽपि तदुन्मुखतां भजन्ते, ततः सत्तर्कसुदागमसदुरूप दइशद्वेषिण एवं ।

Aham, ato viśvottīrṇo viśvātmā ca aham iti | *sa ca ayam māyāndhānāṁ na utpadyate sattarkādīnām abhāvāt vaiṣṇavādyā hi tāvanmātra eva āgame rāgatattvena niyamitā iti na ūrdhvadarśane lapi tadunmukhatāṁ bhajante, tataḥ sattarkasudāgamasadurūpa daishadveṣiṇ evaṁ* |

"I am Śiva, I am both transcendent and immanent", this kind of conviction, however, does not arise in those blinded by *māyā*, because they lack right reasoning (*sat-tarka*), etc. Vaiṣṇavas and others are restricted to their own scriptures by the principle of attachment (*rága*). For this very reason, they show no interest in studying superior āgamas in spite of their being available. In this way, they show jealousy in regard to right reasoning, right scriptures (āgama), and the correct instruction of a teacher.

Any form of attachment is an illusion, and attachment is one of the five daughters of *māyā*. Some Vaiṣṇavites are deeply attached to their scriptures and beliefs. This attachment takes on the form of Envy. Their envy is so intense that they label the principles of *advaita* as a demonic philosophy, which, according to them, Śiva manifested on Earth to lead astray those with demonic tendencies. This, they argue, ensures that those with unholy inclinations stray, leaving only the virtuous to worship Viṣṇu. According to their perspective, Śiva is a rapist and is obviously inferior to Viṣṇu.
However, the masters of the Śaiva tradition do not criticise them; they remain indifferent because they understand that all of this is merely a play orchestrated by Śiva. As Bhaṭṭa Nārāyaṇa sings:

O Lord Śiva, You conceal the joy of the knowledge of oneness for those who are ignorant, and You reveal the joy of the knowledge of oneness for those who deserve. So, in both ways You create misunderstanding and You destroy misunderstanding.

(*Stava Chintāmaṇi* 72)

Slightly lower in the category are those who merely study the *Āgamic* scriptures but remain confined to studying alone. About them, Śiva remarks:

वेदागमपुराणज्ञः परमार्थं न वेत्ति यः।
विडम्बकस्य तस्यापि तत् सर्वं काकभाषितम्।। ८६ ।।
इदं ज्ञानमिदं ज्ञेयमिति चिन्तासमाकुलाः।
पठन्त्यहर्निशं देवि परतत्त्वपराङ्खाः ।। ६० ।।
वाक्यच्छन्दोनिबन्धेन काव्यालङ्कारशोभिना ।
चिन्तया दुःखिता मूढास्तिष्ठन्ति व्याकुलेन्द्रियाः ।। ६१।।

vedāgamapurāṇajñaḥ paramārthaṁ na vetti yaḥ /
viḍambakasya tasyāpi tat sarvaṁ kākabhāṣitam // 89 //

idaṁ jñānamidaṁ jñeyamiti cintāsamākulāḥ |
paṭhantyaharniśaṁ devi paratatvaparāṅmukhāḥ || 60 ||
vākyacchandonibandhena kāvyālaṅkāraśobhinā |
cintayā duḥkhitā mūḍhāstiṣṭhanti vyākulendriyāḥ || 61 ||

Those who have read the Vedas, Āgamas, and Purānas, yet know nothing of the truth of truth—Śiva, the ultimate zenith—are charlatans, their talks mere echoes of crows. With their backs turned on the worthy of being known, they incessantly mull over volumes of books, anxiously saying 'this is to be known', 'this is knowledge' and so on. Embellished with such knowledge of style, syntax, poetry and rhetorical ornaments of the senses and sound, these fools stand confused and fretful.

कथयन्त्युन्मनीभावं स्वयं नानुभवन्ति हि ।
अहङ्कारहताः केचिदुपदेशविवर्जिताः ।। ६३ ।।
पठन्ति वेदशास्त्राणि विवदन्ति परस्परम् ।
न जानन्ति परं तत्त्वं दव पाकरसं यथा ।। ६४ ।।

kathayantyunmanībhāvaṁ svayaṁ nānubhavanti hi |
ahaṅkārahataḥ kecidupadeśavivarjitāḥ || 63 ||
paṭhanti vedaśāstrāṇi vivadanti parasparam |
na jānanti paraṁ tattvaṁ dava pākarasaṁ yathā || 64 ||

They speak of egoless consciousness (*unmanī-avasthā*) but do not experience this state. Some are the victims of Egoism, and some remain deprived of instructions. They chant the Vedas and dispute among themselves but like the spoon that does not know the taste of the honey it holds, they know not the Truth.

(*Kulārnava Tantra* I.89-94)

They cannot achieve liberation because of their pride in knowledge. Reciting verses from scriptures alone does not lead to liberation, as true as the knowledge in them may be. The question remains: do you possess the capability to truly understand this knowledge? Your interpretation is inevitably influenced by your limited understanding. Much like milk poured into a vessel tainted by impurities will spoil, so too will the knowledge from scriptures in an impure mind.

A person was brought to the royal court on charges of murder. When the king asked if he had anything to say in his defence, the person responded, 'Your Majesty, I have committed no crime. I am a Hindu, and I follow the teachings of my scriptures. In my holy book, my God has said, "He who believes himself to be either the murderer or the murdered lacks understanding. One who is in knowledge knows that the Self is incapable of committing murder or falling victim to it."

Instead of attaining liberation through Śiva's knowledge, such people tend to entangle themselves further. They possess the remarkable skill of making everything a tool for strengthening their own bondage. They speak grandly, reciting verses from scriptures, but their words are as fragile as glass; they echo like a parrot, unaware of the true meaning behind their expressions.

I recall a parrot in my home to which I taught the full form of the acronym BODMAS in arithmetic. It would chant it like a poem, 'brackets and order first, then division, multiplication, addition, and subtraction!' However, just like that parrot never applied the rule of BODMAS, never experienced it practically, and had no inkling of its depth, similarly, these individuals bound by knowledge are. They can lecture on the essence of water, but they remain thirsty for lifetimes and die of dehydration. Their discourse is dry, and their knowledge only inflates their ego, strengthening their illusion and distancing them from the truth.

But, if you were to point this out to them, they wouldn't accept it because they not only deceive the world but also themselves. Eighty percent of those who embark on a spiritual journey end up as frauds. They cloak their ignorance in the beautiful attire of verses and quotes borrowed from books, not truly their own. In their arrogance, they harm themselves, and not only do they not stop there, but they also start imparting knowledge to others; thus, the blind leading the blind, both fall into the ditch.

अविद्यायामन्तरे वर्तमानाः स्वयं धीराः पण्डितम्मन्यमानाः ।
दन्द्रम्यमाणाः परियन्ति मूढा अन्धेनैव नीयमाना यथान्धाः ॥

avidyāyāmantre vartamānāḥ svayaṃ dhīrāḥ paṇḍitammanyamānāḥ |
dandamyamāṇāḥ pariyanti mūḍhā andhenev nīyamānā yathāndhāḥ ||

Fools dwelling in darkness, wise in their own conceit, and puffed up with vain knowledge, go round and round staggering to and fro, like blind men led by the blind.

(*Kathā Upaniṣad* I.2.5)

The world is filled with such people. Every other person wants to impart knowledge, every beggar wants to donate millions! Just as these beggars are ridiculous, so are these teachers.

However, they don't stop either; instead, they begin to exploit people. I have encountered individuals appearing to be mystics who lure girls by weaving deceptive narratives about *Śiva-Śakti.* They recite some verses claiming that sexual union is a form of worship, luring innocent girls into trusting them. They then misuse this trust to exploit them sexually and lead them astray.

Just like a vulture. A vulture soars high in the sky, but its gaze is always fixed below, on the scattered remains of flesh. Similarly, these people speak lofty words about God and truth, yet their focus is always on fulfilling bodily desires—on sex and wealth.

These cerebral simpletons need to let go of their delusion that they know everything, and obviously, this is very difficult for them. They have spent their entire lives accumulating knowledge in vain, ruining their lives chasing this futile knowledge. How can they let it go? Therefore they fight for it, argue with you, but it's obvious that all their examples are like parrots'. So, there's no point in saying anything good or bad to them—just pray for them because the prisoner doesn't want to be free! What could be more tragic than this?

The first principle is not to fool yourself—and you are the easiest person to fool. Avoid overestimating your wisdom; if you were truly wise, you wouldn't find yourself in need of reading this book.

The ones who rank at the bottom of this category are those Hindus who portray themselves as devout believers on social media. They participate in grand processions on *Rāma Navamī*, waving large saffron flags, and create videos at Kedāranātha to appear trendy on social media. However, ask them to name any ten *Upaniṣads* or Tantras, and their mouths will remain shut. Spiritual realisation is a distant concept for them; they lack even basic theoretical knowledge.

This issue is particularly prevalent among Hindus. Every Hindu considers themselves an expert in their faith, convinced they know everything about their *Dharma*, and believing what they know to be the ultimate truth. However, it's likely that the vast majority haven't even read the *Bhagavad Gītā* in its entirety, let alone delving into the depths of *Upaniṣads* or Tantrik scriptures. May Śiva illuminate their minds.

There is another category of people who are cursed with knowledge. Two friends went into an orchard. One of them had accumulated a plethora of useless knowledge: let's say he had recently enrolled in the study of engineering at college. He immediately began counting the mango trees there; he counted the sacks and then counted each tree individually, then counted the fruits, so that an estimate could be made of the total value of the entire garden. Meanwhile, his companion made friends with the owner of the garden, silently climbed a tree, and started enjoying eating mangoes.

So, who among them will you consider wiser? Eat mangoes! This will satisfy your hunger. What is the point in counting the trees and leaves? In the same vein, nowadays, intellectually foolish individuals spend their lives chasing after *why* and *how*. They argue about whether God exists or not, which god is superior, which religion is supreme, and so on. However, in reality, the wise are those who befriend that God and find contentment in that ultimate bliss.

Another thing is that to say that Śiva does not exist, questioning His existence in itself, proves His existence. Abhinavagupta writes,

सर्वापह्नवहेवाक-धर्माप्येवं हि वर्तते।
ज्ञानमात्मार्थमित्येतन्नेति मां प्रति भासते॥
अपह्नुतौ साधने वा वस्तूनांआद्यमीदृशम्।
यत्तत्र के प्रमाणानामुपपत्त्युपयोगिते॥

Sarvāpahnavahevākadharmāpyevaṁ hi vartate |
Jñānamātmārthamityetanneti māṁ prati bhāsate ||
Apahnutau sādhane vā vastūnāṁādyamīdṛśam |
Yattatra ke pramāṇānamupapattyupayogite ||

Even if you hold the belief in the non-existence of the supreme reality, and even if you preach a perspective such as, 'Śiva does not exist; consciousness does not exist. I do not believe in their existence,' the very same 'I' persists even amidst such negation. This 'I' is once again Śiva. Therefore, through the negation of all that emanates from Him, through the negation of Śiva himself, you inadvertently prove His existence.

(*Tantrāloka* I.56, 57)

Śiva stands as primordial. He is established as the foundation, the underpinning upon which the intellect rests—whether the intellect engages in negation or affirmation of things, it finds its footing in him. Therefore, proofs are useless in either refuting or acknowledging his existence.

We are not attempting to prove the existence of Śiva here; his existence is self-evident. You exist, you are conscious—this is His evidence. In the previous chapter, we discussed that the innermost Self of everything sentient or insentient, is Śiva. Not only of objective existents but also of imaginative entities that

have no existence in the external world. Whether you imagine a bird whose head is like that of a human or any other fanciful creation, its innermost Self is still Śiva. Because Śiva is the background of everything. Without a knower, the known cannot exist. Both of them are one and the same. If you are experiencing something, if something exists in your experience, it is proof that an experiencer exists. In the upcoming chapters, my sole purpose is for you to realise this experience, to know Him, and to become one with this Śiva completely. Consume that mango, the nectar of wisdom, and then throw away this book as it will serve no purpose afterward.
Śiva says,

अभ्यस्य सर्वशास्त्राणि तत्त्वं ज्ञात्वा हि बुद्धिमान् ।
पलालमिव धान्यार्थी सर्वशास्त्रं परित्यजेत् ॥

abhyasya sarvaśāstrāṇi tattvaṁ jñātvā hi buddhimān |
palālamiva dhānyārthī sarvaśāstraṁ parityajet ||

(*Kulārnava Tantra* I.103)

Practising all the scriptures and knowing their essential Truth the intelligent should leave them like the one seeking grains leaves the husk aside.

Anything besides this realisation is futile. Speaking about Śiva is futile because nothing definitive can be said about them. Whatever you say, the opposite is also true. He is neither dual nor non-dual, neither formless nor with form, neither He or She, because He is both and beyond both. He can only be experienced.

He is known by those who know Him beyond thought, not to those who imagine He can be attained by thought. (*Kena Upaniṣad* II)

Thoughts are limitless. We can think anything. We can imagine crow's milk, we can imagine boys getting pregnant. In our imagination, we can even go inside the black hole. The scope of imagination is vast, yet beyond this imagination, beyond this thought, lies the Śiva. He cannot be understood through intellectual knowledge; instead, intellectual knowledge acts as a hindrance in understanding Him. Therefore, let us use it for dispelling doubts, entering a meditative state, and thereafter abandon it.

The misconception that I am incomplete—this ignorance can only be dispelled through direct experience. I often hear from many of you that you watch my videos, read my books, but then find yourselves caught in the same illusion. And it reminds me of the tale of the bewildered stag.

Once, a majestic stag and a hare stopped by a pond to quench their thirst. As the stag bent down, it caught a glimpse of its reflection in the water, "Behold my muscular body," it proudly said to the hare, "one that can rival even the mightiest of lions." "Witness my magnificent antlers," it continued, "a single thrust of my horns is enough to scatter the entire pride of lions." Just then, they heard the barking of a hunting dog approaching from afar, and as swift as it could, the stag fled.

After the danger subsided, the hare inquired, "If you could defeat even a lion, why did you flee at the mere sound of a dog?" Bowing its head, the stag replied, "Oh dear hare, I know I am strong, but when I hear their barks, I just... can't control myself."

Some of you are like that stag; you know that you are the children of immortal bliss, you know that you are complete, and you understand that all of this is an illusion—a creation of your own making. Yet, you find yourself entangled because you are accumulating mere bookish knowledge to appease your ego, feigning omniscience to console your mind. You refuse to experience reality for yourself because you dwell in the delusion that you already know everything, and when the time comes, you forget everything and make a run.

There's only one way to break free from this entanglement—direct experience. An experience so intense that it shatters this illusion to its core. This is called *Śaktipāt*. This is what *Nirvāṇa* is. This is liberation.

There is also a third category of people who are ensnared by knowledge; I liken them to *Buridan's donkey*. In philosophy, there exists a concept known as Buridan's donkey. It is a hypothetical donkey that is hungry and positioned equidistantly between two equally enticing sources of food. This donkey, unable to arrive at a rational decision due to the balanced allure of both options, becomes paralyzed in that spot and eventually dies of starvation. It remains incapable of deciding which direction to move towards, as it cannot choose one source over the other.

I receive messages and emails from practitioners every day who seem as perplexed as this donkey. They struggle to decide whether they should make Śiva their chosen deity or Kṛṣṇa. They grapple with the choice of following the path of non-duality or duality. When they focus on Śiva in meditation, self-doubt creeps in, questioning if this is the right path for them. Perhaps devotion to Kṛṣṇa would bring more joy. Conversely, while chanting *Hare Kṛṣṇa*, they feel a pull towards Śiva.

These seekers become entangled in various books and diverse philosophies, finding themselves in a state of confusion. They discover contradictory statements in two different scriptures, and spiritually enlightened beings seem to express opposing views. It becomes challenging for them to decide what to pursue, which path to choose. This confusion also stems from their own knowledge. They need to seek a guru, select one person and one path to progress further. As Śiva states,

नाश्रामाः कारणं मुक्तेर्दर्शनानि न कारणम्।
तथैव सर्वशास्त्राणि ज्ञानमेव हि कारणम् ॥
मुक्तिदा गुरुवागेका विद्याः सर्वा विडम्बकाः ।
काष्ठभारश्रमादस्मादेकं सञ्जीवनं परम् ॥

nāśrāmāḥ kāraṇaṁ mukterdarśanāni na kāraṇam |
tathaiva sarvaśāstrāṇi jñānameva hi kāraṇam ||
muktidā guruvāgekā vidyāḥ sarvā viḍambakāḥ |
kāṣṭhabhāraśramādasmādekam sañjīvanaṁ param ||

Neither *Asramas* (four stages of life) nor philosophies or Sciences can provide the means for liberation; only the *Jñana* of all the Śastras can give it. And this *Jñana* can be received through the words of a *Guru*. All other ways are deceptive, oppressive; the knowledge of Truth alone is life-giving.

(*Kulārnava Tantra* I.107)

In recent years, a slew of new spiritual gurus have emerged in the market, claiming that they do not adhere to any particular school of thought, traditional philosophy, or subscribe to any specific ideology. They assert that their "whole work is to confuse you", urging individuals not to believe in any teachings, encouraging them to embark on their own search, to be seekers rather than believers.

This advice, however, is profoundly toxic. Followers of such individuals seldom attain enlightenment. While their words may sound reasonable, it is essential to scrutinise how many people, after listening to them, actually attain spiritual realisation. These gurus do not follow a *guru-disciple* tradition, and they aim to impress followers of every faith, hence their rhetoric. However, the consequence of this is often borne by those who heed their words.

Faith is important. The German physicist Max Planck, whose discovery of energy quanta earned him the Nobel Prize in Physics, famously said, "Anybody who has been seriously engaged in scientific work of any kind realises that over the entrance to the gates of the temple of science are written the words: Ye must have faith."

Even for a sceptic, faith is necessary because without faith in something, giving it your hundred percent becomes impossible. If you lack faith in what I am trying to teach, you won't be able to wholeheartedly follow it, and any task done half-heartedly cannot lead to success. Your lack of success will then convince you that I was wrong.

Consider this scenario: you are trekking to Kedāranātha, but you doubt the existence of a temple like Kedāranātha or the accuracy of the path you were given. The trek is arduous, a ten-mile climb against gravity. In such a situation, you may give up halfway because Kedāranātha is not visible. Your mind will flood you with doubts, suggesting that you were misled. Up to that point, you were already battling physical exhaustion to continue the climb. Now, you have to combat both your body and mind, and it's evident that you will lose. And then, you will tell everyone that my doubt turned out to be true—there is no temple, and the climb was in vain… Giving up halfway, how could you reach there?

Sometimes, we search for something, combing through every room of the house, but fail to locate it. Then, someone suggests checking the table, even though we've already searched there without success. However, upon revisiting and looking again, we manage to find it. So what's the difference between before and now? It's the faith in their words. You must have faith in a guru, a philosophy, an ideal, and then steadfastly follow it until you reach your destination.

Swāmī Vivekānanda used the metaphor of oysters to illustrate this concept. He wrote,

> "There is a pretty Indian fable to the effect that if it rains when the star *Swāti* is in the ascendant, and a drop of rain falls into an oyster, that drop becomes a pearl. The oysters know this, so they come to the surface when that star shines, and wait to catch the precious raindrop. When a drop falls into them, quickly the oysters close their shells and dive down to the bottom of the sea, there to patiently develop the drop into the pearl. We should be like that. First hear, then understand, and then, leaving all distractions, shut your minds to outside influences, and devote yourselves to developing the truth within you. There is the danger of frittering away your energies by taking up an idea only for its novelty, and then giving it up for another that is newer.
>
> Take one thing up and do it, and see the end of it, and before you have seen the end, do not give it up. He who can become mad with an idea, he alone sees light. Those that only take a nibble here and

a nibble there will never attain anything. They may titillate their nerves for a moment, but there it will end. They will be slaves in the hands of nature, and will never get beyond the senses."

Therefore, if, my dear friend, you aspire to glean insights from this book, a yearning for personal transformation stirring within, you must have faith in me. Cast aside all preconceptions—whatever ideas you've accumulated, whatever echoes have reached your ears—and engage with this book in a state of uncluttered receptivity. Will you grant me your trust as I guide you to truth, holding your hand throughout the journey?

This concludes our study of Sūtra Two.

This Sūtra elucidates the concept of bondage more comprehensively. In the previous chapter, we learned that incomplete knowledge is what creates the illusion of incompleteness within you (*āṇava-mala*), and it is a form of bondage. This Sūtra further expounds on that bondage, revealing that such knowledge manifests itself in two forms—*māyīya-mala* and the *karma-mala*.

First, let me explain the meaning of the word *mala*, and then we will proceed further. In the Sanskrit language, *mala* translates to dirt or waste product; impurities. In the Āyurvedic text *Aṣṭāṅga-hṛdaya-saṃhitā*, the term *mala* is used for waste products—urine and faeces, mucus, earwax, phlegm, sweat, and so on.

All the impurities that the body expels are considered *mala*. Similarly, there are three impurities of your true self, which I will now elucidate. It is essential to eliminate these impurities to attain the purest state of being.

You can also understand it this way: you are looking at a mirror, but layers of dirt and dust have accumulated on it, preventing you from seeing yourself clearly. Everything appears blurry and dirty to you—just filth. And you mistakenly identify that dirty and blurry reflection as your true Self.

The dirt, and dust, and grime that have settled on the surface of the mirror—this is *mala*. Three layers of impurities have settled on the mirror. You must clean these layers of dirt, one by one, so that you can perceive your true beauty, so that you can know your true Self.

However, these malas are not separate from you. We use the term *impurities* only to comprehend them, but they are not impurities in the conventional sense of the word. Impurity is what renders a pure thing impure, something distinct from the pure thing, like the mirror and the settled dirt on it are distinct. However, nothing is distinct or separate from you. Therefore, a more accurate way to perceive malas is as distorted perceptions. Śiva covers His eyes with His hands so as not to see the complete truth—you cover your eyes with your hands and then lament about the darkness. This is the reality of your bondage.

So, there are three *malas*: *āṇava-mala, māyīya-mala,* and *karma-mala. āṇava-mala* was explained in the previous chapter. This chapter focuses on *māyīya-mala* and *karma-mala.* I will explain them thoroughly in a few minutes. In the interim, to avoid confusion, here's a concise definition of the three malas.

I. *Āṇava-mala*—The deepest and most fundamental layer. *āṇava-mala* is the root of all three. It is the belief that something is lacking within us, that there exists something beyond us or separate from us that can fulfil us.

II. *Māyīya-mala*—The layer above *āṇava-mala*, *māyīya-mala* is the diplopia that makes us perceive duality, creating the illusion that I and the world are separate. This *mala* creates the deceptive appearance of multiplicity.

III. *Karma-mala*—The outermost layer. *Karma* translates to actions. When actions are motivated by attachment or aversion, they create entanglements, leaving imprints in the mind that reinforce the illusion of duality and incompleteness, and lead to rebirth.

Āṇava-mala expands into *māyīya-mala*, which, in turn, expands into *karma-mala*. This progression extends into various superficial entanglements in our lives. Therefore, *karma-mala* cannot exist without *māyīya-mala*, and *māyīya-mala* cannot exist without *āṇava-mala*.

Now, we will comprehensively explore these three malas, starting from the start. It happened when there was nothing; Śiva was. He was nothing. He was the void. Within this void, lay the infinite universe. All the potential of existence slumbered within this nothingness, for only nothingness can be infinite. The very nature of somethingness implies finitude. The infinite expanse of life, with all its boundless possibilities and vast horizons, cannot be realised or manifested from within the finite bounds of somethingness. Nay, it is only in the void of nothingness, wherein lies the potential.

Śiva is not a person; not the figure you see in the calendar. He is nobody or rather, no-bodiness. Śiva is not a thing; he is nothing or, even more accurately, no-thingness. Nothingness with the seeds of creativity. Yes, within this emptiness, there existed creativity. This creativity was his energy, his Śakti. Creativity is the department of feminine. Therefore, this emptiness can be depicted as the embodiment of both the masculine and feminine, half-man and half-woman, *ardhanārīśvara*. In the emptiness, Śiva and Śakti existed as one in an ecstatic and never-ending cosmic embrace.

In the realm of imagination, we envision them as half man and half woman. But the truth is that even half of infinity is still infinte, half of nothingness is still nothingness. 0 divided by two will remain 0. In reality, Śiva and Śakti are both wholly man and wholly woman. To be more precise, Śiva and Śakti are not two separate entities, but one and the same, indivisible and inseparable. The supposed division between them is a mere fabrication of our own minds, a delusion born from the limitations of our understanding. As Abhinavagupta clarified in the very first chapter of *Tantrāloka:*

शक्तिश्च नाम भावस्य स्वं रूपं मातृकल्पितम्।
तेनाद्वयः स एवापि शक्तिमत्परिकल्पने॥

śaktiśca nāma bhāvasya svaṁ rūpaṁ mātṛkalpitam |
Tenādvayaḥ sa evāpi śaktimatparikalpane ||

She, whose name is Śakti, is in fact the quintessential essence, the heart of Śiva . The disparity between the two is merely a product of the cognitive distinctions, the intellectual perceptions of the observers, as in reality, no actual distinction exists. For Śiva, the possessor and wielder of his beloved Śakti, and She are truly one and the same.

(*Tantrāloka* I.68)

The analogy of fire can illuminate your understanding of this idea. Fire has the power to emit both heat and light, two seemingly distinct energies that are intimately intertwined with the essence of fire. The energy of heat, and the energy of light cannot exist without fire, and fire cannot exist without the energy of heat and light. Just as fire cannot be separated from its thermal energy (of heat and light), it is impossible to separate Śiva from his energy. In fact, Śakti is the very being of Śiva and is inseparable from him. Just as heat and light are integral to the nature of fire, Śakti is integral to the nature of Śiva.

Now, fire possesses many subtle energies such as chemical energy, heat energy, internal energy, and others, all of which fall under the all-encompassing umbrella of thermal energy. Yet, they are all one with the fire and inseparable from its being. Similarly, Śiva possesses and wields countless energies like consciousness, ecstasy, will, knowledge, action, and more, yet all these energies are subsumed under his overarching energy of absolute freedom (*svātantrya-śakti*). In this way, just as the different energies in fire cannot be separated from its essence, Śiva's energies cannot be separated from his essential nature. To create distinctions between them would be both illogical and useless. It is impossible to conceive of Śiva without Śakti, or Śakti without Śiva. Such an exercise would be a futile intellectual gymnastic, devoid of logic or utility.

Śiva was complete. He lacked nothing, desired nothing, for he was all. The opposite of completeness is desire. Desire arises when we feel incomplete. When a void is created within us, we seek to fill it, and that is desire. For example, if you desire a person, it means that you feel incomplete within yourself. There is a void within you that you are trying to fill with the desire for that person. Desire is incompleteness. Therefore, desire and completeness cannot coexist, just as darkness and light cannot coexist. Darkness is simply the absence of light, and desire is simply the absence of completeness. Thus, desire cannot arise within that which is complete. It is impossible for desire to arise within completeness.

However, Śiva is omnipotent; there is nothing that is impossible for him. If something is impossible for you, it means you are not omnipotent. Omnipotent means having all powers within you. If there are things beyond your power, over which you have no authority, in such a case, you cannot be omnipotent. If you are unable to desire, if you don't have the power of will within you, you cannot be omnipotent.

Another point to consider is that the absence of desire within Śiva is also against non-duality. If there is no desire within him, it implies that the element of desire is separate from him. We acknowledge the existence of desire, and if this element is not present in Śiva, it suggests that it is distinct and separate from him, thereby implying that Śiva is not everything. This introduces duality and gives rise to the notion of multiplicity. If Śiva is considered only complete, then he cannot be incomplete; where would the element of incompleteness go then? Hence, this argument refutes the concept of non-duality.

The third point is that if the arising of desire within Śiva is impossible, it means that Śiva is not absolutely free. He is confined within certain limits, operating within defined boundaries that allows certain actions while prohibiting others. This contradicts freedom. Should Śiva be incapable of desire, it signifies a limitation, a bondage on his part. The impossibility of desire within him directly challenges his independence. We must remember that whatever we say about Śiva, the opposite is also true. Śiva is all-knowing, eternal, omnipresent, omnipotent, and complete. However, the contrary is also true. Śiva is not all-knowing, not eternal, not omnipresent, not omnipotent, and not complete.

Nothing is excluded from His being. In the *Kāmikā Tantra*, it is stated that Śiva is *sarvākriti*, possessing all formations of the world, and He is *nirākriti*, possessing no formation at all. Śiva is the most beautiful; one of His names is *Nitya-sundara*, meaning eternal beauty that never fades. However, Śiva is also the most fearsome; his *Kāla-Bhairava* form in the cremation ground starkly contrasts with his beauty. He is the embodiment of tranquillity, deep in meditation, yet engages in a fierce *tāṇḍava*, residing in the state of cosmic dance as *Natarāja*. Śiva is all-knowing; he understands the workings of every mind. Despite this omniscience, he remains the innocent and compassionate *Bholenātha* (the innocent God). He exists both transcendent and immanent simultaneously, encompassing the entire universe while also existing beyond it. He is everything and nothing at the same time. This is His freedom.

If someone were to ask me who Śiva is in a single sentence, I would say that He is the one who is absolutely free. Yes, the opposite is also true; He chose to bind Himself by becoming you and me. However, even His choice to enter into bondage reflects His inherent freedom. That's why in Tantras, the primary form attributed to Him, the one who created the Tantras, is called *Svacchaṃda Nāth*. *Svacchaṃda* means self-willed, spontaneous, completely independent—beyond all confinements and limitations. And if someone asks me what the world is in a single sentence, I would say that the world is Śiva's way of expressing His freedom.

So, Śiva conceived a desire, and from that desire emerged the seed of the universe. The expression of Śiva's inherent freedom was this desire, and desire creates the seed of the illusion of an existence outside of oneself. Śiva was in a state of completeness, and from within that completeness, a desire arose, and then he became incomplete. Now, to fulfil himself, he needs something. What he needs appears to be outside of him, not within. Because if it were within, he would be complete. So, in pursuit of completeness, he diverts his attention outward from within himself. In doing so, he brings this diverse universe into existence. Our consciousness of the universe is what brings it into existence. The universe appears to be outside of you, but it is not. It seems outside because you are experiencing incompleteness within yourself, and thus, you seek something outside of you that will make you complete. Therefore, you divert your consciousness outward, and the outward flow of consciousness creates the universe. I will elaborate on this in the fifth chapter. Desire serves as the seed of *āṇava-mala*, meaning incompleteness. Because if you harbour a desire for something, you are acknowledging that there is something you lack.

Thus far, it has been established that Śiva brought forth a desire as an expression of his absolute freedom. But what was the nature of this yearning? What did Śiva seek? It was a yearning to experience his own self, to taste the honeyed nectar, the bliss of his own being.

Suppose, if you will, that you had never viewed your own eyes, nor even seen their reflection. You are living in an era before the invention of mirrors. Yet all who lay eyes on you remark that none possess eyes as beautiful as yours. Your yearning to behold your own beauty would be inescapable, compelling you to peer into water or search for a reflective surface.

Similarly, Śiva was stirred by a yearning to taste the honey of his own nature, to experience the pure ecstasy that is himself. His very essence is ecstasy, and so he desires to taste the sweetness of his own nature. Sugar yearns to taste its own sweetness. As I see it, the grand creation, in all its myriad forms, is but an endeavour of sugar to savour its own sweetness.

Śiva savours his own ecstasy, his own glory by becoming mirror-like. In the tradition, there exists a beautiful analogy of a mirror.

दर्पणबिम्बे यद्वन् नगरग्रामादिचित्रमविभागि।
भाति विभागेनैव च परस्परं दर्पणादपि च ॥
विमलतमपरमभैरबोधात् तद्वत् विभागगशून्यमपि।
अन्योन्यं च ततोऽपि च विभक्तमाभापि जगदेतत् ॥

darpaṇabimbe yadvan nagaragrāmādicitramavibhāgi |
bhāti vibhāgenaiva ca parasparaṃ darpaṇādapi ca ||
vimalatamaparamabhairabodhāt tadvat vibhāgaghaśūnyamapi |
anyonyaṃ ca tato'pi ca vibhaktamābhāpi jagadetat ||

Just as in a clear mirror, varied images of city, village, etc. appear as different from one another and from the mirror, though they are non-different from the mirror, even so the world, though non-different from purest consciousness of *Parama Bhairava* (Śiva), appears as different both in respect of its varied objects and that universal consciousness. Just as reflection in a mirror is not something different from the mirror, but appears as different, even so creation is not different from the creator and yet appears as different.

(*Paramārthasāra*, 12-13)

It must be noted that this analogy is not exact, for in the case of a mirror, there must always exist an external object for it to reflect. That is, the process of reflection necessitates the presence of three distinct entities: the mirror itself, the reflection, and the object being reflected. However, in the case of Śiva, it is his own self, his own ideation that is being reflected as the universe. There are no distinctions to be made between the mirror, the reflection, and the object. Śiva becomes the mirror, reflecting his own Self. The reflection is none other than himself, manifesting in his immanent form. Whereas a mirror reflects only visual images, Śiva's mirror reflects visuals, taste, sounds, and everything that exists.

We have hastily skimmed through this matter. Let us return to where we were. The world, it has not yet come to be, only the urge has been stirred. The fulfilment of any desire requires three steps. First, the desire itself, second, knowledge or a plan, and third, the execution of that plan or the action required. Thus, following the birth of desire, the element of knowledge was called forth.

The analogy of an embryo can illuminate our understanding of this idea. Let us assume that this creation is an infant, and you are its creator, its parent. To this point, you possess only the desire to create a life within you. The child, it exists as a fertilised egg within your uterus. The embryo has yet to manifest, to develop limbs or any form of appendage, only a seed. That seed, still it resides within you, lifeless, bereft of independent existence. Until now, your existence reigns supreme, you are the one who is, not the child, for it has not yet come into being. At present, the child exists only as a seed and remains within you. Similarly, up until this stage, the world exists only as a seed, just a faint idea. Until now, the unmanifest, the transcendent remains dominant, not the immanent.

At this stage, Śiva experiences the *aham idam* state, that is, *I am everything, I am the world.* He does not perceive a separate existence of the world. The emphasis is on 'I'. All that exists is 'I', with only a faint awareness of the world.

Now comes the second stage, the stage of knowledge, or ideation. You can understand this stage in this way. Some months have passed, and the embryo is thriving within your womb, and the sound of its heartbeat resounds. Its separate existence has begun to be felt, though it still remains a part of you. At this stage, you experience that what lies within my womb is my expansion, it is me.

This is what Śiva experiences in this stage, *idam aham—this is my expansion; it is me*. Although the emphasis now shifts more towards this (*idam*), the oneness of this and I remains inseparable.

The third stage marks the stage of *kriyā* or action, the emergence of the child. The seed that was has now developed into a distinct existence. It has come out of your body. Now, you are experiencing the separate existence of that creation within your lap. You are now hearing its cries, smelling the odour of its diapers, and acknowledging that this is not me! Its separate existence has now become prominent. It is as much of a separate existence as you are. You experience—*I am me, and this is this! aham aham idam idam!* Yet, even in this awareness, you feel, you know that the baby is still a part of you, no matter how different it may appear. It has emerged from you. It is still you.

This is what Śiva experiences in this stage: *aham aham idam idam—I am me, and this is this!* Both 'I' and 'this' have equally distinct existences. The desire and incompleteness brought forth a separate existence, something distinct from Śiva, not within him. It manifests as a means for Śiva to fulfil his desires, but it is ultimately a delusion—a self-induced amnesia. Nothing has truly become separate from Śiva; he has merely forgotten that 'this' is also him. Similar to how ostriches respond to danger by burying their heads in the sand or in a hole. The threat doesn't vanish; they simply become unaware of it, as their sight and hearing are cut off from the danger.

Similarly, Śiva, through his own volition, becomes oblivious and forgetful that he is everything, bringing forth the existence of this world. Much like an ostrich burying its head in the sand, Śiva conceals himself—we will explore that further in this chapter.

So, this analogy of the child in the womb is simply for the sake of simplification. It's not entirely accurate. Unlike a child, despite being created by the mother, is separate from her, the world is not separate from Śiva. It is sort of like how someone forms a fist by bringing together five fingers. The fist is created by them; they are the creator, but it's not separate from them, unlike a mother and her child. The fist may appear separate, but it cannot be separate. Similarly, Śiva creates this world by combining his five energies. His creation may appear separate from him, but it is not.

And a slightly more precise analogy would be of a dancer and his dance. Just as the dancer and his creation, the dance, are one, similarly, Śiva and the world are one. This is why He is depicted as *Naṭarāja*—a dancer, the king of dancers! He is not portrayed as a sculptor, painter, or poet because after the creation of a sculpture, painting, or poem, they become separate from the creator. However, this world, after creation, does not become separate from Śiva. This world has no independent existence, no independent identity. It is created from Śiva and by Śiva, much like a dancer and his dance. The dance is created from the dancer and by the dancer; they are one. When the dance stops, the dancer also disappears.

The second point is that the progression of desire, knowledge, and action did not occur sequentially; instead, they unfolded concurrently. Until that stage, the concept of time was nonexistent. Therefore, asserting a chronological sequence becomes meaningless in a reality devoid of time. It is only for the sake of intellectual comprehension, we have delineated these processes into distinct stages. Each of these stages (*tattvas*), represents dimensions of experience realised both by myself and the sages during meditation. These stages can be accessed by anyone through spiritual practices.

As one enters the stage of action and firmly grounds oneself in that state, the title of *Mantra* is conferred. Ascending further and establishing oneself in the stage of knowledge or ideation elevates one to the status of *Mantreśvara*. Advancing further to the stage of will, one attains the designation of *Mantra-Maheśvara*. Finally, the pinnacle is reached in the stage of *Śiva-Śakti,* where one becomes Śiva himself.

Let's proceed now. Thus far, the creation of a separate existence has occurred—creation separate from Śiva. By having it, by becoming one with it, Śiva can satiate his desires and complete his incompleteness, or so he believes. This marks the point where Śiva's energy of absolute freedom transforms into the energy of bondage. *Svātantrya-śakti* becomes *māyā-śakti*. The plant of *māyā* has now sprouted into existence. *Māyā* or *māyīya-mala* is the illusion of multiplicity. Forget everything you've been told or read about the word *māyā* so far. *māyā* has a singular meaning—multiplicity. It is the belief that there is something separate from you. I and you are separate, I and the world are separate, I and Śiva are separate. Where there is the experience of two instead of one, there is *māyā*. The sages of the Vedas proclaim, "This belongs to me, that does not; this is yours, that is not. Such divisions arise from the narrow-minded. However, those with a broad and generous mindset perceive the entire world as one family, their own family" (*ayaṁ nijaḥ paro veti gaṇanā laghucetasām, udāracaritānāṁ tu vasudhaiva kuṭumbakam*). And for the enlightened, the entirety of the world merges into a singular entity, one being, their own being.

It happened. In the land of Bihar, there was a man known for his unwavering devotion. He remained in constant communion with the divine and preferred to maintain a silent demeanour. Due to his peculiar behaviour, he became a subject of ridicule among the masses, labelled as a lunatic in the eyes of the world.

One fateful day, after seeking alms from the villagers, he sat down next to a stray dog to have his meal. The gathered onlookers witnessed an extraordinary spectacle as the holy man and the canine companion engaged in a remarkable display of brotherhood. They shared their food, taking turns to feed each other and enjoying the meal together as life-long companions.

As this scene unfolded, a ripple of amusement swept through the crowd, and laughter erupted from some of the people. Mockery and derision surrounded the holy man as they considered him a madman. However, undeterred by their scorn, he uttered words, cutting through their mocking chorus:

"Why do you find amusement in this sight?
Śiva rests beside Śiva;
Śiva feeds Śiva;
So, why do you laugh, O Śiva?
For everything that exists, in its entirety, is nothing but Śiva."

Once, within the temple of *Dakṣiṇeśvara Kālī*, two wandering sadhus arrived—one was a father, and the other was his son. In this peculiar pair, the son had achieved enlightenment, while the father remained trapped in the veil of ignorance. They found themselves seated together in the very chamber where Śrī Rāmakṛṣṇa resided, engaging in a conversation with the revered Tantrik mystic. Meanwhile, as their discourse continued, a cobra stealthily emerged from a rat-hole and sank its venomous fangs into the son's flesh.

This sudden turn of events instilled terror in the father's heart, and his desperate plea echoed through the chamber's hallowed halls, beckoning anyone who would lend an ear.

However, the son remained composed, perplexing the father even further with his tranquillity. Seeking an explanation for his serene demeanour, the father inquired, and the son responded with laughter, his words illuminating the depth and essence of his understanding. He asked, **"Who is the snake, and whom has it bitten?"** Through his realisation of the underlying oneness beyond māyā, he was unable to perceive any duality or distinction between the serpent and himself.

Māyā is the second impurity and the sixth element (1. *Śiva,* 2. *Śakti,* 3. *Icchā,* 4. *Jñāna,* 5. *Kriyā,* and 6. *Māyā*). Now, this *māyā,* which has just sprouted from the seed, begins to bear fruit. It yields five fruits. Or, to put it another way, māyā possesses five weapons or tools through which it intensifies the illusion of diversity within Śiva. Just as a mechanic works through his tools, *māyā* operates through these tools, strengthening the illusion of diversity.

These tools are *kalā, rāga, vidyā, kāla,* and *niyati.*

Let's briefly explore these five elements. Earlier, I used an example that, similar to an ostrich burying its head in the sand, Śiva also covers himself to feel powerless. When Śiva veils himself, these are the five blankets he uses—*kalā, rāga, vidyā, kāla, and niyati.*

Śiva brought forth something separate and apart from himself, something that was not Him, in order to seek and fulfil his desire. However, a predicament, a problem arose: he was all powerful. He was imbued with five unlimited powers. The first being the ability to be omnipresent, simultaneously spanning every corner of existence. The second power bestowed upon him eternity, the capability to transcend the confines of time, existing simultaneously in the past, present, and future. The third power graced him with omniscience, infinite depth of knowledge. With the fourth power, he remained in a tranquil state of contentment, an inner completeness that resonated through his very being. Lastly, the fifth power granted him omnipotence. the freedom to effortlessly bend reality to his will, empowering him to accomplish anything his heart desired.

It was necessary for Śiva to limit his own powers so that he could play the game of pursuing his desires and their fulfilment. If he truly desired to experience multiplicity and perceive something separate from himself, it became essential to restrict these powers. For this, he created the five elements of *kalā, rāga, vidyā, kāla,* and *niyati.*

These elements acted as blankets, partially veiling his powers. The power to know everything, omniscience, transformed into the power of limited knowledge—incomplete knowledge. Omnipotence was now the power of performing limited actions. The power of perfection and eternal contentment was veiled, giving way to incompleteness and constant yearning.

Thus, Śiva, who had now become a limited soul, always felt dissatisfied, thirsty, constantly seeking something to satisfy His yearning. This reflects your current condition; you might think, "I need to lose weight; if I don't reduce my weight and get physically fit, everyone will say I'm unattractive. No one will like me." or "I need to have a sexual relationship with a girl; otherwise, people will mock me, saying I remained a virgin." or "I need love in my life, a relationship with a woman, or else I'll die single." This illustrates the power of constant yearning, and its developed form is attachment. We become attached to someone or something because we mistakenly feel we cannot live without them, that without them, we are incomplete. Due to this feeling of incompleteness, we fear losing others; we fear being left, rejected. A sense of void is felt, a deep sucking hole in our hearts when someone or something we are attached to leaves us. However, the reality is that we are eternally complete and perfect.

Then, His power of eternal existence was veiled into temporary existence, experience of time. Due to this power, the limited Śiva thinks thoughts like, 'I am 19 years old; next year, I will turn 20.' He contemplates, 'I was born 19 years ago; before that, I did not exist.' He worries about the future and keeps recalling the happenings of the past, while in reality, He is eternal. Time does not actually exist. However, He has forgotten this truth because He has veiled His power of timeless existence.

Then, the power of omnipresence transforms into the power of being limited in space, thinking, "I am only in one place and not everywhere." When these divine powers, which make Śiva totally free, are veiled and take the form of limitations and bondage, they are known as *kalā, vidyā, rāga, kāla,* and *niyati.*

In other words, just as we wear 3D glasses to enjoy a movie in a realistic way, similarly, Śiva wears 5D glasses to experience this divided existence, this cosmic illusion, *māyā*, in a realistic manner. These 5 dimensions are *kalā, rāga, vidyā, kāla,* and *niyati.*

Kalā is what prevents Śiva from accomplishing everything. *Vidyā* is what veils his omniscience. *Rāga*, attachment, is what limits his completeness, his contentment. Why? Because attachment arises when you are not complete, not satisfied, when you feel something is lacking. *Kāla*, time, is what limits his eternity, his timeless nature. *Niyati* is what restricts his omnipresence. It is the limitation of place. In reality, you are everywhere, but due to *niyati*, you are only in one place and nowhere else. It may sound strange, even untrue, but it is also mentioned in the *Bhagavad Gītā* by Lord Kṛṣṇa.

अच्छेद्योऽयमदाह्योऽयमक्लेद्योऽशोष्य एव च ।
नित्य: सर्वगत: स्थाणुरचलोऽयं सनातन: ॥

acchedyo'yam adāhyo'yam akledyo'śoṣya eva cha |
nityaḥ sarvagataḥ sthāṇurachalo'yaṁ sanātanaḥ ||

> The soul, the *ātmā,* is beyond the reach of being cut, burned, dampened, or dried up. You are beyond the reach of time, everywhere at once, unchanging, immovable, and eternal.
>
> (*Bhagavad Gītā* II.24)

Niyati is what limits Śiva in time and space, and on what basis does it limit? It does so on the basis of cause and effect. Upon reaching the element of *niyati*, *karma-mala* sprouts. This *karma-mala* is one of the three malas, or impurities, that cause bondage. *Malas* will be explained shortly.

Karma means actions. Everything we do is *karma.* Forget whatever you have heard or read about *karma.* The only meaning of *karma* is the actions performed by us. Action, work, activity—that is *karma.* And how does the bondage of *karma* form? It forms when it intensifies the feelings of duality, multiplicity, or incompleteness within us, becoming a form of bondage. This impure *karma*, which causes bondage, we will refer to as *karma-mala* from now on.

Karma-mala is inseparable from attachment (*rāga*). Without attachment, the possibility of *karma-mala* is eliminated. Attachment is the root of karmic entanglements. It is the firm belief that I need something to fulfil myself, something external, like a soulmate, etc. Or I need to be separate from something, to distance myself, or renounce something to attain completeness. This too is attachment. Here, the energy of attachment is flowing in the opposite direction. It is commonly called aversion—the belief that we cannot be complete until certain things are ended or avoided. The more intense attachments or aversions we have, the more intense our actions will be, like a lover who believes "I cannot live without him!" The emotion that inspires us to do a certain task, the more extreme it is, the stronger our bondage to that action will be.

Imagine this scenario: You and your friends have gathered on a rooftop of a building for an evening get-together, enjoying the vibrant atmosphere and panoramic views. Among them, you find yourself caught in the middle of an intense argument between two of your friends, escalating quickly.

Feeling the need to intervene and defuse the situation, you step forward, driven by concern and a desire to restore harmony. As you reach out to physically separate the individuals by force, an unexpected misstep occurs, causing one of them to lose balance and teeter on the edge of the rooftop. Unaware of their precarious position, they tragically fall from the rooftop, resulting in their death.

It was your push (though unintended) that inadvertently caused this unfortunate chain of events, despite your original intention to resolve the conflict.

Consider another scenario: Within your friend circle, there exists a strong aversion in you towards someone—a former girlfriend who had left you feeling betrayed. Over the course of several months, your hatred towards her has been steadily growing. You patiently await the opportune moment, a chance to exact your revenge. One evening, you, your friends, and she find yourselves on a rooftop, gathering for an evening get-together. Suddenly, an intense argument erupts between her and another member of the group.

Viewing this situation as the perfect opportunity, you step forward pretending to physically intervene and forcefully separate the individuals. Fuelled by your animosity, you deliberately push her, causing her to tumble from the rooftop's edge, resulting in her death.

Once again, it was your push, your actions, that caused a death.

In both scenarios, you pushed someone, causing them to fall from the rooftop and ultimately resulting in their death. However, these actions are not equivalent. It is not difficult to discern which of the two actions would result in greater bondage and produce the most terrible outcome. By *bondage*, I am not referring to worldly or social punishments, such as legal charges or imprisonment.

The consequence for the individual who tragically lost their life would be the same in both cases: death resulting from falling off the rooftop. However, the effect on you depends on the nature of your intentions in each scenario. It is not solely about what you have done but also how you have done it. The intensity of bondage you experience is determined not only by the outcome but more so by the degree of aversion or attachment present. To put it in another way, the determining factor in whether an action becomes enslaving or liberating lies in the root of the action rather than its fruit.

Only the actions that arise spontaneously, from the depths of our being, as an expression of our true nature, devoid of personal motives of gain or loss, carry no binding effect.
As Kṛṣṇa has expressed in the *Gītā*.

कर्मण्येवाधिकारस्ते मा फलेषु कदाचन ।
मा कर्मफलहेतुर्भूर्मा ते सङ्गोऽस्त्वकर्मणि ॥

karmaṇy-evādhikāras te mā phaleṣhu kadāchana |
mā karma-phala-hetur bhūr mā te saṅgo 'stvakarmaṇi ||

You have a right to perform your prescribed duties, but you are not entitled to the fruits of your actions. Never consider yourself to be the cause of the results of your activities, nor be attached to inaction.

योगस्थ: कुरु कर्माणि सङ्गं त्यक्त्वा धनञ्जय ।
सिद्ध्यसिद्ध्यो: समो भूत्वा समत्वं योग उच्यते ॥

yoga-sthaḥ kuru karmāṇi saṅgaṁ tyaktvā dhanañjaya |
siddhy-asiddhyoḥ samo bhūtvā samatvaṁ yoga uchyate ||

Be steadfast in the performance of your duty, O Dhanañjaya, abandoning attachment to success and failure. Such equanimity is called yoga.

(*Bhagavad Gītā* II.47, 48)

There exists a faint celestial body, a star known as *Arundhatī*, or Alcor in the English tongue. Nestled within the vast expanse of

Ursa Major's constellation, it resides adjacent to a more visible and luminous star known as *Vasiṣṭha* or Mizar.

In Hinduism, a code is offered to spouses, advising them to look upon the luminous *Arundhatī* whenever they encounter challenges in their married life. The tales resonate with the belief that she, as the beloved consort of *Maharṣi Vasiṣṭha*, exemplified the essence of an ideal wife. With unwavering loyalty, devotion, and an obeisance that knows no bounds, she adorned her life, thereby transcending mortal existence and ascending to the heavens, where her luminous essence was embodied by a star. Thus, this culture nurtures a tradition wherein married pairs are told to revere *Arundhatī* as their celestial compass, devoutly treading the path set forth by her.

So, the *Arundhatī* star is not easily visible in the sky because it is small and faint. It does not capture our attention easily. Instead, our attention is initially drawn to *Vasiṣṭha*, a larger, more visible, and brighter star located adjacent to *Arundhatī*. If you want someone to see *Arundhatī*, you should first direct their attention to *Vasiṣṭha*. You need to tell them to focus on this larger, more visible, and radiant star, which is easier to notice. Once they have found *Vasiṣṭha*, you can then ask them to shift their gaze towards the fainter star shining beside it, which is *Arundhatī*. This is the usual method for locating the luminary in the night sky.

In the same manner, these impurities are. Impurity of action is like the *Vasiṣṭha* star. It is more gross. Therefore, attention is first brought to it. It is the effect. To infer the cause, to reach the cause, one has to start from the effect. Now, the subtle form of the *karma-mala* is the *māyīya-mala.* The cause of the *karma-mala* is the *māyīya-mala*. As I clarified earlier, *māyīya-mala* is the impurity that makes us perceive diversity, creating the illusion that I and the world are separate. It is *māyīya-mala* that causes attachment (*rāga*).

If you stop believing the world as separate from yourself, the existence of attachment or aversion will cease. The desire to acquire something arises when we perceive it as different from us. If you realise that it is not separate from you but rather a part of your own being, then attachment will naturally fade away. Just as you are never attracted to your own finger because you know it is a part of your body and not separate from you.

The most effective way to overcome the *karma-mala* is to address the root cause: becoming completely assured that there is nothing outside of you that you need to acquire to become complete. Nor is there anything that needs to be subtracted to make you pure. Considering oneself as incomplete, inferior, limited, or separate from the world is the greatest sin. If you can eliminate this mindset, even if only to a small extent, performing actions without any selfish motive will become easy for you, and thus, you will become free from *karma.*

In a distant village stood a monastery, its ancient walls guarding a community of devout monks who adhered to a humble existence, venturing out each day to beg for sustenance. Amidst their routine, a monk, on his alms-seeking path, witnessed a cruel landlord brutally beating a fellow man. Filled with compassion, he intervened, pleading with the tormentor to cease his onslaught. Yet, the landlord's heart simmered with rage, and he redirected his anger towards the innocent monk, relentlessly beating him until he lay lifeless upon the earth.

News of this atrocity reached the monastery, prompting a hasty pilgrimage of concerned brethren to the scene of the tragedy. With utmost care, they carried their fallen comrade back to the monastery, gently placing him on a bed. The monk remained motionless, while his brethren encircled him, their sorrow evident in their pained expressions. Some sought solace in fanning the motionless figure, hoping to revive his dormant spirit.

After a time, a notion emerged among the mournful assembly—a notion whispered in hushed tones. Perhaps, they thought, a small offering of milk could stir the unconscious monk back to life. Without hesitation, they poured milk into his parched lips, coaxing him towards consciousness. With a gradual return to awareness, he flickered his eyes open, taking in the familiar faces surrounding him.

A curious brother, eager to gauge the extent of the monk's lucidity, leaned in closely and shouted into his ear, demanding, "Brother, who committed this atrocity upon you? Who unleashed such violence?" With a voice barely above a whisper, the holy man responded, "Brother, it is he who, in this moment, offers me milk, who laid upon me this torment." "The one who now quenches my thirst with the milk of compassion, it is none other than he who delivered the blows that left me unconscious."

If you embrace this perspective in life, recognizing both friends and foes as a single entity, and blurring the lines between *you* and *me*, the chains of causality, or *karma-mala*, will naturally begin to dissolve.

However, everything ultimately comes back to the *āṇava-mala*. It is the *Sharingan* that causes the genjutsu of multiplicity. Among all three impurities, it is the subtlest and the root of all. It is the true *Arundhatī* star that, so you can perceive, your attention was first directed to the grosser stars of *māyā* and *karma*.

Āṇava-mala is the unfulfillment, which, as I explained earlier, originated within you, within Śiva at the beginning of creation. It is the *āṇava-mala* that causes you to perceive yourself as incomplete.

It is the belief that something is lacking, something is missing, or something is inherently wrong with you—a belief that hinders you from believing yourself as Śiva and seeing yourself as Śiva.

When you lack contentment and a sense of completeness within yourself, you feel compelled to search for something external, outside of yourself, that can bring you (a sense of) completeness. You believe that once you obtain it, you will achieve totality and completeness. This creates the illusion of duality. Simply believing in the existence of something separate from your being gives rise to *māyā*, the illusion of duality. By acknowledging the existence of something apart from you, *māyā* takes form. Remember this: you are everything that exists. However, you fragment your essence, dividing it between the internal and the external, the 'I' and the 'world'. In this fragmentation, *māyā* flourishes. When you become conscious of a reality outside of you, you bring forth (the illusion of) a reality outside of you.

This is extroversion. Extrovert means turning outward, fixing your gaze on what's beyond you. The root of *extrovert* stems from the Latin *extra*, meaning *outside*, and *vertere*, meaning *to turn*.

I'm not discussing some personality type that revels in socialising, partying, and needless chatter. The extroversion I'm referring to is how the world sprang forth. Śiva, he became extroverted and birthed the supposed existence separate from himself. He sought completeness by turning outward, away from his own being. This gave rise to *āṇava-mala*, the Original sin, the root of all enslavements.

Extroversion enslaves. And introversion, frees.

Long ago, when the *Kali Yuga* began, Śiva manifested himself on Mount Kailāśa, amidst the sacred peaks that kissed the heavens. He sought to restore the teachings of the Tantras, lost amidst the ravages of the *Kali Yuga*. To the sage Durvāsā, he imparted this long-forgotten, ancient science. At Kailāśa, during initiation, Śiva entrusted Durvāsā with the task of spreading the sacred wisdom throughout the vast universe, to anyone who was worthy. Having completed his teachings, Śiva vanished from sight.

Durvāsā, consumed by his yearning for a deserving disciple, embarked upon a quest to find one who could bear the weight of initiation, but his efforts were in vain. It was no ordinary initiation; it was practical, wherein the teachings were made clear through direct realisation. The disciples underwent spiritual experiences, transcending mind and intellect, and achieving instantaneous enlightenment. Disheartened by his fruitless search, Durvāsā turned inward (introversion) and, by becoming one with the world, he brought forth three sons and a daughter, created from his own thoughts. Such occurrences, far from being unheard of, finds affirmation within the Sūtra '*śaktisandhāne śarīrotpattih*' of this very scripture. Having created them, Durvāsā fully initiated them into the enigmatic secrets of the Tantras.

Following in their father's footsteps, Durvāsā's sons, too, created mind-born offspring and guided them into the realm of the Tantras. Thus, fifteen siddhas were brought forth through the power of the mind. However, when the fifteenth siddha attempted to create a mind-born son, he faced failure. He had not fully turned inward, remaining entangled in the illusion that the world existed separate from himself (extroversion). Bound by the chains of āṇava-mala, he failed to realise that everything existed within himself, that he was whole and complete. Consequently, his endeavour of creating a mind-born heir met with disappointment. Driven by an ardent desire, he sought solace in this world, discovering a radiant woman who possessed every virtue. Love blossomed, and he sought her father's blessing for their union. Together, they bore a son named Saṁgamāditya, and from that point forward, sons who were initiated into the Tantras were born biologically.

Incidentally, Saṁgamāditya's great-great-grandson became the disciple of Vasugupta, the mystical luminary who discovered the scripture that currently lies open before you.

We were immersed in a deep discussion, tracing the path through which Śiva unfolded and transformed into the cosmos—a progression composed of precise steps. So far, I have shed light on the creation of *kalā, rāga, vidyā, kāla, and niyati*, as they veiled the five infinite powers of Śiva. Each stage of this wondrous creation is a tattva or element, totaling thirty-six in number. Niyati serves as the precursor to the twelfth element, *puruṣa* or the individual soul. *Puruṣa* is Śiva, bound by the hypnotic influence of three impurities. *Puruṣa* is the constrained, limited state of Śiva. When Śiva succumbs to the sway of *māyā*, He takes on the identity of puruṣa. Following puruṣa, the remaining twenty-four elements come into existence. I shall expound upon them thoroughly within the pages of my forthcoming book. For now, a mere mention of these elements shall suffice.

12. *puruṣa* — limited Śiva (individual consciousness/self, knowing subject, witness, seer, pure awareness, jīva, kṣetrajña)
13. *prakṛti* — nature, the primordial substance, matter/energy, manifests as all lower tattva:

The 3 Inner Organs (antaḥkaraṇa)

14. intelligence (*buddhi*) — reason, discrimination between truth and illusion, knowing, intelligence.
15. ego (*ahaṁkāra*) — the I AM sense, identity, the felt sense of individuality.
16. mind (*manas*) — memories (that manifest in the form of, thought, sense-process, perception, preferences, remembrance (past) & imagination (future)

The Organs of Knowing (jñānendriya)

17. ears (śrotra) — hearing
18. skin *(tvak)* — touch
19. eyes *(cakṣus)* — sight
20. tongue *(rasanā)* — taste
21. nose *(ghrāṇa)* — smell

The Organs of Action (karmendriya)

22. mouth *(vāk)* — speech
23. hands *(pāni)* — manipulation
24. feet *(pāda)* — locomotion
25. genitals *(upastha)* — reproduction
26. bowels *(pāyu)* — excretion

The 5 Subtle Elements (tanmātra)

27. sound *(śabda)*
28. touch *(sparśa)*
29. form *(rūpa)*
30. taste *(rasa)*
31. smell *(gandha)*

The 5 Great Elements (mahā-bhūta)

32. ether *(ākāśa)*
33. air *(vāyu)*
34. fire *(agni)*
35. water *(jala)*

Having elucidated the triad of impurities—āṇava, *māyā*, and *karma*—that veil one's remembrance of their true self, I now draw this discourse to a close. In substantiating my credibility, I shall quote the sacred verbiage of both divinity and sages.

मलप्रध्वस्तचैतन्यं कलाविद्यासमाश्रितम् ।
रागेण रञ्जितात्मानं कालेन कलितं तथा ॥
नियत्या यमितं भूयः पुंभावेनोपबृं हितम् ।
प्रधानाशयसंपन्नं गुणत्रयसमन्वितम् ॥
बुद्धितत्त्वसमासीनमहङ्कारसमावृतम् ।
मनसा बुद्धिकर्माक्षैस्तन्मात्रैः स्थूलभूतकैः ॥

malapradhvashchaitanyaṁ kalāvidyāsamāśritam |
rāgeṇa rañjitātmānaṁ kālena kalitaṁ tathā ||
niyatyā yamitaṁ bhūyaḥ puṁbhāvenopabṛṁ hitam |

pradhānāśayasaṁpannaṁ guṇatrayasamanvitam ||
buddhitattvasamāsīnamahaṅkārasamāvṛtam |
manasā buddhikarmākṣaistanmātraiḥ sthūlabhūtakaiḥ ||

Caitanya (consciousness; recognition of true self) is suppressed by *mala* (i.e., āṇava-*mala*) and provided with *kalā* and *vidyā*, is tainted by *raga*, limited in respect of *kāla* (time), restrained by *niyati*. magnified by the sense of being a *puruṣa* (an empirical self), furnished with the disposition of *prakṛti*, endowed with the three gunas (*rajas, tamas and sattva*), *buddhi*, *ahāmkara*, and manas, *jñānendriyas* (organs of sense) and *karmendriyas* (organs of action), *tanmātras*, and the gross elements.

(*Svacchaṃda Tantra* II, 39-41)

धर्माधर्मात्मकं कर्म सुखदुःखादिलक्षणम् ।

dharmādharmātmakaṁ karma sukhaduḥkhādilakṣaṇam |

He (the jīva) does good and bad deeds which bring about pleasure and pain.

(*Mālinīvijaya Tantra* I, 24)

भिन्नवेद्यप्रथात्रैव मायाख्यं जन्मभोगदम् ।
कर्तर्यबोधे कामं च मायाशक्त्यंव तत्त्रयम् ... ॥

bhinnavedyaprathātraiva māyākhyaṁ janmabhogadam |
kartaryabodhe kāmaṁ ca māyāśaktyaṁva tattrayam ... ||

When there is ignorance of real Self, then *āṇava-mala* being present, there arise *māyīya-mala* bringing about a sense of difference in respect of every object, and *karma-mala* which brings about birth and experience of pleasure and pain (*bhoga*). All the three malas are brought about by the *māyā-śakti* of Śiva.

(Īśvara-*pratyabhijñā* III.2.5)

Alternative Viewpoint

Bhairava illuminated an alternate interpretation of this Sūtra within the depths of my intellect. In the previous interpretation, He revealed the expanses of ignorance. In this interpretation, he is enlightening us about true knowledge. This nuanced interpretation is equally worth understanding and deserves further explanation. In this interpretation, the meanings of the remaining three words will be the same as in the previous interpretation, with the only difference being the interpretation of the word *kalā*, which will take on a different meaning.

Yoni—Vagina; In this case, the vagina of the divine mother; the origin of all existence—the source from which this world of illusion emerges.

Varga— A multitude of similar things, whether animate or inanimate; a class, family, or group. In this case, everything—the trees, plants, animals, mountains, houses, rivers, and beyond—that came forth from the vagina of the divine mother.

Kalā—A part or portion of the whole.

Kalā also translates to a distinct part, portion, division or segment within a larger whole, that adds to the overall understanding or composition of the entirety.

For example, in the Bṛhadāraṇyakopaniṣad I.5.14. The sixteen parts of the moon are referred to by the word *kalā*. (The moon waxes and wanes in periods of fifteen days; each day it gains or loses one *kalā*. The sixteenth *kalā* is the *amṛtakalā* which never dies, even at the dark of the moon.)

Śariram—The body, or form.

|| YONIVARGAḤ KALĀŚARĪRAM ||3||

(Just as your hands, feet, brain, lungs, and heart came forth from your mother's vagina, a multitude of parts found their beginning, all tracing back to a shared origin—the vagina. However, all of these, this group, this multitude of similar things originating from a shared source, the vagina, are parts of a single body—your physical body. Similarly,) **Everything,** (—the trees, plants, animals, mountains, houses, rivers, and beyond—) **that came forth from the universal vagina** (the *yoni* of the divine mother) **are parts of a single body** (—your real, cosmic body).

In the preceding chapter, I clarified that the first two Sūtras are meant to be read together, as one—*chaitanyamaatmaajnaanambandhah.* This is the correct way to read these Sūtras. Both of them should become one. Similarly, the correct way to live in the world is to become one with it, with a sense of non-duality. Live by making yourself one with the world. This is liberation, this is true knowledge.

If you create divisions between yourself and the world, between me and you, between mine and yours, it will become a bondage. Śiva is saying that the knowledge that you and I are separate, that everything is separate, is the cause of bondage. Just as if we read those two Sūtras separately, we are creating duality, and then, that *jñānaṁ* (knowledge) which arises from this duality, creates duality, and is bondage.

Now in this Sūtra, he is enlightening us about true knowledge, which arises from oneness and becomes freedom:

"everything—the trees, plants, animals, mountains, houses, rivers, and beyond—that came forth from the universal vagina, the yoni of the divine mother, are parts of a single body—your real, cosmic body."

Everything that exists is a part of me; nay, I am everything. I am the plant; I am also the tree and the book that lies open before you—I am that too. It is important for us to understand that we are not separate; we must relinquish our flawed understanding of Self and discard our limited identifications. Instead, we must embrace the idea that I am the entirety of humanity; this vast humanity is my identity; nay, it extends beyond humanity to encompass animals, birds, and nature itself. Consciousness is singular, infinite;

how can there be two infinities? And when we realise this, all our futile worries, greed, jealousy, and fear of death vanish. Once you recognize that you are everything, that everything is a part of your physical being, you treat everyone with care as you would yourself. You do not exploit anything for the pleasure of your physical body. And in this way, the world naturally becomes beautiful.

I used to title myself 'Lonewolf' after my name. This word held great significance for me; it has a dual meaning. Firstly, it signifies an introvert, as I explained a while ago. Secondly, the root 'lone' implies being alone, and for me, it means being truly alone in this entire world. Because I perceive myself as alone; no one else seems to exist for me. I only see myself in everything around me. Kṛṣṇa sings:

विद्याविनयसम्पन्ने ब्राह्मणे गवि हस्तिनि ।
शुनि चैव श्वपाके च पण्डिता: समदर्शिन: ॥

vidyā-vinaya-sampanne brāhmaṇe gavi hastini |
śhuni chaiva śhva-pāke cha paṇḍitāḥ sama-darśhinaḥ ||

He is a true sage, an enlightened being, knowledgeable in the scriptures, who sees with equal vision a gentle and learned brāhmaṇa, a cow, an elephant, a dog or a dog eater.

(*Bhagavad Gītā* V.18)

In the same way, I see myself in all of you. In that dog walking down the street, I see my own self, and the earthworm wriggling on the ground—I'm that too. I am alone; I am the entirety of this universe. There is no one else in this world except me. If I am causing harm to someone, I am, in fact, harming myself. If I am helping someone else, I am helping myself. If someone is suffering because of me, I too will not find happiness. This is the reality. The law of *karma* operates on this very principle. Whatever you think you are doing to others, you are actually doing to yourself. What I am giving to you will ultimately return to me because there is no one else. If you mistreat someone, it will return to you in the future. Why? Because the doer and the one it is done to are one and the same.

How simple it is. I established the singularity of consciousness in the first chapter itself. Bondage occurs because you consider a limited entity as yourself. The moment everything becomes your identity, all your limitations cease to exist.

To experience this truth, live as you would after experiencing it; do what you would do after realising that everything is a part of your own being. You would take care of everything as if they are parts of your own body. You would feed the birds and animals and take care of nature. You would not harm anyone for the sake of the pleasures of your physical body.

You must continuously remind yourself that we are all one; be mindful of this truth at all times. Only when you remain steadfast in this conviction will it truly transform into reality. See others as if they are a part of yourself. Recognize your own soul in every being. We are not just brothers; we are one. Every moment, remind yourself of this, and you will notice that your behaviour towards others has changed. You will never harbour anger towards anyone, nor wish harm upon them. The feeling of jealousy will dissipate because who is jealous of one's own self? You will start to love the whole world; the fear of death, the emotion of hatred, and pride will all cease within you. In the end, you will merge into that ultimate consciousness.

Some people might argue that since chicken is also a part of my own body, what's wrong with eating it? No, if you truly believed that the bird and you are one, this self-centred thought would never cross your mind. You still only worry about the pleasures and pain of this body, the concerns of this stomach, not the body of that bird. Because you don't truly believe in this. So, it's essential for you to remain authentic and genuinely strive to realise the entire world as your body.

This matter will serve as one of the central themes of the book, receiving repeated emphasis, especially in the chapter dedicated to the fourteenth aphorism.

This concludes our study of Sūtra Three.

CHAPTER FOUR

ज्ञानाधिष्ठानं मातृका ॥४॥

|| jñānādhiṣṭhānam mātṛkā || 4 ||

***Mātṛkā* serves as the base, the breeding ground of (incomplete) knowledge.**

In the second chapter, Śiva enlightened us about knowledge. He clarified how knowledge frees us and, paradoxically, is also the means of bondage. If knowing something makes you believe that you are an incomplete, enslaved being, requiring something or someone else to achieve completeness and contentment—that knowledge is bondage. Ignorance is not bondage; knowledge itself is the bondage.

There was a lion that was raised in a herd of donkeys. His mother was pregnant, and one day, she went out to hunt. Her instincts led her to a herd of donkeys. In the throes of the hunt, she felt a sudden pain in her belly, and she crumpled to the earth. In the midst of her agony, her cub was born, but alas, she did not survive.

Thus, the baby lion grew up among the donkeys, and from his childhood, he was instilled with the belief that he too was a donkey. Growing up, he emulated their behaviour, mimicking their eating habits, and whenever the silhouette of another lion loomed on the horizon, his blood would run cold, and he would retreat into the shadows, for he believed himself to be naught but a lowly donkey. He suffered the constant fear of predatory lions lurking nearby.

One day, a fellow lion could no longer stand to witness this misplaced identity. He seized the lion-donkey and, with genuine curiosity, inquired, "Why, pray tell, do you flee from your own kind?" To this, the lion-donkey quivered and responded, "I am a donkey, and you lions would surely devour me."

The fellow lion chuckled softly and said, "Come with me," guiding him to the edge of a crystal-clear pond.

There, the lion-donkey gazed into the water's reflection and was struck by a revelation. He was not a donkey; he was a majestic lion. This newfound awareness instantly dissolved his lingering fears, shedding the illusory cloak of donkey-hood, liberating him from his self-imposed limitations. Now, unburdened by the shackles of fear, he stood tall, a lion among lions, free to roam the savanna with the majestic grace and dignity that had been his birthright all along.

That which had ensnared the lion was also knowledge; the knowledge that he is a donkey. And, that which freed the lion was also knowledge; the knowledge that he is a lion. Knowledge serves as both the cause of bondage and freedom. In this Sūtra, Śiva specifically refers to the knowledge that creates bondage. Śiva enlightens us about the foundation of this knowledge, the breeding ground from which it sprouts. First, a dissection of its meaning, word by word.

Jñāna, translates to knowledge.

Adhiṣṭhānam translates to a seat or foundation, conveying meanings such as basis, substratum, ground, platform, or support. It refers to the breeding ground or fundamental principle upon which something is built or established. The breeding ground of the roots of the tree of knowledge—the knowledge that makes you believe that you are an incomplete, enslaved being. The tree, whose shoots are the illusion of multiplicity, where grows the branches of karmic entanglements. This is what is being referred to.

And what is the breeding ground of this tree? *Mātṛkā*.

Mātṛkā translates to mother, the mother who is unknown, whom we do not understand completely. For a more literal understanding, we can dissect the word into two parts. *Mātṛ* means mother. For example, *mātṛbhūmi* means motherland (formed by combining *mātṛ* with *bhūmi*, which means land or earth), and *-kā*. The suffix *-kā* in Sanskrit indicates that whatever word it has been attached to at the end is unknown or not understood.

Interestingly, the suffix *-kā* is also a common way to indicate the feminine gender in Sanskrit! Perhaps our sages also believed that women cannot be understood!

Jokes aside, this Sūtra reveals to us that the source of this knowledge, the foundation of this knowledge, is the Mother—Śakti, the Primeval Power, the wife of Lord Śiva. Why Mother? When you become one with Śiva, then that goddess becomes your energy, not your mother. At present, She is your mother, meaning the one who gave birth to you. However, that which is eternal and changeless cannot have a mother because it was never born. That which never dies never took birth. It is a universal law that one who is born will die, and one who dies must have been born at some point.

In your present state, you are not that eternal one. Right now, you consider yourself an individual, who was born some years ago and will die (maybe not—you never truly consider that you are going to die), who is reading this book, with the desire to know their true Self. The day this individual realises their true self, they will be no more; they will cease to exist.

This person, whether it be Suyash, Suleman, or Simon, can never become Śiva. A person can never become free, but you become free from this person. Either you can identify with this person or with your true self, i.e., Śiva, but you cannot identify with both simultaneously. Without letting go of one identity, you cannot embrace another. Without letting go of this person, you cannot touch the Śiva state. Siddhārtha Gautama and Buddha were not the same. Buddha emerged only after Siddhārtha Gautama's death.

So, this individual, this person, this bound soul, will one day meet its end; it is inevitable. And whoever meets their end, it is certain that they were born. And whoever is born has a mother. And that mother is none other than *mātṛkā*.

As long as I am identified with Suyash, I am at the level of my lower self. Until then, the Primeval Power is my Mother, and for me, she is *mātṛkā*, as she has given birth to me, the individual, whom she remains unknown to; otherwise, I was the unborn Śiva, for whom nothing remains unknown. However, when I am in my true Śiva state, She is not my mother; She is my power, my heart. She is Suyash's mother and Śiva's consort, and Suyash can never become Śiva. So, because this Sūtra is referring to the knowledge that keeps one in the state of individuality, the Primeval Power is referred to here as the Mother.

The Mother cannot be understood. Understanding Her means becoming Śiva, and She is not Śiva's mother. The Primeval Power has two aspects: one that we do not understand and one that we do understand. Although both are one and the same, it's just that after understanding a thing, it completely transforms for us, and it transforms us. When we remain ignorant towards it, it is something else, and when we realise it, it becomes something else. And so do we.

Just like when we don't understand that we are lions, until then we remain as donkeys, and when we realise that we are lions, then we transform from donkeys to lions.

When we don't understand Mother, She keeps us bound. And when we do understand Her, She sets us free. Mother is our inherent power of freedom (*svātantrya-śakti*). You are Śiva, and you have forgotten your freedom. Forgetting your freedom is also your freedom, because forgetting it was your choice. Without this power, the power of freedom, you cannot forget your independent nature and become confined in the form of an individual. So, this power of freedom is also the power of bondage. You are currently in the state of a limited soul, bound because of your power of freedom.

The only difference between a liberated one and a bound soul is that the liberated one knows and understands that it is my own freedom that I have chosen bondage. Whereas a bound soul is oblivious to this fact. They never take responsibility for their suffering; the reason for their suffering is always someone else. They believe someone else made them depressed, or if they are sad or feel hurt, it is because of someone else—their ex-boyfriend, their boss, their parents, or whatnot. They do not understand their power of freedom; hence, their power remains *mātṛkā* for them, keeping them bound.

Our higher reality is Śiva, and the lower reality is the individual soul—an emergent property of mind, intellect, and ego. The individual soul perceives itself as bound and experiences the world. This is our current reality, so the *mātṛkā-śakti* is functioning. *Mātṛkā* brings us from the higher reality to the lower reality. When we are in the higher reality, the *svātantrya-śakti* (power of freedom) functions. However, you feel incapable of returning to the higher reality because you haven't fully understood your own power; you are unaware of your abilities. This unawareness of one's own power is *mātṛkā*.

I should clarify that it is not accurate to say that you do not know your powers. You do know your powers, but you know them incorrectly. You do not know that you can do everything; instead, you believe that you cannot do everything, but you can accomplish certain things. You are not aware that you are complete and content within yourself; instead, you think you are dissatisfied, but you can find contentment if certain conditions occur, such as your parents being happy or finding the right partner. You do not know that you are everywhere at once; instead, you believe you can only be in one place at a time but can book a plane ticket and travel wherever you wish. You do not know that you are Śiva, but you know that you cannot be Śiva because you are Mr. So & So, the son of Mr. So & So Sr. You know your powers, but not in the right way; it's a misunderstanding. And when these powers are misunderstood, they are called *mātṛkā*'

And this serves as the base, the breeding ground of āṇava-*mala*, *māyīya-mala*, and *karma-mala.*

Alternative Viewpoint

The term *mātṛkā* holds another meaning, another interpretation. Although it's a profoundly intricate philosophy, I will keep the explanation simple for now, delving into its depths in another volume. *Mātṛkā* is the energy that pervades within the letters. She is the source, the heart of everything made of words, every book, and mantras. In a literal sense, *mātṛkā* can also be translated as 'she who gave rise to all mantras and Tantras.' The depiction of the Goddess in Tantra often shows her adorned with a garland of half a hundred skulls—these fifty skulls symbolise the fifty alphabets of the Sanskrit language. The use of skulls is intentional as they represent the pronunciation of these letters, emanating from the head, as the sounds are articulated through moving the tongue and lips in certain ways. Just as the English language has twenty-six alphabets, the Sanskrit language has fifty of them.

अ (*a*), आ (*ā*), इ (*i*), ई (*ī*), उ (*u*), ऊ (*ū*), ए (*e*), ऐ (*ai*), ओ (*o*), औ (*au*), ऋ (*ṛ*), अं (*aṁ*), अ: (*aḥ*), क (*ka*), ख (*kha*), ग (*ga*), घ (*gha*), ड़ (*ṛa*), च (*ca*), छ (*cha*), ज (*ja*), झ (*jha*), ञ (ña), ट (*ṭa*), ठ (*ṭha*), ड (*ḍa*), ढ (*ḍha*), ण (*ṇa*), त (*ta*), थ (*tha*), द (*da*), ध (*dha*), न (*na*), प (*pa*), फ (*pha*), ब (*ba*), भ (*bha*), म (*ma*), य (*ya*), र (*ra*), ल (*la*), व (*va*), श (*ś*a), ष (*ṣa*), स (*sa*), ह (*ha*), क्ष (*kṣa*), त्र (*tra*), ज्ञ (*jña*), श्र (*śra*), ड़ (*ṛa*), ढ़ (*ṛha*).

Sanskrit is the world's oldest language, and over time, it has undergone variations. It has various scripts like *Śiddhaṁ, Śāradā, Devanāgarī*, with *Devanāgarī* being the most well-known. Due to these variations, there may be one or more additional or fewer characters in different scripts, but generally, they consist of about fifty letters. These characters are like ornaments or external adornments; inherently powerless, they derive energy from *mātṛkā*, who wears them. These alphabets combine to form words, and words create sentences. Since Sanskrit is the mother of all languages, and this philosophy originated at a time when no other languages existed, Sanskrit alphabets are metaphorically depicted as a necklace around the goddess's neck. However, this truth holds for every language. Whatever language you communicate in becomes the foundation of incomplete knowledge.

So, *mātṛkā* serves as the base, the breeding ground of (incomplete) knowledge.

This implies that language, constructed from words, formed by letters, and powered by the *mātṛkā* serves as the foundation of incomplete knowledge.

Interestingly, some neuroscience research suggests that the brain regions responsible for language processing are also involved in regulating heart rate, hormones, immune system function, and breathing. So, even at a very superficial level, what you say and hear contributes significantly to your entanglements and sorrows.

Consider, for example, a married couple who, after several years of marriage, rarely find happiness with each other. Here, too, the major cause is often language and communication issues, creating misunderstandings, misinterpretations, and frustration.

Observing your own life closely, you'll find that words play a significant role in your entanglements. Human life often revolves around the fear of what others will say. *Lōg kyā kahēṅge?* becomes their biggest concern. People may forcefully arrange marriages for their daughters, whether or not the girl is happy in that relationship, just to avoid negative comments. They fear people talking about their daughter not getting married and instead having an affair, etc. They may not be content in their own marital relationships, yet they can't opt for a divorce because of societal judgments. They desire to do something, yet they refrain, fearing what people will say.

Some wish to live a simple life without any pretence, yet they can't gather the courage; the fear prevails—what will others say? They want to see and experience things, but they hold back, wondering what people will say. Living freely becomes a distant dream because of the constant worry about societal opinions. They can't escape the concern of what people will say.

Will you keep listening to what others say? Is your entire life meant to pass according to the judgement of others? What will you achieve by this? When you breathe your last breath and these same people carry your coffin, they will say, 'Poor soul, this is how he went!' Your entire life will have gone thinking about what people will say. You won't be able to do anything. You won't even truly live your life.

And who are these people? What is their value? What is their self-worth? Today, they applaud your praises; tomorrow, they hurl abuses. The same people. It doesn't take long for them to change; there is no integrity in them. Do they have any substance? Is there any stability in them? None of their words hold any value. Their praise, their honour is not free. When they show respect, they expect something in return. It's a negotiation. They say, follow our norms, and we will give you respect. If you want more respect, follow our norms even more. If you want us to call you a great soul, then unquestionably follow our norms to the letter.

And for their words of praises, we have completely confined ourselves. We can do anything for their validation. In China, for thousands of years, women lived in crippled conditions. Small iron shoes were placed on the feet of little girls so that their feet wouldn't grow larger. Having small feet was a symbol of beauty, a sign of nobility. So small that truly noble women had to walk with the support of two other women because with feet so cramped, they couldn't manage a large body. The whole body grew larger, but the feet remained incredibly small. However, women were willing to endure this because the smallness of their feet garnered praise.

Even today, women are willing to do anything for compliments. Their lips are painted red, they apply fake blush to appear as if they are in love or sexually interested, all to attract attention. They wear heels and mini skirts to make their legs appear longer because, in the animal kingdom, long legs are a sign that the female is ready to breed. All things considered beautiful are merely mind tricks to evoke sexual attraction in the opposite gender. Women are knowingly or unknowingly ready to do all this because it earns them praise.Yes, if they do it of their own free will, I have no problem, but the reality is that they are not making these choices without compulsion. If they don't wear makeup, if they don't wear heels, their entire confidence shatters; they feel inferior. Is this freedom? No. They feel inferior because they worry about what people will say; people's words bind them, whether they accept it or not.

And the source of these words is *mātṛkā.*

Rudyard Kipling, the author of *The Jungle Book*, wrote "Words are, of course, the most powerful drug used by mankind."

Words deeply impact us. For instance, in our village, there used to be an elderly couple whose son served in the army. Every year or two, he would send them letters, assuring them of his well-being. However, someone misinformed them that their son had become a martyr. Given the limited means of long-distance communication at the time, the words, despite being false, took a toll, causing both parents to pass away within a month.

Another incident involves a girl I know who was in a long-term relationship with her lover. Words reached her, alleging betrayal by her beloved. The impact of these untrue words was profound, sparking a heated confrontation that eventually led to a painful breakup. Later, it was revealed that the words were false and entirely baseless. However, her former lover moved on and got married to someone else, while the girl spiraled into mental illness, attempting suicide multiple times.

These incidents highlight the tragic outcomes that can result from words. If we take these words just as words, as a distinct pattern of sound, without connecting them with objects, similar to how we take words of a language we don't understand, then they will have no impact on us whatsoever. For example, if I were to verbally abuse you, you might react strongly, even violently. However, if I were to abuse you in a language you don't understand, using even the harshest and most vulgar words but with a smile, you would merely look at me with curiosity. And since I'm smiling, you would likely smile too.

The point is, we are troubled by words when we associate them with the objects they refer to. By maintaining a separation between the words and the objects they are referring to, ninety percent of problems will disappear.

Now, it's one thing to be influenced by the words of others; it's superficial. *Mātṛkā*, however, operates on a much profounder level. Whatever words you verbalise or conceive mentally define you. You become those words, and they become your identity, creating boundaries and limitations. In Sanskrit, we express it as *yat bhāvo tat bhavati*, meaning you become what you think. In fact, your thoughts make you who you are.

Pause for a moment and consider a state where all thoughts come to a halt. In that moment, who are you? No ready answers surface. You can't say that you are a Hindu, or a Muslim, or a man, or a woman. All thoughts have vanished—names, countries, genders—all words cease to exist. You can't even articulate your own name. Language itself dissolves, making it impossible for you to identify with your nationality or ethnicity. In the absence of thought, who are you?

Patañjali writes in his *Yoga Sūtras*,

योगश्चित्तवृत्तिनिरोधः ॥
तदा द्रष्टु स्वरूपेऽवस्थानम् ॥
वृत्तिसारूप्यमितरत्र ॥

yogaścittavṛttinirodhaḥ ||
tadā draṣṭuḥ svarūpe 'vasthānam ||
vṛttisārūpyamitaratra ||

Yoga is the cessation of thoughts
Then the seer abides in itself, resting in its true nature.
At other times, the seer identifies with the thoughts.

(*Yoga Sūtras* I.2-4)

The current state of being that you're experiencing, as a limited entity, is shaped by your thoughts. Once your thoughts cease, you will become rooted in your true Self. In that consciousness, which is absolutely free. But right now, you are in ignorance, having become a limited being. Why? Because you are identified with your thoughts. These thoughts are constructed from words, and those words are formed by letters energised by *mātṛkā*. Now, you might have gained a slight understanding of the depth of how *mātṛkā* serves as the foundation of bondage.

We perceive multiplicity, and words play a significant role in creating and maintaining this illusion.

In the vast and arid savannas of Namibia, there exists a tribe called the Himba. These are people who are incapable of distinguishing between green and blue colours. It's not because they are colour-blind. No, they can see and understand various shades of green, but they cannot differentiate between blue and green. The colour blue doesn't exist for them because in their language, there is no specific word for the colour blue. It's not that their language lacks a term for the colour blue because they can't see it, or because there is a certain defect in their eyes, but rather, they cannot see it as separate from green because there is no distinct word for it in their language. They use the same word to describe both blue and green. When they look at the sky or the sea, they see the same colour as the leaves on a tree.

This is an incredibly fascinating example that tells us how the words we use to describe the world around us can shape our perceptions and create the illusion of diversity.

We immediately create imaginary divisions of reality and connect them with words, giving them a name. This one is Muslim, that one is Hindu; this is a snake, that is a plant—no, it just is. Simply become conscious of that existence; don't label it. The act of labelling leads to the division of things. When we were children, we only saw a tree; then we started seeing branches, twigs, dry and fresh leaves, flowers, fruits, etc.—we created an infinite division of a single tree. And this is what reinforces the illusion of multiplicity (*māyā*). We will delve into this in the next chapter.

शब्दराशिसमुत्थस्य शक्तिवर्गस्य भोग्यताम् ।
कलाविलुप्तविभवो गतः सन्स पशुः स्मृतः ॥

śabdārāśisamutthasya śaktivarṇasya bhogyatām |
kalāviluptavibhavo gataḥ sans pashuḥ smṛtaḥ ||

Being deprived of his glory by *kalā*, he (the individual) becomes a victim of the group of Powers arising from the multitude of words, and thus he is known as the bound one (*paśu*).

(*Spanda-Kārikās* III.13)

This concludes our study of Sūtra Four.

CHAPTER FIVE

उद्यमो भैरवः ॥५॥

|| Udyamo Bhairavaḥ || 5 ||

(Active) **Effort is *Bhairava.***

Names fall into one of two categories: those that provide information about the entity they represent, conveying a specific meaning that imparts a clear understanding upon hearing them. The other type of name has no connection whatsoever with the object it represents.

For example, consider *Felis domestica*, the scientific name for a domestic cat, which serves two purposes:

1. It indicates that the entity belongs to the cat family, using *Felis* to denote a group of animals related to the cat family.
2. It specifies that the cat is domesticated, as *domestica* means domestic.

On the other hand, if a cat is named *Bubbles*, it doesn't convey any relevant information; it's a name without purpose. This is because bubbles are thin spheres of liquid enclosing air or gas, typically producing a spherical shape due to surface tension, and it holds no connection to the feline.

Naming for humans also often falls into this second category because parents name their child based on their own preferences without having any idea about the child's nature.

My father used to share a story with me about a boy named Thithpaal. This name had no meaning, which troubled him deep inside. One day, this inner turmoil drove him to leave his home in search of answers about whether our names influence us in any way.

As he walked a short distance, he came across a maid sweeping outside someone else's house. Thithpaal approached her and asked for her name, and she replied, "Rājeśvarī (the Goddess of kings)". Continuing on his path, Thithpaal encountered a beggar. He asked the beggar for his name, and the beggar replied, "Kubera (the God of wealth)".

Pressing further, Thithpaal stumbled upon a funeral procession, where four individuals carried a deceased person on their shoulders. He asked them for the name of the dead, and the mourners responded, "His name was Amar (immortal)".

Thithpaal returned home content and at peace with his own name.

So, human names lack meaning; they are mere beautiful words chosen by the parents. In contrast, divine names carry meanings that reveal the essence of their bearers. Bhairava, a name not chosen arbitrarily, reflects the sages' deep understanding of the nature of supreme reality. This name is rich with interpretations and stands as one of two words in the Sūtra, deserving a concise comprehension. As Bhairava is my chosen deity, it is both my pleasure and privilege to illuminate the essence of His name through my words. To me, there exists no beauty more greater than this. Instead of delving into the labyrinth of Sanskrit grammar and explaining the literal meanings behind each interpretation, I shall, in simple words, describe the manifold meanings of Bhairava as penned in our sacred texts.

1. The first meaning of the name Bhairava is that which lifts us beyond fear, tears, and sorrow. Until we experience the reality of this world and our own reality, fear (*bhaya*, means fear) remains our companion, fear of death, and fear of death is the root of all other fears. If you fear disgrace,

it is also connected to the fear of death because disrespect means social rejection. You fear that you will be separated from your herd, from those who know you and those who love you, and for a solitary animal that has strayed from the herd, surviving alone in the wilderness is as difficult as navigating a maze in complete darkness.

So, from this fear, the abyss of sorrow, and the wailing (*rava* translates to screaming or crying out loudly), He elevates you; hence, He is called Bhairava. Our screams emerge when we feel trapped, when we are overwhelmed by fear. Every creature screams; in fact, even plants emit ultrasonic signals when they are in great fear or distress, such as when their stems are damaged. He who takes us above and beyond this crying, screaming, suffering, and fear (*vyutthāna*, meaning transcendence—literally, *intensely rising up or away from*), He is Bhairava, and how does He make us transcend this suffering?

2. The first syllable in Bhairava can have two different meanings: fear (*bhaya*), as mentioned earlier, and the refulgent light (*bha*) of consciousness. This light, the illumination of consciousness, enlightens everything. Just as the sun in the external world transforms the darkness of night into the brightness of morning, similarly, this light of consciousness transforms the darkness of ignorance into the brilliance of enlightenment.

   The meaning of the syllable *rava* can also be resonance or vibration (according to the *Brahma Yāmala*). One can also think of it as the power of self-consciousness—*vimarśa śakti.* Therefore, Bhairava means the resonance of consciousness that pervades everything, and that's how He lifts us above the sufferings of this world.
3. In a person's life, there comes a time when they shatter completely. They begin to harbour resentment towards the world. They feel the weight of their bonds, realising

that for every grain of pleasure, they endure mountains of sorrow. Yet, despite knowing this, they find no other choice but to chase after pleasures. Everything they love, everything they cherish, is snatched away. They spend their entire life chasing success, tirelessly making efforts, only to be stripped of everything by death in the end. And they reincarnate, empty-handed, naked, and the race begins anew. Much like Sisyphus, who was forced to roll a boulder up a hill for eternity.

After this realisation, fear grips them. They want to break free from this cycle of existence, yearning for freedom. A scream emanates from within, a scream for liberation from this worldly bondage. This is true renunciation. Renunciation is when the knowledge of worldly bondage emerges from within you. It doesn't let you live for even a moment in it. The longing for liberation intensifies within, like the desperate gasp for breath by a drowning person. This desire for liberation, the fear of the world, the scream for liberation from the world—this is Bhairava.

4. The resolution born within us in the face of the fears of the world—the manifestations that arise in our hearts—that is Bhairava. When we are afraid of the world, our hearts automatically turn towards the divine. In the Mahābhārata, Kunti prays to Lord Kṛṣṇa, *vipadaḥ santu tāḥ śaśvat tatra tatra jagadguro bhavato darśanaṃ yatsyādapunarbhavadarśanam*—may calamities come again and again so that we can witness Your divine presence repeatedly, as seeing You ensures liberation from the cycle of birth and death.

So, when the world instills fear, a contemplation arises within us—a call is heard in our hearts, the call of the divine, the call of Bhairava. Our minds, then, detach from the world, we leave everything behind, and our attachment to life diminishes, marking the beginning of our spiritual journey. This is the divine initiation—*śaktipāt*. Bhairava is *śaktipāt*.

5. For those who fear the world, those who dread the ceaseless cycle of birth and death, Bhairava is their benefactor. That's another reason why His name is Bhairava. He eradicates your fears; He doesn't assist you in escaping from life; instead, He teaches you to confront life. He makes you resilient, he makes you fearless. He doesn't succumb to your hardships; instead, he empowers you so much that you can face your hardships. Ultimately, He reveals to you that the world is your own creation, dissipating your fears forever.
6. The name Bhairava has another meaning. *Bhera* means time *(bhāṇi-nakṣatrāṇi īrayati prerayati iti bheraḥ)*; it is time that propels celestial bodies such as stars, planets, and other cosmic entities in motion. Time inspires their movement. Hence, time is referred to as Bhera. However, the great yogis are called *bheravāḥ* because their power is such that they cause the existence of time to dry out for them. They make time wither; they sap the life out of time *(bheraṁ śoṣyanti iti bheravāḥ)*. They have advanced in meditation to such an extent that time holds no sway over them. They have transcended the limitations of time and space, remaining in a state of deep meditation known as *kāla-grāsa-samādhi*—a transcendental state where time ceases to exist. Such yogis are called *bheravāḥ*.

   And, *tāsām ayam prakaṭa iti bhairava*, He who manifests in front of these yogis is Bhairava. Because he manifests in the *samādhi* experienced by these yogis, He is given the name Bhairava.
7. The name Bhairava also serves as a title, signifying his mastery and lordship over the four goddesses—*khecharī, gocarī, dikcharī,* and *bhucarī*. In Sanskrit, the collective group of these four goddesses is termed as *bhīrava*. Thus,

Bhairava is the appellation bestowed upon the one who holds dominion over them. A more detailed exploration of these four goddesses awaits in the forthcoming chapter.

8. The eighth facet of the name Bhairava is frightening. He is frightening because he brings about the end of our worldly existence, including all our identifications, actions, and inclinations. In Vārāṇasī, it is said that those who meet their death near the banks of the river Ganga, Bhairava liberates them from the cycles of birth and death. However, the consequences of one's actions persist, awaiting them in the next life. If an individual has engaged in a lifetime of negative deeds without a trace of self-realisation, and now, as they approach death, they arrive near the river in the hopes of being liberated without facing the consequences, it seems unjust. Hence, it is said that before liberating someone, Bhairava makes them endure the consequences of their actions. In a split second, they feel the infinite pain of eternal hell, reaping the results of all their past deeds. This torment, this process, is *bhairavī yātna.*

   Now, when one is engaged in such a frightening task, the appearance must match. Hence, the terrifying form of Bhairava. One glance at him can make a person dizzy because it signifies the end of our limited existence—all that which we hold dear, cling to, and do not wish to let go. Bhairava snatches away all that from us, and that's why he appears frightening.

9. The ninth meaning of the name Bhairava is the One who sustains and maintains this world, the universe, by becoming one with it and filling it with His consciousness. This world exists because we are aware of it; we have imbued it with our consciousness. If we were to become unconscious, the existence of this world would cease. Everything in this world exists because it is one with our consciousness, filled by it, and sustained through our awareness.

Bhairava Himself is protected by this world, which, in turn, is maintained by Him. This world is an expression of Bhairava, just as this book is an expression of what is happening within me—a manifestation. If I didn't write this book, the events within me would never come to light, never manifest. For its existence, this expression was necessary. Similarly, if this world did not exist, we wouldn't understand Bhairava because we wouldn't exist. Bhairava would have no manifested existence. This world, as I always say, is Śiva's attempt to taste His own sweetness, to savour His own bliss.

10. And finally, the meaning of the name Bhairava is one who creates, destroys, and preserves. *Bha* signifies *bharana*, which means to create, to form, to fill the world with one's consciousness. *Ra* stands for *raman*, implying playing, sustaining the world, maintaining it. As long as we are engaging with this world, its existence remains. And *va* stands for *vamana*, meaning to puke out, expel, emit, taking the world out of one's consciousness. So, Bhairava is derived from these three words: *bharana* (to create), *ramana* (to protect), and *vamana* (to emit or disgorge).

Therefore, in Tantra, we refer to Lord Śiva as Bhairava. There can be no better name for that supreme reality. Now, before delving into the meaning of this aphorism, let me provide scriptural evidence that what I have mentioned above is revealed by Bhairava himself to those sages who have experienced Bhairava. These are not merely my theories but divine revelations passed down through generations to us Tāntrikas.

viśvaṁ bibharti pūraṇadhāraṇayogena tena ca śriyate |
savimarśatayā rava rūpataśca saṁsārabhīruhitakṛcca ||
saṁsārabhītijanitādravātparāmarśato'pi hṛdi jātaḥ |
prakaṭībhūtaṁ bhavabhayavimarśanaṁ śaktipātato yena ||

He who carries the whole universe, who nourishes and supports it, and who is carried by it. He is the sound who by his power of awareness, protects those who are frightened by the world of transmigration.

Nakṣatraprerakakālatattvasaṁśoṣakāriṇo ye ca |
Kālagrāsasamādhānarasikamanaḥsu teṣu ca prakaṭaḥ ||
Saṅkocipaśujanabhiye yāsāṁ ravaṇaṁ svakaraṇadevīnām |
Antarbahiścaturvidhakhecaryādikagaṇasyāpi ||
Tasya svāmī saṁsāravṛttivighaṭanamahābhīmaḥ |
Bhairava iti gurubhirimairanvarthaiḥ saṁstutaḥ śāstre ||

Bhairava reveals Himself to yogins (in their hearts) who are capable of drying up the stream of time which is the mover of the planetary system. (This they do by virtue of stopping the functions of breathing-in and breathing-out, *prāna* and *apāna*, and redirecting the breath via the *suṣumnā*) and thus by getting the bliss of equipoise of mind. In scriptures grand teachers have explained the derivation of the name Bhairava significantly as the Divine Being who as the frightful mighty agent is responsible for removing the evil of worldliness which is the cause of bringing contraction to the Self so as to remove it away from Śiva to place it down to the level of animality by means of bringing limitation to the range of the senses operating externally and four forces, namely, (*khecharī, gocarī, dikcharī,* and *bhucarī*) operating internally.

(*Tantrāloka* I.96-100)

bhayā sarvam ravayati sarvado-vyāpako' khile |
iti bhairava-śabdasya santatoccāranācchivaḥ ||

Bhairava is one who with fear (*bhayā*) makes everything resound (*ravayati*), and who pervades the entire universe. He who utters this word Bhairava unceasingly becomes Śiva.

(*Vijñāna Bhairava Tantra* 130)

The second word of this verse is *udyama*. This word is profound, encompassing various meanings within itself. *Udyama*, in Sanskrit, generally translates to strenuous or assiduous effort, exertion, diligence, and perseverance. For instance, a verse from the *Pañcatantra*, states, *udyamena hi sidhyanti kāryāṇi na manorathaiḥ*, translating to strenuous efforts alone bring success; not mere wishes.

Kaliḍāsa also used the term *udyama* specifically to denote arduous efforts or penance, as evident in one of his masterpieces, *Kumārasambhava*. A line from this epic goes, *niśamya caināṃ tapase kṛtodyamām*, which translates to, *having heard her (Pārvatī), resolute in her strenuous efforts...*

In this sentence, Kaliḍāsa describes the intense penance and diligence of Mother Pārvatī to attain Śiva. She abstained from both food and drink, enduring heavy snowfall during the cold season to engage in night-long meditation. Chanting the "*Oṁ Namaḥ Śivāyaḥ*" mantra, she immersed her body in water up to her throat, meditating within the icy water on severe cold nights. As the weather turned hot, she continued her meditation outside, surrounded by blazing fires in the scorching afternoon sun. Her unwavering dedication and extreme exertion were directed entirely towards attaining Śiva.

The first meaning of this verse is inherently clear—**Bhairava is attained through intense and robust efforts**. In this world, everything is attained through effort,

Udyamena hi sidhyanti kāryāṇi na manorathaiḥ; 'strenuous efforts alone bring success; not mere wishes'. Even a competitive exam in India, to select candidates for various administrative positions within the government (UPSC), requires extreme efforts to crack . I am from Bihar , a region in India where the majority of children prepare for such competitive exams. I have seen their hard work . They come from villages and underprivileged backgrounds. Their parents struggle to earn a two-square meal, engaging in labour, farming, and various odd jobs to support their children. Despite financial hardships, they manage to educate their children, often sacrificing their own meals. Then, these youngsters are sent to cities for exam preparation. Some families sell their lands or mortgage their homes to send them to the city. Millions of children leave their homes with the hope that they will return to their villages adorned in the coveted uniform, but out of a million aspirants, only about a thousand manage to crack the administrative exam.

In the city, they manage their studies in a small room, sometimes even smaller than the average person's bathroom. They cook, study, and sleep in that cramped space. I have personally witnessed how they study under a flickering light bulb during rainy nights, rainwater pouring into their rooms from damaged roofs. When so much effort is put into cracking a competitive exam, how can one expect the truth to be obtained so easily?

Many people approach me, expressing that they exert arduous efforts and diligently practice meditation. However, despite their endeavours, they find themselves not experiencing a connection with God or attaining enlightenment. Yet I observe that their faces don't reflect arduous efforts. For them, spiritual activities, prayer, and meditation appear to be mere ornamental displays. They believe they have everything in life—home, wife, good income—so a little prayer should suffice. They manage to take out some time in the day, maybe half an hour or an hour, to perform prayers or recite a couple of hymns, but is this enough to attain the truth?

I consistently emphasise that just as much effort and dedication is required in spiritual practices and meditation as one puts into their job, source of income, or academic pursuits if they are a student. Without surpassing the effort invested in these aspects, achieving enlightenment becomes very difficult. Yes, your mind will become calmer, your life will be okay, and there will be less stress, but the possibility of attaining Śiva is minimal.

During my days of practising meditation, I found myself in a state of detachment from formal education. The process of dropping out from school was gradual. Initially, I attended school for four days, and on the other two days, I would feign stomach pain as an excuse for my absence. Then it progressed to 3 days in school and 3 days absent, then 2 days in school and 4 days absent, continuing like this until, by the time I reached the ninth grade, I attended school only for five days.

Devoting extensive periods to meditation, I engaged in continuous sessions lasting 5-7 hours, twice a day. During the remaining time, I would either immerse myself in drawing or delve into books. Unable to express myself in front of people, I found expression through my art, while my quest for truth led me deep into the pages of books. Even after a year of this routine, I achieved no results… other than arthritis! Yet, despite the excruciating pain in my knees, I persevered in meditating in the lotus position for extended periods.

It was only then that I had one of my earlier spiritual experiences. One night, as I was meditating in the prayer room as usual, hours passed, and then, for the first time, I understood that I was not the body. It happened that when I opened my eyes, it was half past two in the night, and I was sitting in a meditative posture, but my body had fallen back. However, I felt no fear or anxiety, and when I closed my eyes again and opened them, I was back in my body, lying down. The clock confirmed it was half past two in the night, dispelling any doubts that it was a mere dream. That night, I realised that reality surpasses the boundaries of our imagination.

Efforts are essential, but it's important to understand that efforts are of two types: active and passive, direct and indirect; And, there exists a third type that falls somewhere in between. For instance, reciting a mantra, performing noble and selfless actions, practising breathing exercises, or engaging in worship—

these are indirect efforts toward attaining truth. This falls under the category of *āṇavopāya*—the path to attaining the divine, where distinctions exist between me and the deity I am meditating on, or between me and the mantra I am chanting, etc. This path is considered the lowest, as it is indirect. Worshipping an idol and chanting mantras are methods employed to purify the mind. We undertake these practices to free our minds from thoughts that create differences, to clear such thoughts that I am separate from the rest of the world. Through idol worship or selfless actions, we strive to purify our minds of such divisive thoughts. Both the devotee and the object of devotion experience a sense of oneness through worship. Chanting mantras eradicates thoughts that create differences. With selfless actions, we feel one with all living beings, finding joy in their happiness and feeling their sorrows. We rise above thoughts that create differences. This is also achieved through breathing exercises. Once the mind is purified, we progress to *śaktopāya,* where both duality and non-duality coexist. Here, we meditate on ourselves, contemplating "Who am I?"—Here also there is a difference between the unknown entity we connect with using terms like 'who' and 'what,' and our own Self. Although both are referring to the same entity, therefore, both duality and non-duality coexist here. Pure thoughts are crucial for this technique—thoughts that do not create differences.

However, *śaktopāya* does not fall under the category of active effort either; it lies between the direct and indirect, between active and passive effort.

In this Sūtra, the term *udyama* specifically refers to active effort. It is the effort that directly unites us with Bhairava, happening instantaneously. There are reasons behind my assertion. Firstly, this volume of the Śiva *Sūtras* is based on *śāmbhavopāya. Śāmbhavopāya,* meaning active and direct effort, aligns you immediately with Bhairava. This is the pathless path.

The second reason is that in this context, the meaning of *udyama* is *unmajjanarūpaḥ*—as also stated by *Kṣemarāja*. *Unmajjanarūpaḥ* translates to a sudden emergence, instantaneous. It is the effort that makes you one with Bhairava instantaneously, and that's why this effort is Bhairava. *Udyamao Bhairava.*

Understand this: you yourself are God, and this truth cannot be attained through actions. You might feel that I am contradicting myself, but please understand carefully. Enlightenment is not the result of hard work; it cannot be. After enlightenment, you become limitless, merging with the source of infinite knowledge and bliss. Therefore, it's evident that this cannot be the outcome of limited efforts. Actions and reactions are equally proportional. The more effort you exert, the more results you achieve, neither less nor more. Your effort is limited; whether you meditate for seven years or a lifetime, it remains finite. In such a scenario, the result of that limited effort should also be finite, not limitless. If the obtained result is limitless—infinitive knowledge and bliss—it can never be, and never was, the result of your limited and finite efforts. In reality, it has always been yours; it was not attained through your efforts.

The effort you put in was just to realise that the truth has always been mine; it was never separate from me. Effort was required to prepare the body and mind. The sun is visible; there was no effort to make it rise; the effort was to remove the cataract from the eyes. However, it's possible that this effort was already made in a past life. That's why some commentators do not believe that in this verse, *udyama* means efforts, at all. They argue that *udyama* means instantaneous, sudden emergence, and they are correct.

Enlightenment is that moment when the fruit separates from the branch, the process of the fruit ripening is not enlightenment. The moment it disconnects from the branch is enlightenment. And it is spontaneous, it is instantaneous, it is sudden. Once it separates from the branch, the earth automatically draws it into its lap, just like when the moment of enlightenment occurs, Bhairava draws you into his embrace.

And it can happen now, it can happen in this very moment if you have ripened enough, and if your effort is active and direct. What does active effort mean? The word *udyama* in this aphorism can be interpreted in another way. The word is formed from *ut* + *yam*. *Ut* means up, upwards, and *yam* means to raise, to hold. Therefore, *udyama* means lifting up, raising up, elevation of consciousness.

Active effort is when you elevate your consciousness and hold it there. At that moment, you instantly become one with the truth. There is no need for any meditative absorption. Maharṣi Aṣṭāvakra speaks of this active effort, stating:

निःसंगो निष्क्रियोऽसि तं स्वप्रकाशो निरंजनः ।
अयमेव हि ते बन्धः समाधिमनुतिष्ठसि ॥

niḥsaṅgo niṣkriyo'si taṁ svaprakāśo nirañjanaḥ |
ayameva hi te bandhaḥ samādhimanutiṣṭhasi ||

You are unattached, still, self-effulgent and without any blemish.
This indeed is your bondage that you have to practise *samādhi*.

We are inherently free. Yet, we aspire to attain *samādhi*—the cessation of mental fluctuations, or pursue various spiritual experiences. However, such endeavours give birth to the notion that we are bound, not inherently free, and that we must experience *samādhi* to achieve freedom. These efforts reinforce the belief that we are not already free. As long as we perceive ourselves as bound, freedom remains elusive.

Putting in active effort means raising up your consciousness and holding it there. Where exactly is *up*? Bhairava resides on Mount Kailāśa. It is there that he imparted the teachings of Tantra to Goddess Pārvatī. In *Sanātana Dharma*, the peak of Kailāśa is considered the highest, even surpassing Mount Everest. While thousands have conquered Everest's summit, none have conquered Mount Kailāśa. Symbolically, Kailāśa represents the pinnacle of consciousness. Near Kailāśa, there are two water bodies: Rākṣasa Tāla and Mānasarovar. Initially, one was nearly circular like the sun, and the other had a crescent moon shape. Over time, their shapes changed, but the symbolism remains clear.

In yogic and Tāntrika principles, the sun and moon represent *piṅgalā* and *iḍā nāḍīs*. The central channel, called *suṣumṇā nāḍī*, flows between them, leading us to Śiva. *iḍā*, on the left side, is associated with the moon, while *piṅgalā*, on the right, is associated with the sun. Interestingly, Mānasarovar, resembling a crescent moon, is on the left, and Rākṣasa Tāla, with a circular sun-like shape, is on the right. The path to Mount Kailāśa goes between them.

Now, why is the highest pinnacle of consciousness symbolised as a mountain? When one sees the world from an elevated perspective or from the summit of a mountain, clarity emerges. Everything unfolds before the observer in its true form. In contrast, standing at ground level provides only a limited view of what lies directly ahead; to grasp the entirety, ascending to a higher perspective becomes necessary.

Focusing only on a small aspect of something hinders a complete understanding. If we analogize this world to a jungle, one must climb to an elevated vantage point (such as a treetop or hill) to comprehend its true structure, identify landmarks, and navigate effectively through the complexities. Otherwise, one may find oneself meandering in circles.

Similarly, maintaining consciousness at an elevated state is essential. This is why Bhairav is always portrayed atop the world's highest mountain. Positioned there, He perceives reality, as it is. Worship is bestowed upon Him, and He impartially regards both gods and demons because, from His perspective, the concepts of good and evil dissolve into a broader, all-encompassing understanding.

How can we practically maintain consciousness in an elevated state? The answer to this question is properly found in the next aphorism, but the explanation of the aphorism seems incomplete here, so I will provide the answer to this question right here. As an illustration, consider this image of snow-covered rocky mountains. I have zoomed in to highlight specific details, showcasing the structure, material, form, and colours (given the print is in colour). However, by focusing on these details, one might miss the bigger picture. When we step back and zoom out a bit, disregarding specific details and observing the whole, Śiva, hidden within, becomes apparent…

If you cannot see it, it means you are currently entangled in specifics. Thus, let's step back a bit more, zoom out a little further, so that we do not get entangled in specific forms, structures, etc.

I am reminded of a tale, perhaps encountered in my readings, which unfolds in Athens, Greece, involving a philosopher—possibly Socrates. There came a moment when this philosopher vanished without a trace, causing concern from his wife, family, friends, and disciples. Their concerted efforts to locate him spanned the entirety of Athens. After two days of relentless searching, they discovered him beneath a tree, his head inclined upwards, seemingly in a deep contemplation. Though his eyes were open, they remained fixed, as a stone. While he looked in a direction, it was not towards anything specific, and his body was motionless, with a tranquil expression on his face. He breathed; he was alive. The nature of his state—whether he was entranced or oblivious to his surroundings—remained unclear. People attempted to rouse him, calling his name loudly, and only then did he return to awareness.

Upon inquiry about his activities, Socrates responded with uncertainty, "I do not know how I arrived here. The last I can recall is that I was observing the stars, looking at the sky. I kept watching, and watching, and gradually, the stars started disappearing. The sky also disappeared. Everything disappeared. I felt at peace." Beyond this point, he found himself unable to recall any further details of the experience.

In the tale of Socrates, the state in which he transcended is referred to as *bhairavī mudrā*. We will delve into this in the next chapter. It is a practice that can be considered an active effort, to some extent. You can try it, and if you are persistent enough, this practice will bring you instantly face to face with the truth. The moment you perform it correctly, you will confront the truth directly.

What to do?

Simply observe things as they are, without any filters. When you remain aware without applying filters, your ego diminishes, and you become one with everything.

You need to become aware without any choice, be it towards the sky, towards plants, or towards one's own body—just stay attentive, stay aware. There is no need for interference there, like saying I don't want this, this person is not good, and so on. Just remain aware, reserve judgement only where necessary, where a decision needs to be made. Otherwise, just stay aware. Without liking or disliking anything. And refrain from attaching words and names to existence.

This one is Muslim, that one is Hindu; this is a snake, that is a plant—no, it just is. Simply become conscious of that existence; don't label it. The act of labelling leads to the division of things. When we were children, we only saw a tree; then we started seeing branches, twigs, dry and fresh leaves, flowers, fruits, etc.—we created an infinite division of a single tree.

This strengthens *māyā*. The point at which the fruit separates from the tree is the boundary of that fruit, and there is no place for separations and boundaries in this technique.

We have established certain imaginary boundaries to differentiate the fruit from the branch, the branch from the trunk, but all of them are inherently one, and there is no true separation. We have delineated boundaries to differentiate that up to this point, it is a tree, beyond which the tree ends, and the ground begins. Or, beyond this point, the tree ends, and the sky begins. Yet, the tree and the ground are intimately connected; they exist because of each other. Every moment, the roots absorb water and nutrients from the soil—a process crucial for the tree's growth, development, and overall metabolic functions.

Simultaneously, the leaves and branches, upon falling, decompose with the help of microorganisms, enriching the soil and making it more fertile. This enriched soil allows the tree to absorb nutrients again. The presence of tree roots in the soil prevents soil erosion, as they stabilise soil particles and form a network that binds the soil together. Anyone who observes will find that the tree and the soil beneath function like a single organism.

Trees also serve as natural windbreaks, reducing wind speed at ground level. This windbreak effect significantly impacts local climates by shielding against soil erosion and preserving soil moisture. The interconnectedness between the trunk, the sky, clouds, and the surrounding climate is so intricate and interdependent that any attempt to segregate them is merely superficial, lacking depth. I will shed some light on this connection so that you can perceive things from my vantage point.

Around people, there is a coolness, and it's not just because their branches and leaves provide us shade and protection from the sun, no. The leaves of trees release moisture into the atmosphere, and this process is called transpiration. Think of it as the forest's breath. The leaves release water vapour, creating a refreshing ambience and contributing to the formation of clouds that bring life-giving rainfall.

Clouds and trees share an even deeper connection. Trees release tiny scented molecules into the air, known as volatile organic compounds or VOCs, giving the forest its fresh fragrance. Now, here's the fascinating part: a significant portion of these fragrant compounds transforms into tiny particles called aerosols. Think of aerosols as invisible dust in the air.

These minuscule aerosols act like magic seeds for clouds. When there's a sufficient amount of them in the sky, they attract water droplets. These water droplets gather around the aerosols, forming clouds. And clouds, as we know, bring rain.

Trees and animals are also intricately connected. The carbon dioxide we exhale is breathed in by the plants, and the oxygen they exhale is vital for our lives. Without it, we are nothing. In this world, everything is interconnected, much like the various organs of a body. Everything functions together as inseparable limbs of one universal being.

Consider your body with its many organs and the millions of cells that form them, and then think about the countless microorganisms that are a part of your body, necessary for its proper functioning. All these elements come together to form your body, and you recognize them as an inseparable part of yourself. Right now, you consider your body as yourself, and so these organs, limbs, and microorganisms constitute your identity. They are a part of yourself. So, why stop at the boundaries of our skin? Beyond our physical bodies, we are intimately connected to the trees, the earth, the sky, the sun, and everything in the universe. What prevents us from embracing oneness with the entire world? Why do we create divisions and boundaries?

There is no place for division and boundaries in this technique. A similar method is found in the *Vijñāna Bhairav Tantra* (59), where Lord Śiva instructs, "Direct your gaze towards something and let go of all boundaries associated with it. Through this, you will merge with that and become one with the entirety of existence". Boundaries attribute a name and form to anything. If you remove the boundaries of a country from the world map, neither its name nor its form remains. Similarly, in this world, boundaries define everything, and due to a distinct form, we assign a name to it because we need words to refer to it. As mentioned earlier, there is no difference between the leaf and the tree's trunk, but we separate a portion of the tree, give it boundaries, and due to these boundaries, it takes on a distinct form, and we name it a leaf. This name and form are bondage. Giving something a distinct form, by separating a portion from the whole, automatically assigns it a name, and it works vice versa; when you assign a name to something, it automatically separates that portion from the whole and gives it a distinct form. Name and form are essentially the same thing; both are different types of labelling—audible labelling, and visual labelling. Giving a name and form to something separates it from existence and gives rise to the illusion of diversity—*māyā*.

Śiva is saying, discard the boundaries, *bhittis tyakatva*, *bhittis* meaning enclosures of a particular shape and its characteristics. Remove all kinds of enclosures, walls, and boundaries, as they are purely imaginative. They have no real existence; you have created these boundaries only for easy communication or understanding.

And when you look at something without these enclosures, you will truly become one with it, because now there are no boundaries left to prevent you from becoming one with it. When you see without these boundaries, there will be no movement in the eyes, and there is no need to let the eyes move, because if the eyes are moving, it means you are dividing existence into fragments, seeing one part before the other. You are not seeing the world as a whole. Your focus is now on the tree, then the eyes move to look at a stone; this should not happen. When the tree and the stone are one, why move the eye? Just look at the tree, remove all the enclosures, and it becomes one with the entirety of existence. Because it was a tree, now it is not; it has no name or form now, no boundary separating it from the world. So, the eyes will not move.

And when the eyes remain still, the flow of thoughts naturally ceases. There exists an inherent connection between thoughts and the movement of the eyes. The second point is that without a name and form, something is simply pure existence; there is no possibility of any thought or contemplation about it. It simply is; you cannot think about it. If it had a particular form, a name, or if it were made of a particular substance, then you could think about it in various ways. You might want to steal it, do something with it, sell it, or think about its value—many things are possible. But in pure existence, no thoughts or contemplation are possible. Pure existence dissolves every name, form, substance, and, therefore, stops all thoughts. And there is no possibility for the eyes to move from one part to another; because there are no parts, no enclosures, you have taken it as a whole. Thus you become one with it in the end.

You must understand that this is not concentrating on a single thing. Generally, concentration means limiting oneself to a particular object. When you attempt to focus on a single object, in reality, you are resisting the rest, other countless things. And this creates a conflict. A battle. Half of your energy is consumed in this struggle. Every type of conflict creates tension; tension is when you are constantly applying force. Your constant force is engaged in keeping your attention away from everything else except that one thing. So, this is a state of tension. It is necessary at times, but we are not discussing concentration here. I am talking about a state that is not limited to a single object, that is not at war with anything; and because there is no resistance, no stress, you become capable of high levels of alertness. Śiva says,

"Wherever the mind goes, whether outside or within, there itself is the state of Śiva. Since He is all-pervading, where else could the mind go?"

However, I am still asserting that the eyes should not move. Why? Isn't keeping the eyes still the same as concentrating? You can divide the practice of this method into two parts—one that you can do anytime, anywhere while living life. Whether you're on the metro, in the park, or during a 10-15 minute break in the office, in fact, it would be best to do this every hour by taking out 10-15 minutes. In this variation, there is no need to keep the eyes focused on a single object; everything else remains the same. Look without any boundaries, and look in a way that the identity of the observer is not left.

Aside from this, take at least half an hour each day to sit somewhere without moving your eyes, focusing on a single object, as I explained above. In this variation, the eyes should remain still. This approach is for beginners. As you progress, you will reach a state where heightened awareness persists, regardless of whatever or wherever you are looking.

Likewise when you gaze at a mango tree, don't think of it as a mango tree. Avoid assigning labels; simply observe it as existence. Otherwise, boundaries will persist, and you'll inevitably project your memories onto it. Any knowledge you've amassed about the mango tree will be superimposed, and your preconceived beliefs will overshadow it. For you, it won't remain something new, something marvellous. And neither will the observer cease to exist. Because the one observing is having his beliefs thrust upon the object he is observing. So, the observer remains. Either the observer can exist, or the observed. If both exist, it's *māyā*. We have to perceive without the observer. The observer is the past, conditioned with upbringing, filters, always seeing from that conditioned perspective, hence having likes and dislikes, distinctions of Hindu-Muslim, concepts of purity-impurity, and everything else.

All I am saying is that you must observe without the observer. Because you are the observer, therefore, the one you are observing is distinct from you; in this scenario, non-duality cannot exist. Be aware, observe the entire surrounding environment, stay present, watch, notice the beautiful birds, observe humans—just observe. Be alert while doing so. However, in this observation, there should be no interference, no judgement, no decision, no desire, no attachment of thoughts. Do you understand the point?

Complete attentiveness is required. When you are completely focused, entirely present and involved, there is no 'I' left; 'I' exists only where there is a difference, where there is a veil. If you are wholly involved, 'I' is not there; 'I' ceases to exist, just like in a flow state. Do you understand? Become so aware that there is no mind or ego left. Only when the observer, the act of observing, and the observed become one, that is true involvement, true awareness. Then that awareness, that involvement, that attentiveness becomes infinite, and gradually, the realisation of non-duality begins. You become one with Bhairava.

This concludes our study of Sūtra Five.

CHAPTER SIX

पराचः कामाननुयन्ति बालाः ते मृत्योर्यन्ति विततस्य पाशम् ।
अथ धीरा अमृतत्वं विदित्वा ध्रुवमध्रुवेष्विह न प्रार्थयन्ते ॥

parācaḥ kāmānanuyanti bālāḥ te mṛtyoryanti vitatasya pāśam |
atha dhīrā amṛtatvaṃ viditvā dhruvamadhruveṣviha na prārthayante ||

The creator designed the sense organs with a fundamental inclination outward, towards material objects. Hence, man sees only external appearances alone (he sees only outside himself and not within himself). Only a select few, possessing wisdom, choose to redirect their gaze inward, into the depths of their being, and thereby taste immortality.

(Kaṭha Upaniṣad IV.1*)*

शक्तिचक्रसंधाने विश्वसंहारः ॥६॥

|| ŚAKTICAKRASAṂDHĀNE VIŚVASAṂHĀRAḤ || 6 ||

Dissolve the host of ***śaktis*** **into one another, make them one, and the world outside will disappear.**

I shall commence my commentary on this thread with a prayer.

We extol the praises of that Śaṅkara (Śiva), whose mere opening and closing of eyelids bring forth the appearance and dissolution of the entire world, and who serves as the source of the majestic powers of the host of śaktis (śakti-cakra).

(*Spanda-Kārikās* I.1)

The significance of this prayer will become clear to you later. Before that, let's dissect the aphorism's meaning word by word:

Śakti-cakra—The Sanskrit word *cakra* has two meanings. In common language, we use the word *cakra* for a wheel, like the one on a bicycle. The English word *circum* or circle is derived from *cakram* itself. So, one meaning of *cakra* is a wheel, circle, disc, cycle, etc. The seven *cakras* are also related to this, namely—*mūlādhāra* (root) *cakra*, *svādhiṣṭhāna* (sacral) *cakra*, *maṇipūra* (solar plexus) *cakra*, *anāhata* (heart) *cakra*, *viśuddha* (throat) *cakra*, *ājñā* (third eye) *cakra*, and *sahasrāra* (crown) *cakra*. Much has been said about them elsewhere, and you are likely familiar with them, so I won't elaborate further. The second meaning of *cakra* is an army, a troop, a host, multitude, or collection. It is essentially a collective noun, usually used in the sense of a military unit.

Army of what? Of energies. *śakti* means energy, or power. Although there is only one energy, one power, the power of absolute freedom, as we learned in the last few chapters. But that power has many functions. Based on those functions, we categorise them into different aspects and give them different names. Like fire, for instance, has many powers—such as the power to cook, the power to provide light, the power to make ashes, the power to run a steam engine, etc. However, they all are different aspects of the same thermal energy. Similarly, all powers are different aspects of that power of absolute freedom. Various classifications have been made based on different criteria to fully understand that primordial power. The study of these classifications is essential for advancing our understanding of the inner world and for practising meditations that harness various forms of energy for practical purposes. Although power is one, it takes different forms. In this particular Sūtra, we will break it down into four parts, to facilitate easy understanding: *khecarī, gocarī, dikcarī* aur *bhūcarī*. We will understand them further in this chapter.

Here, the host of *śaktis* is being addressed through the term *śakti-cakra*. The next word, *saṃdhān*, literally means, holding together, uniting, joining, tying, binding, or merging. It also refers to the act of concentrating and focusing one's attention towards a specific target, in this case, to such an extent that you become one with it.

We are discussing the four divisions of the primordial power here, which need to be unified once again. And when this is accomplished, what will happen?

Viśvasaṃhāraḥ—The dissolution of the entire world. The world will disappear for us. Be mindful of the wordings—the world is not being destroyed but disappearing. We will delve into this further.

śakticakrasaṃdhāne viśvasaṃhāraḥ ||

dissolve the host of śaktis into one another, make them one, and the world outside will disappear.

Now, let me elucidate this. We are expanding from the centre. Our centre is consciousness, the very source of our existence. In reality, this is who we are. This consciousness limited itself, and the mind came into existence. From that mind, the senses emerged, and those senses brought forth this external world made of water, land, fire, sky, and air. Essentially, these are the fourfold expansions.

Don't consider them as separate from each other; they are much like the telescoping mechanism in a tripod, radio antennas, or a telescope. Telescoping refers to the ability of an object to slide or extend into itself. Just as pulling radio antennas makes them longer, they have multiple sections that fit into each other. This allows for easy adjustment of the length.

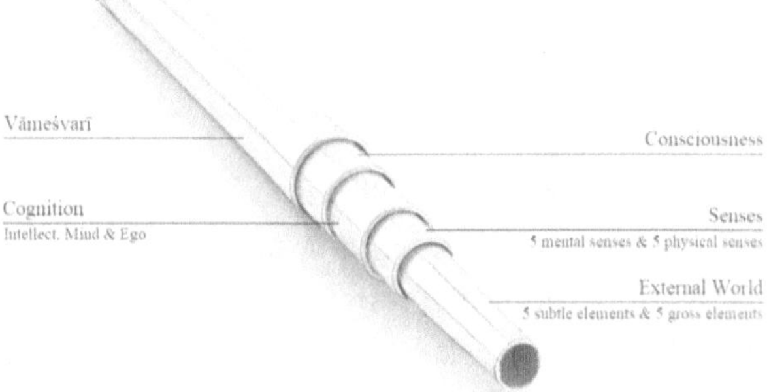

Similarly, within singular consciousness, all these aspects are contained. When the creation of the world occurs, they emerge one by one, interconnected. And when merged back into each other, the world disappears. Indeed, everything perceivable stems from consciousness, residing therein, much like the myriad vibrant hues of a peacock feather residing within the egg.

To further illustrate, think of it like the nested structure of Russian dolls. Russian dolls fit one inside the other. Open one doll, and another one comes out from inside; open that one, and a third doll comes out, and so on. Similarly, from consciousness emerges the mind, from the mind, the senses, and from the senses, the outer world. In the end, all these layers fit into each other like Russian dolls: the external world in the senses, the senses in the mind, and the mind in consciousness. Each of these aspects—consciousness, mind, senses, and the outer world—is governed by a distinct power, or energy dwelling within them. These four powers are known as *khecarī, gocarī, dikcarī* aur *bhūcarī.*

All four of these names share the suffix *-carī,* derived from the Sanskrit word *carati,* which means to roam, dwell, move, or function (within whatever the suffix is added to). Let's now delve into each of these powers one by one.

Khecarī—The term *kha* translates to open space, the sky, the cosmos, or emptiness. If we explore the origin of this term, it leads us back to the ancient Vedic era when ox-drawn carts were prevalent. The design of these carts featured a chassis with two wheels and a stationary axle connecting them. While the wheels rotated, the axle remained static, facilitating the cart's functioning. If the axle were to rotate with the wheels, the entire cart would overturn. Therefore, the axle connecting the wheels had to remain static while the wheels rotated. Hence, there was a deliberate gap, an empty space, between the axle and the wheel—referred to as *kha*. This space allowed the wheels to rotate independently and facilitated smooth wheel rotation during the cart's movement.

In the *Upaniṣads*, there are discourses on the existence of a cosmic space within the heart. Allow me to quote a few verses. The *Brahma Upaniṣad* says:

*hṛdyākāśe tadvijñānamākāśaṁ tatsuṣiramākāśaṁ tadvedyam**
hṛdyākāśaṁ yasminnidam saṁcarati vicarati yasminnidam**
sarvamotam protam** | *saṁ vibhoḥ prajā jñāyeran* | *na tatra devā*
ṛṣayaḥ pitara īśate pratibuddhaḥ sarvaviditi ||

Within the recess of the heart is that space (void, ākāśa) of consciousness-that with many openings, the aim of knowledge, within the space of the heart in which all this (universe outside) evolves and moves about, in which all this is warped and woofed (as it were). (Who knows this), knows fully all creation. There the gods, the sages, the ancestors have no control, for being fully awakened, one becomes the knower of all truth.

The *Bṛhadāraṇyaka Upaniṣad* (IV.4.22) says:

sa vā eṣa mahānaja ātmā yo'yaṁ vijñānamayaḥ prāṇeṣu ya
eṣo'ntarhṛdaya ākāśastasmiñchete sarvasya vaśī sarvasyeśānaḥ
sarvasyādhipatiḥ sa na sādhunā karmaṇā bhūyānno evāsādhunā
kaniyāneṣa sarveśvara eṣa bhūtādhipatireṣa bhūtapāla
eṣa seturvidharaṇa eṣāṁ lokānāmasaṁbhedāya tametaṁ

vedānuvacanena brāhmaṇā vividishanti yajñena dānena tapasā'nāśakenaitameva viditvā munirbhavati ||

That great, unborn Self, which is filled with consciousness and which dwells in the midst of the organs, lies in the space (void, *ākāśa*) within the heart. It is the controller of all, the lord of all, the ruler of all. It does not become greater through good deeds or smaller through evil deeds. It is the lord of all, the ruler of all beings, the protector of all beings. It is the dam that serves as the boundary to keep the different worlds apart. The brahmins seek to realise It through the study of the Vedas, through sacrifices, through gifts and through austerity which does not lead to annihilation. Knowing It alone one becomes a sage.

And as you read, this cosmic space is absolute consciousness, or Brahman, Śiva."

The *Chāndogya Upaniṣad* says:

yad vai tad brahmetīdhaṁ vāva tadyo'yam bahirdhā puruṣādākāśo yo vai sa bahirdhā puruṣādākāśaḥ || ayam vāva sa yo'yamantaḥ puruṣa akāśo yo vai so'ntaḥ puruṣa ākāśaḥ ||

The Śiva or Brahman which has been thus described is the same as the (physical) space (void, *ākāśa*) outside a person. The space which is outside a person is the same as that which is inside a person. The space which is inside a person is the space within the heart. The space which is within the heart is omnipresent and unchanging. He who knows this obtains full and unchanging prosperity…

So, *kha* means that gap, which lies between two thoughts, between two breaths. *kha* means the Brahman, the inner space within the heart, symbolised by the moving sky. And the suffix *-carī* has already been explained to mean 'to dwell,' 'to move in,' or 'to function in.'

Abhinavagupta, in his commentary on *Parātriśikā*, has elucidated the *khecarī* energy quite comprehensively. I will quote him here,

> *"The meaning of khecarī is as follows. That* śakti *is khecarī, who abides in kha, i.e. brahma which is identical with herself roams about, i.e. functions in various ways (carati). This khecarī in her universal aspect functions (carati) in three ways. She (as gocarī) brings about a knowledge of objects, (as dikcarī) effects movements, such as grasping, relinquishing, etc., (as bhūcarī) exists in the form of objective existents. Thus, this khecarī exists as gocarī in the form of antaḥkaraṇa (the inner psychic apparatus), as dikcarī in the form of bahiṣkaraṇa (i.e. outer senses), as bhūcarī in the form of objective existents, as (the colour) blue, etc., or subjective existents as pleasure, etc.*
>
> *Similarly, in the individual aspects, the* śaktis *that are known successively as vyomacarī in the void (of consciousness) in which the distinction between subject and object has not yet appeared, as gocarī in the form of antaḥkaraṇa in which there is just appearance of knowledge, as dikcarī in the form of the outer senses suggesting the appearance of diversity in which state there is diversity of the knower from the knowable object, as bhūcarī in the form of bhāvas or existents in which there is preponderance of clear diversity in the objects, are in reality, according to the principle enunciated, non-distinct from khecarī which abides in the essential nature i.e. anuttara. Thus that śakti of the Supreme Lord is only one."*
>
> *(Parātriśikā Vivaraṇa,* pp. 38-39*)*

Abhinavagupta, in his commentary, has elucidated that *gocarī*, *dikcarī*, and *bhūcarī* are also forms of *khecarī*, and this is because, as I explained earlier, they emanate from *khecarī*. Just as within a Russian doll, there are multiple layers that fit together, similarly, within *khecarī* resides *gocarī*, within *gocarī* resides *dikcarī*, and within *dikcarī* resides *bhūcarī*.

Khecarī is the power that is one with absolute consciousness, one with the Brahman of the Vedas, and one with the Śiva of the Tantras. It is at the centre of our identity. Even beyond *khecarī*, sometimes in the scriptures, another form of energy is recognized—*chidgagancarī*—who dwells in the infinite space of consciousness. She is the purest and most subtle, even more than *khecarī*. She is also referred to as *vāmeśvarī*, meaning the Goddess who emits or vomits the universe, bringing it forth from herself. And *cakreśvarī* because She is the mistress of the host of *śaktis*. Experiencing Her while residing in the physical body is not possible. No one who experienced Her directly stayed to write or teach about Her. We only have an understanding of Her through inference. We know that there is a power that is above and beyond all, and that's all we know about Her. And it is not necessary for us to know more.

So, She who functions in the consciousness is *khecarī*.

In the tradition of *hatha yoga* and *kuṇḍalinī yoga*, where efforts are made to awaken the *cakras* and *kuṇḍalinī* energy through various physical asanas (postures) and *mudrās* (physiological gestures), there exists a specific *mudrā*—the *khecarī mudrā*. This *mudrā* is purely physiological, involving the curling back of the tongue into the mouth.

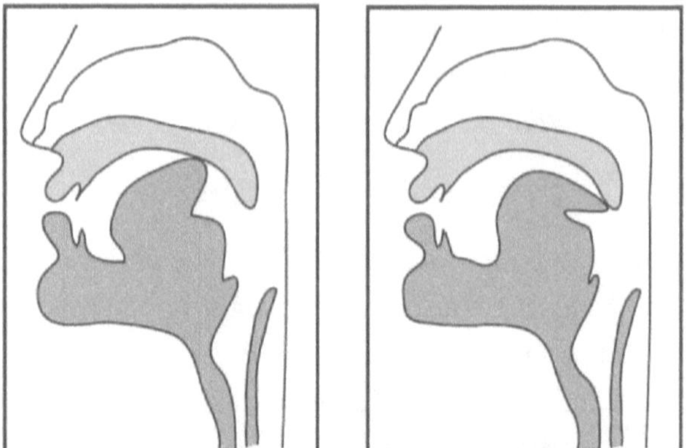

Symbolically, it holds profound meaning. The moment we were born, at that very instant, we turned outward in search of completeness. Our tongue, the first to venture out in search of fulfilment, sought the mother's breast for nourishment. The infant, driven by hunger, the primal drive, was motivated to find fulfilment externally. It was incomplete, and it searched outwardly for completeness. Hunger was the first factor that compelled us to seek our completeness outside ourselves.

Consciousness was identified with the body, and naturally, bodily needs are such that consciousness turns outward; it has to. You need food, you need water to drink—these are your physical needs, and they can only be fulfilled in the world. Therefore, consciousness naturally moves through the senses toward the outside world. If a child were self-sufficient from birth, without the need for nourishment, it would not instinctively turn toward its mother and seek her breast. As a result, the *khecarī* would never manifest into *gocarī, dikcarī*, and then *bhūcarī.*

Gocarī is she who functions in cognition. *Go*, meaning rays, beams, rays of cognition. Those rays which first illuminate something, marking the initial step towards outward manifestation. It is the point from where the flow of our consciousness turns outward. The river Ganges symbolises the flow of consciousness in India, and the place from where the Ganges originates, where it begins flowing towards the world, is called *Gomukh*. Here too, the root is the same: *go*, meaning rays of cognition. It serves as a symbol of *gocarī* in the physical world—the point from which the stream of consciousness begins its outward journey.

Up to the point of *khecarī*, there was no distinction between subject and object. However, as soon as *khecarī* limits itself and becomes *gocarī*, that's when the distinction begins. *Gocarī* functions in the dimensions of the mind, or to be more precise, in intellect, mind, and ego. These three make up the entire psychological process.

When she further conceals her nature, this energy becomes *dikcarī*. *Dik*, meaning spatial directions. There are ten directions—*Ūrdhva* (Upward), *Īśāna* (Northeast), *Pūrva* (East), *Āgneya* (Southeast), *Dakṣiṇa* (South), *Nairṛtya* (Southwest), *Paścima* (West), *Vāyavya* (Northwest), *Uttar* (North), *Adho* (Downward). And one perceives these directions through external senses, five *jñānendriyas* (mental senses) and five *karmendriyas* (sense organs that deal with bodily functions). The senses of hearing, touch, sight, taste, and smell; and the organs of speech (*vāk*), dexterity (*pāṇi*), locomotion (*pād*), generation (*upashtam*), and excretion (*pāyu*). *Dikcarī* functions in these external senses. In this state of *śakti,* there is a diversity felt, of the knower from the knowable object. We have almost become extroverted in this state. Just one step remains. This process is completed when finally, completely clouding her undifferentiated nature and appearing as *bhūcarī*, she who dwells or functions in the earth, she takes the form of the differentiated objective existence. *Bhu*, meaning earth, this world of multiplicity that is physically tangible—trees, humans, objects, etc. These are made up of five subtle elements and five gross elements: smell, taste, appearance, touch, and sound; And earth, water, fire, air, and space. *Bhūcarī-śakti* functions in these. Here, the distinction becomes crystal clear between the subject and object, between myself and the world. And the flow of consciousness becomes totally extroverted.

As I was saying, if a child were self-sufficient from birth, without the need for nourishment, it wouldn't be extroverted. Here, nourishment is symbolic, referring to that essential substance we need to feel complete or at least believe that we need because we don't inherently feel fulfilled. Extending the tongue outward or keeping the tip of the tongue facing outside symbolises the extroverted flow of consciousness. When practising the *khecarī mudrā* and curling the tongue back into the mouth, it conveys the end of seeking; one has become content within oneself. They have found the source of their completeness, their nourishment, where it can really be found—inwards. And so, their flow of consciousness has become introverted.

As discussed multiple times before, our completeness cannot be found outward. Completeness will only be found within, so turn your gaze inwards. This is precisely what the *khecarī mudrā* signifies. Now, let me make it clear that this doesn't mean that the physiological gesture we are performing by curling our tongue back into the mouth is useless or foolish. No. You need to understand that these mudras, these specific physiological poses, trigger certain changes within us. And the changes happening within us are sometimes expressed in the form of these physiological poses.

Whenever I experience the arousal of *kuṇḍalinī* (coiled-up energy) within, there have been instances where my tongue naturally curls inward. It is mentioned in the texts of yoga that this tongue-curling expression is specifically for awakening *kuṇḍalinī* energy. I never intentionally practised it, but through other spiritual practices, whenever my energy awakened, this gesture spontaneously occurred. I will clarify *kuṇḍalinī* energy and its connection with this particular sūtra at the end of our discussion.

When certain internal processes are happening, they are also physiologically expressed. Similarly, certain physiological expressions can trigger internal processes. To further illustrate, think of a TV antenna. In our childhood, when we watched TV and the signal got disrupted, someone would adjust the TV antenna. By placing it in a particular pose, it would catch the satellite signal, and the network signal would become clear. Similarly, these physiological expressions, like curling the tongue, are symbolic, yes, but can simultaneously trigger specific processes within.

Another physiological hand gesture (*mudrā*), for example, involves forming the symbol of the vagina with the hands (*yoni mudrā*), often utilised in Tantric rituals. When you practise and master this gesture, you realise that performing it immediately connects you with the universal vagina, or the source of the entire cosmos.

In all the ancient traditional paintings of Lord Śiva, you will invariably find him surrounded by his attendants or energies. He stands in the midst, and a circle of energies surrounds him from all sides. Wherever he goes, these beings accompany him. This too is symbolic. Śiva is us—our consciousness, our Self—and wherever consciousness traverses in the physical world, he is always accompanied by this assemblage of energies: the mind, the senses, the organs of action, and the objective existents.

You are presently with me, aware of this book. Pay attention to the fact that you are perceiving this book—its odour, flavour, appearance, tactility, and sound; and earth, water, fire, air, and space—all of these are active, meaning the *bhūcarī* energy is with you. And be mindful that they are entering through your senses. In other words, the *dikcarī* energy is also with you, and the power of your cognition (*gocarī*) is present and active, allowing you to cognize this book. And all these are happening on the canvas of consciousness, meaning the *khecarī* energy. Wherever you go, wherever the stream of consciousness flows, this assemblage of energies will accompany you, and you are always at their centre. Now these energies are inert in themselves, like the chess pieces, and as the moon borrows its radiance from the sun, these energies derive consciousness from the Self.

That principle (that consciousness, Śiva), should be examined with great care and reverence by which this group of senses, though insentient, acts as a sentient force by itself, and along with the inner group of senses, goes towards objects, takes pleasure in their maintenance, and withdraws into itself, because this natural freedom of it prevails everywhere.

(*Spanda-Kārikās*, I.6-7)

The eighteen hands of *Svacchaṃda Bhairava* manifest to bestow life upon all these energies or, one might say, control them like chess pieces. Why eighteen hands? Because they encompass the mind, intellect, and ego; the senses of hearing, touch, sight, taste, and smell; as well as the organs of speech, dexterity, locomotion, generation, and excretion; and smell, taste, appearance, touch, and sound—all together add up to eighteen.

This elucidates the concept of the *śakti-cakra*. The Sūtra says to *dissolve the host of śaktis into one another, to unify them, and the world outside will disappear.*

In essence, redirect the outward flow of consciousness towards the inner self; merge the river back into its source. Much like the telescoping mechanism example mentioned earlier. Pulling it extends various sections outward, making it longer; similarly, retract it inwards, merge each section into one another, until they become one. Place the first Russian doll inside the second, the second within the third, and the third within the fourth, until they all become one. In the same way merge the *bhūcarī* with *dikcarī*, the *dikcarī* with *gocarī*, and the *gocarī* with *khecarī*, causing the world to disappear. You can make this happen only when you turn inward.

Your outwardness creates the world for you, while your inwardness dissolves it. You might remember that I initiated my commentary on this aphorism with a prayer, *"We extol the praises of that Śaṅkara (Śiva), whose mere opening and closing of eyelids bring forth the appearance and dissolution of the entire world, and who serves as the source of the majestic powers of the host of śaktis (śakti-cakra)."*

Now, you might have started to understand its significance. Closing the eyes is a symbol of turning inward, where you draw back the external world, your senses, and your mind into consciousness. Opening the eyes is a symbol of turning outward, where you allow these streams to flow back into the external realm. By turning your gaze inwards the world becomes one with consciousness. And as we understood, Śiva is the source of these energies, controlling and infusing life into them with his eighteen hands.

To convey the understanding of this concept in the Vedāntic tradition, an analogy is often presented, that of a spider—*yathorṇanābhiḥ sṛjate gṛhṇate ca*—as the spider creates and absorbs back (its web)… So do we project forth this universe and absorb it back within us.

We are like spiders.
We weave our lives and then move along in them.
We are like the dreamer who dreams and then lives that dream.
And in the end, we draw our world back into ourselves.

Here, if it has not already been made clear, we're not talking about the destruction of the world, as often described in Abrahamic religions with depictions of fire raining down, earthquakes, lightning striking, and the earth splitting apart—No. Śaivism says that we, ourselves, project the world outwards, and it is us who ultimately retract it back within us.

Now, the question arises: how can we become introverted? So far, we have made it clear that unifying the host of energies in this context means becoming introverted. Now the question is, how do we achieve this?

Kṣemarāja and all other traditional commentators have kept the method secret. According to Kṣemarāja, "This comes into experience only by devotion to the lotus feet of a genuine guru." As for the non-traditional commentators, they have misunderstood the entire Sūtra and written whatever came to their minds. As for me, I revealed a method in the previous chapter.

Just look; don't look at something. Just look—without boundaries, without moving your eyes—and in a short while, you will realise that the distinction between subject and object has vanished. Because enclosures have disappeared. In other words, the gaze has now turned inwards. This is not a religious practice but a scientific method. Another reason why it works is that when you don't get entangled in the particulars of the outside world, you become aware of your inner Self. You start to see the bigger picture; I used an illustration in the previous chapter. Let's use another illustration this time.

What did you first see in this image? Half of you will perceive the portrait of a young girl looking in the same direction you are now. She has fair cheeks, and her left ear and cheek are oriented towards you, etc. If you look at her particulars like this, you will miss the hidden old woman in the photo. Within this image, an old woman is also concealed. If you saw the old woman first, then a young girl is also hidden there. Try to just look at the picture without delving into the details. Just see it in its entirety, not focusing on any specific part but absorbing the whole. Take a moment, look without trying to find something. If you attempt to find that old woman/young lady, you will never discover her. Simply observe. Stare at it. Gaze for a moment without actively searching, and that old woman/young lady will reveal itself to you. Once you see her, then continue reading.

She was right there. The cheeks and mouth of the young girl were the nose of the old woman, in case you still haven't found her.

So, what happened? Your eyes cannot fixate on one point, so if you concentrate on the young woman's figure, your eyes will become fatigued. Suddenly, your eyes will shift from that figure, and in that moment, you become aware of the second figure hidden within the young woman in the same patterns. The magic lies in the fact that when you become conscious of the old woman, you can't see the young woman. But you know that both are there now. When you are aware of one, the other self-vanishes. When you are aware of the other, the first self-vanishes.

That's precisely why the Sūtra is saying that the external world will disappear once you dissolve the host of śaktis into one another. The world outside will dissolve. Either the external world can remain, or consciousness can. Either we can be extroverted or introverted; both cannot happen simultaneously.

When you are observing the world, you are looking outward: the stream of consciousness is flowing outward. Your attention is fixed on the external world. Keep staring at it continuously. Your eyes will tire; they will want to move. But there is nothing to move towards. And upon finding nothing to move towards, suddenly the gaze will turn inwards. This is the only possibility.

You have forced your consciousness to fall back, to retreat, to merge with the source. And when you enter the self, the end of the world will happen; the world will not be there.

The twentieth Sūtra of *Pratyabhijñāhṛdyam* says:

तदा प्रकाशानन्दसारमहामन्त्रवीर्यात्मकपूर्णाहंतावे शात्सदासर्वसर्गसं हार
कारिनिजसंविद्देवताचक्रेश्वरताप्राप्तिर्भवतीति शिवम् ॥

tadā prakāśānanda-sāra-mahā-mantra-vīryātmaka-pūrṇāhantāve śātsadā-sarvasarga-saṁ hārakāri-nija-saṁvid-devatā-cakreśvara-tāprāptirbhavatīti śivam ||

When one enters the Self, which is light and bliss, one attains Lordship over the *śakti-cakra* that creates and dissolves the universe.

(*Pratyabhijñāhṛdyam* 20)

In the successful culmination of this practice, the state you attain is called the *bhairavī mudrā*. In this state, your eyes are wide open, yet you are not registering anything external. You remain fully aware of yourself, but you are looking outwards—*antarlakṣyō bahirdṛṣṭih*. All your energies are functioning, but they have become one. The state that Socrates entered, as I narrated in the previous chapter, is precisely this.

When you consistently exist in this state—speaking, eating, walking, laughing—you ascend to the highest state, the *khecarī mudrā*. I always abide in this state, and so do the yogis of the highest order.

There is another traditional method for unifying the host of *śaktis*. While various meditation practices serve this purpose, either directly or indirectly, these two methods are direct, active, and fall under *śāmbhavopāya*. One is artificial, and the other is natural. The earlier discussion was about the artificial method, where we intentionally induce this state. By staring outwards, we forced the flow of consciousness inward—this is an artificial process. However this state can also be induced differently—naturally, during moments of emotional outbursts, such as intense anger, overwhelming fear, or when one feels like a hungry lion chasing its prey; even during a sneeze…

क्षुताद्यन्ते भये शोके गह्वरे वारणद्रुते । कुतूहले क्षुधाद्यन्ते ब्रह्मसत्ता समीपगा ॥

kṣutādyante bhaye śoke gahvare vāraṇa-drute | kutūhale kṣhudhādyante brahma-sattā samīpagā ||

At the beginning and end of sneezing, in a state of fear or sorrow, (standing) on top of an abyss or while fleeing from a battlefield, at the moment of intense curiosity, at the beginning or end of hunger; such a state comes close to the reality of Brahman.

कामक्रोधलोभमोहमदमात्सर्यगोचरे । बुद्धिं निस्तिमितां कृत्वा तत्तत्त्वमवशिष्यते ॥

kāma-krodha-lobha-moha-mada-mātsarya-gocare | buddhiṁ nistimtāṁ kṛtvā tattvamavaśiṣyate ||

If one makes one's mind stable in the various states of desire, anger, greed, delusion, intoxication or envy, then the Reality alone will remain (which is underlying them).

(*Vijñāna Bhairava Tantra* 118, 101)

You might wonder how one can attain introvertedness or enlightenment through a sneeze, but that's the specialty of the path of Śiva. Even seemingly ordinary things are utilised as devices here because, no matter how trivial they may seem, they are not. They are very complex, their inner mechanisms are delicate. Take sneezing, for example. Firstly, it doesn't happen at your will. When a sneeze has to come, it will, and you can't do anything to bring it about. This holds true for intense fear or pain as well; you can't control them according to your will. So, you have to wait for them, and that moment passes very quickly. You must catch them at the beginning because once they are in motion, you can't do anything. The bullet has left the gun; now nothing can be done. The energy is on its way to being released, and it won't stop. Can you stop a sneeze midway? No. So, you have to catch it at the beginning. And that moment happens very quickly. The duration between triggering and the bullet leaving the gun is very short. So, if you're not alert, you won't be able to catch it. If you want to use this method, stay alert to these moments beforehand, all the time. And, of course, there will be many unsuccessful attempts initially, so persist with it for a few months.

Become fully alert and conscious as soon as you sense a sneeze coming on. If you recall, at the moment a sneeze begins, all thoughts stop. Whenever you've had a sneeze, your thoughts have ceased, and you become one with the source of intense energy. Similarly, during a panic attack, thoughts suddenly halt, and you feel an intense surge of energy, or when a dog is chasing you, etc.

In such moments, two things happen: thoughts come to a standstill, and you unify with an intense energy source within you. Now, add one more thing—consciousness—and enlightenment will instantly manifest. At the very least, you'll catch a glimpse of your inner Self. The host of energies within you will converge, even if only for a moment.

Thoughts are the hindrance. Therefore, if thoughts disappear in any way, what needs to happen will happen. But thoughts need to vanish, and you need to remain conscious. Thoughts can and do disappear even in sleep; when you become unconscious or when you are on drugs, thoughts vanish, but along with thoughts, consciousness also disappears. This state we are talking about is thoughtless consciousness. You can be thoughtless and unconscious; then it's meaningless. You can be conscious with thoughts, like you are now, but that too is useless. Bring these two things together—consciousness and thoughtlessness. When they two become one, what is worthy of attainment is attained.

So, as soon as such a moment arrives, like a sneeze, become aware and fully alert in that very instant. It will happen that the sneeze disappears. A sneeze doesn't occur when you are completely alert to it. Also, a sneeze doesn't occur when your eyes are wide open. So, to make it easy, consciously keep your eyes open in that moment when the sneeze is about a fraction of a second away and stay conscious. You will find that the sneeze has disappeared, but the energy that was about to be released will merge with your consciousness, like a flash of lightning, and you will become super conscious—attaining that introverted state. Similarly, if an intense fear arises within you, immediately become alert, close your eyes, and become conscious. The fear will disappear, and the energy about to be released will merge with consciousness, and what is worthy of attainment is attained.

To better understand this process of becoming conscious in these moments, an analogy is given: retract your focus, breath, emotions, to the centre, much like a tortoise draws in its limbs and head inward, sensing fear. This is the alertness we are talking about. As soon as that moment occurs—the beginning of a sneeze, a panic attack, etc.—immediately retract your mind, senses, and feelings to the centre, become completely alert. It's challenging to express this properly in words. It can only be understood by doing.

And in the successful culmination of this practice... *one attains Lordship over the* śakti-*cakra that creates and dissolves the universe.*

Various commentators have linked the seven *cakras* of the subtle body and *kuṇḍalinī* with this Sūtra. However, I choose not to delve into that interpretation because, in the practice of *śāmbhavopāya,* there is no room for imagining the diverse colours of lotus flowers on different parts of the body. I am not dismissing those interpretations; they represent a unique yogic technique with its own merits. It's just that they do not belong in this volume, and specifically, this Sūtra. Although the ultimate goal remains the same—the union of *kuṇḍalinī* with Śiva—the difference lies in perspective and approach.

Every spiritual practice, in one way or another, awakens *kuṇḍalinī.* Some approaches are direct, while others are indirect. The method outlined in this Sūtra is the most direct and active approach. Unlike traditional *kuṇḍalinī yoga*, with externalised practices, such as physically curling the tongue back into the mouth, here, everything is internalised. The attempt is to induce those states actively, like entering *khecarī mudra* directly, rather than indirectly triggering them through external practices. The paths are many, but the goal remains the same.

The term *cakra* carries yet another layer of meaning. Śiva has meticulously chosen words to encapsulate multiple layers of meanings within the least amount of words. As discussed earlier, one meaning of *cakra* is a wheel, circle, disc, cycle, etc. It can carry the same connotation as the word cycle in the water cycle—a recurring cycle. In this interpretation, *cakra* denotes a recurring, repetitive, or continuous sequence of events or processes; thus, *śakti-cakra* can be translated as the recurring cycle of *śaktis*. The expansion of *khecarī* into *bhūcarī* is the process of creation, and the retraction of *bhūcarī* into *khecarī* represents dissolution. This wheel of creation and dissolution keeps spinning eternally, and that's also why it is referred to as the *śakti-cakra*.

This concludes our study of Sūtra Six.

CHAPTER SEVEN

जाग्रत्स्वप्नसुषुप्तभेदे तुर्याभोगसम्भवः ॥७॥

|| JĀGRATSVAPNASUṢUPTABHEDE TURYĀBHOGASAMBHAVAḤ || 7 ||

If one can discern (between the Self and nonself) **in the states of waking, dreaming, and deep sleep, the experience, the enjoyment of *Turiya* becomes possible.**

ज्ञानं जाग्रत् ॥८॥

|| JÑĀNAM JĀGRAT || 8 ||

The waking state is external knowledge, based on cognitive activities.

स्वप्नो विकल्पाः ॥९॥

|| SVAPNO VIKALPĀḤ || 9 ||

Dreaming is a state of mental constructs.

अविवेको माया सौषुप्तम् ॥१०॥

|| AVIVEKO MĀYĀ SAUṢUPTAM || 10 ||

Deep sleep is a state of non-discernment and self-concealment.

त्रितयभोक्ता वीरेशः ॥११॥

|| TRITAYABHOKTĀ VĪREŚAḤ || 11 ||

***Vīresha* is the experiencer of the three states.**

In these aphorisms, Śiva imparts another method to attain enlightenment. First, a dissection of its meaning, word by word. There are three states—*jāgrat* (waking), *svapna* (dream), and *suṣupti* (deep sleep)—in which we exist. *Jāgrat* is the state you are currently in, the waking state, where the conscious mind is active. It is the state where you can consciously think, solve maths problems, accumulate information—essentially, the state in which you are presently listening to me is *jāgrat*. And you are identified with this state; your identity changes in each state, and your idea of Self is never constant.

In the wakeful state, your identity is shaped by things around you that you know or cognize through your senses. Your family, your profession, your position in the office—these all become different facets of your identity. For example, a person identifies as a husband when cognizing his spouse, and as a school teacher when teaching children. Behaviour, way of speaking, everything changes in front of a spouse compared to in front of children at school. When the school principal enters the classroom, the identity shifts to that of a subordinate, and behaviour adjusts accordingly. The idea of Self in the waking state is rooted in external knowledge, relying on cognition through the senses. Therefore, Śiva further states, *jñānam jāgrat*—the waking state is external knowledge, based on cognitive activities.

To become identified with the state of wakefulness—and with the knowledge derived from sensory perceptions—is not intelligent. These identifications that seem so real now dissolve in the state of dreaming (*svapna*, meaning the state where we see dreams while sleeping). When sleep begins to take over, we enter the state of dreaming from wakefulness. During the school going days, when mother would wake us up in the morning or when the alarm went off, sometimes it wasn't clear when we fell back asleep. It felt like we had packed our bags and put on our uniforms; everything seemed so real, but it was just imagination. When consciousness returned, it was quite disappointing. That state was the state of dreaming.

The other day, I dreamt that I was Lord Śiva, dancing exuberantly on the snow clad mountains. It was a profoundly joyful experience, but the state it was in was purely imaginative; it was the dream state. Śiva has defined it further, *svapno vikalpāḥ*, meaning dreaming is a state of mental constructs (*vikalpa*). What is *vikalpa*? Patañjali writes,

शब्दज्ञानानुपाती वस्तुशून्यो विकल्पः

śabda-jñāna-anupātī vastu-śūnyo vikalpaḥ

Vikalpa is the knowledge, based on words devoid of any objective reality.

(*Yoga Sūtras* I.9)

Vikalpa means imagination, or fantasy. It lacks any grounding in reality. (and its source is *mātṛkā*, as I elucidated earlier because the basis of *vikalpa* is words, concepts, which have no connection with objective reality).

So, the state of dreams is purely imaginative. Whatever or whoever we are currently identifying with in this waking state disappears when we enter the state of a dream. In a dream, we can become anything—even a giraffe or a butterfly. Master Zhuang, a Chinese philosopher who lived around 2300 years ago, is known to have written, "Once upon a time, I, Zhuangzi, dreamt I was a butterfly, fluttering hither and thither, a veritable butterfly, enjoying itself to the full of its bent, and not knowing it was Zhuangzi. Suddenly I awoke and came to myself, the veritable Zhuangzi. Now I do not know whether it was then I dreamt I was a butterfly or whether I am now a butterfly dreaming I am a man."

And this is a valid question: how do we know that even this waking state is not a dream? Who knows if some other entity—a butterfly or a giraffe—might be dreaming that it is you? And of course, each dream feels real until one awakens from it. So, as soon as we transition from wakefulness to the dream state, our identification changes. We become identified with that dream, with those imaginations, those fantasies, which have no real basis. And these identifications are not permanent either; they also dissolve in the state of deep sleep.

The third state is the state of deep sleep (*suṣupti*, meaning sound sleep or the state of profound slumber). However, understanding what deep sleep truly entails proves to be quite challenging. In the words of Śiva, *aviveko māyā sauṣuptam*—deep sleep is a state of non-discernment and self-concealment.

The identifications we cherish in the waking state—where do they go in the state of deep sleep? Where do the body, name, form, spouse, children, and social status disappear to? All of these vanish, yet identification persists. Why? Because there is no discernment. We become one with that state of unawareness, with that unconsciousness. Yes, thoughts have ceased, all identifications have disappeared, but consciousness has also disappeared. If consciousness were present, deep sleep would transform into enlightenment, into the state of *samādhi*—when discernment is present, if awareness is there. The goal is to be wakeful even while sound asleep. However, this is a very difficult goal to achieve.

Abuddha, the non-enlightened, is awake in the state of wakefulness. Buddha, the semi-enlightened state is the transcendence of wakefulness into the realm of dreaming. Prabuddha, fully enlightened, witnesses wakefulness manifesting even within the depths of deep sleep. And Suprabuddha, the perfectly enlightened state, is attained by remaining wakeful even in the fourth state.

(Paraphrased, *Mālinīvijaya* II.43)

When you remain wakeful even within the depths of sleep, it is an enlightened state—not completely enlightened, but what is referred to as *samādhi*. Perfect enlightenment reflects in every state, not just when your eyes are closed, and you are motionless like a starfish.

Another thing is that these three states have their own waking, dreaming, and deep sleep. It means each state has its three sub-states. So, 3x3 equals a total of 9 states. Like wakefulness has three states:

1. Waking in wakefulness *(jāgrat jāgrat)*—This is the normal waking state, where you consciously live life, staying in the present moment.
2. Dreaming in wakefulness *(jāgrat svapna)*—This is the state where the predominance is of your thoughts, where you are daydreaming, not living in objective reality, but rather being absorbed in your thoughts, in the worries of the future and memories of the past.
3. Deep sleep in wakefulness *(jāgrat suṣupti)*—This is the most degraded state, unfortunately inhabited by the majority. If at least you remain awake in the wakeful state, we can do something, but people are asleep all the time. They lack awareness. Even when awake, they are not truly conscious, so how can they remain awake while sleeping? Their waking state is also a form of deep sleep. For ninety-nine percent of people, life is like that of robots—mechanical and animal-like. When a dog chases another dog, it has no awareness of its actions. It is completely under the control of its instincts, chemicals, and hormones released by its brain. This is the condition of the majority. Waking up in the morning like robots, getting hypnotised by their phones, brushing without any awareness, and heading to work—all done without consciousness. When we were children, there was awareness; everything was new, and the world seemed colourful. But then we were placed into school, where everything became mechanical. The world started to seem dull and boring. By the time we reach college, a significant number of students commit suicide. Suicide is a process—a gradual diminishing of awareness. From school to college, it was happening gradually. Some

committed suicide, and some became zombies. To some extent, we are all zombies, under the control of our minds, unaware. Some a little less, some a little more, but this condition is universal.

So, when we lack wakefulness even in our waking state, how can we hope for wakefulness and awareness in deep sleep? But that is the goal…

There are three states of dreaming, as well:

1. Dreaming in Dream (*svapna svapna*)—This is your normal dreaming state where there is no self-awareness, and you are not aware that you are dreaming.
2. Wakefulness in Dream (*svapna jāgrat*)—Wakefulness in a dream occurs when you are aware that you are dreaming and can often control or influence the dream. This can be considered a state of lucid dreaming or a variation of it.
3. Deep Sleep in Dream (*svapna suṣupti*)—This state serves as a transition point between dream and deep sleep. These are dreams that you experience but don't retain any memory of upon waking up. Only a faint, blurry, hazy impression remains after waking up in the morning.

And lastly, there are three states of deep sleep:

1. Dream in deep sleep (*suṣupti svapna*)—It too serves as a transitional point, just at the border of dream and deep sleep but on that side of the border which belongs to the realm of deep sleep. The state of *svapna suṣupti* is on the opposite side of the border, belonging to the realm of dreams. It is that state of deep slumber from which, upon waking, only a faint memory remains that I was soundly asleep.
2. Deep sleep in deep sleep (*suṣupti suṣupti*) —When you are completely in deep sleep, no thoughts, no awareness, nothing. Nothing is remembered after waking up—it is that state.

3. And finally, wakefulness in deep sleep (*suṣupti jāgrat*)—This state is akin to *samādhi*, in *Mālinīvijaya*, Śiva refers to this state as *Prabuddha*—enlightened.

As mentioned earlier:

Abuddha, the non-enlightened, is awake in the state of wakefulness. Buddha, the semi-enlightened state is the transcendence of wakefulness into the realm of dreaming. Prabuddha, fully enlightened, witnesses wakefulness manifesting even within the depths of deep sleep. And Suprabuddha, the perfectly enlightened state, is attained by remaining wakeful in the fourth state.

(Paraphrased, *Mālinīvijaya* II.43)

So, the Sūtra is: *jāgratsvapnasuṣuptabhede turyābhogasambhavaḥ*, If we can remain aware during the states of waking, dreaming, and deep sleep, if we can discern the difference (*bheda*, meaning difference, distinction, or discernment) between reality and illusion, and if we can distinguish that we are not the dream-self but rather observing it, that we have not become the unconscious sleep but are distinct from it and are the experiencer of deep sleep. If we can do this, then the experience, the enjoyment of *Turiya* becomes possible.

Ābhoga, denotes a state of enjoyment or rapturous experience, and *sambhava*, means the potential, production, or coming into existence.

If one can discern between the Self and nonself in the states of waking, dreaming, and deep sleep, the experience, the enjoyment of Turiya becomes possible.

What is *Turiya*? *Turiya* simply means the fourth, the transcendental. It is a state that underlies the other three states. It is the experience of these three states, experiencing wakefulness, dreams, and deep sleep. *Turiya* is not actually a state; it is the name of that witness—*Turiya* is consciousness, elucidated in the first chapter. It is completely free, forever, transcendental. *Turiya* is our true identity, unchanging across all three states. What more can be said about it?

In the *Māṇḍūkya Upaniṣad*, there is a verse, my favourite, which gives an analogy of two birds sitting on the same tree. One is peacefully perched on the upper branch, neither moving nor flying, neither sad nor happy, unaffected by comings and goings—just sitting in tranquillity. The one on the lower branch is restless, caught up in many dreams, busy in the world of pleasure and pain. These two birds are within you, and you are that tree. The bird at peace, steady and still, merely observing, is the witness—the consciousness. It is this distinction that you need to discern.

To maintain discernment between the two, a profound effort is required. It necessitates robust and consistent endeavours. It necessitates *udyam*—as the fifth Sūtra instructs—*udyamo bhairavaḥ.*

Moving forward, Śiva asserts, *tritayabhoktā vīreśah*, meaning that he is the courageous one, The Lord of Heros, who is capable of enjoying the three.

Vīreśah is a Sanskrit term composed of *vīr*, meaning courageous, hero or warrior, and *eśa,* denoting lord or ruler. Thus, *vīreśah* translates to 'The Lord of Heros', 'The Lord of Warriors', or 'The Most Courageous' in English.

Vīreśah is one epithet of Lord Śiva. Those who attain enlightenment are called *vīreśah* or *mahāvīra* because this is the greatest valour. The greatest conquest is when you achieve victory over yourself. If you achieve victory in the material world, you are brave, but if you achieve victory over yourself, you are *vīreśah*, the Lord of Gallants, The Most Courageous.

He who conquers himself is the mightiest warrior.—Confucius
Would you have the greatest empire? Rule over yourself.—
Publilius Syrus

Vīreśah is *tritiya bhoktā*—the experiencer of the three states. Understand the distinction. *Bhoktā* translates to the one who perceives, experiences—the enjoying self. Here, *bhoktā* refers to the enjoyer of the three states (*tritiya* means three). Those who are not enlightened identify themselves with the illusion; when they dream, the dreaming Self and the dreaming world become their reality. They are not the experiencers there; they have become the dream itself. The outside observer might say that a person is dreaming, but for the one in that state, the dream has become their reality. Similarly, in the deep sleep state, unconscious slumber becomes their reality. And in the same way, in the waking state, this world becomes their identity. You must be the witness, observe, experience, but do not identify yourself. Differentiate, stay aware in all states of existence. Though, as of now, you are not even truly aware in the waking state.

Therefore, you should begin by being wakeful in the waking state first. Start from the day when you are truly aware, awake—from today itself. From today onward, strive to be even more aware, intensely living in the present. When thoughts arise, observe them; when there are sensations, witness them; do not lose consciousness. Initiate this practice immediately after you are done reading. Don't delay. Start this experiment as soon as you wake up in the morning with the first ray of awareness. There might be a 0.001 percent chance of success; hence, attempt it a thousand times, and perhaps you will succeed once. Even if this one endeavour is successful, you will realise that all those hundreds and thousands of efforts were worthwhile. If even for a moment you feel that what is in motion are not you, you are what is motionless; filled with desires is not you, you are the one without desires forever; perishable is not you, you are eternal, immortal, everlasting; if you reach this state of discernment even for a moment—if you become *vīreśah*, if you reach the state of Śiva even for a moment—then you have opened the door to ultimate freedom, even if it's just for a moment. After this, the journey becomes easier because all the difficulties, all the doubts, end only with the taste of this state.

So, begin from the waking state during the day, and gradually, you will be able to maintain this awareness even in the state of your dreams and deep sleep.

When we succeed in manifesting the witness, even in the state beyond dreaming, the exuberant experience of the fourth state becomes possible. Based on my personal experiences, the waking and dream states are essentially the same. The state you find yourself in as you read this book might be termed the waking state, but is this state any different than a dream? You are continuously dreaming—dreaming at night and dreaming throughout the day. At any moment during the day, if you close your eyes and relax, you will sense the ongoing dream within your mind. Whether you are driving, brushing your teeth, seemingly awake, within your mind, thoughts, memories, imagination, and fictitious scenarios are continuously playing out—that is the dream. The mind creates the objective world, and the mind creates the dream world as well, so their creators and materials are the same.

It feels more real at night because it gets overshadowed by the burden of our day-to-day tasks in the morning. However, this dream state is continuous, like stars always present in the sky. They just fade with the brilliance of the morning sun, similarly...

Why I mentioned this will become clear later. So, how do we go about this? Let me teach you the method I used in my initial days.

The same has also been elucidated by Śiva in the *Vijñāna Bhairava*. If any method has been imparted, whether in any religion, by any prophet or spiritual teacher, for the attainment of enlightenment, and if that method is genuinely effective, it is bound to be found in *Vijñāna Bhairava*. No new method can be invented; Śiva has taught them all. The method that I personally practised is as follows:

अतत्त्वमिन्द्रजालाभमिदं सर्वमवस्थितम् । किं तत्त्वमिन्द्रजालस्य इति
दार्ढ्याच्छमं व्रजेत् ॥

atatvamindrājalābhamidaṃ sarvamavasthitam | kiṃ
tattvamindrājalasya iti dārdhyācchamaṃ vrajet ||

'All this universe is without reality, an illusion, a magic show, for what reality is a magic show?' By firmly contemplating in this manner, one attains peace.

(*Vijñāna Bhairava Tantra* 133)

Constant contemplation is required. With firm conviction, consistently keeping in mind that this entire world is merely a dream, an illusion.

First, thoroughly understand that this is the truth: the world is indeed like a magic show, a dream. Then, you must begin to act, to pretend, to behave as if this entire world is just a dream. Whatever you are doing, it must be done with the awareness that it's all a dream. Remember that you are in a state of dreaming. While eating, contemplate that it's a dream. While walking, remember it's a dream. Even while reading this book, maintain this awareness that you are watching a dream, and the consciousness is revealing these secrets to the mind to wake you up. Every moment, every second, every hour of the day, whenever you regain awareness—this is all just a dream.

Everything we call real is made of things that cannot be regarded as real.—Neils Bohr (Physicist)

Begin with the waking state. Usually, when you are in a dream, you don't remember that it is a dream; you feel like it is reality. But what is the reason for this? Why do you feel that it is reality? It's because all day long you have been thinking that everything is real. Everything is happening in actuality. And this has become your attitude, a fixed outlook towards the world. Right now, I am genuinely reading this book; it's not an illusion. In a little while, I will actually drink water, talk to real people, everything is happening in reality—It is from this perspective that you are viewing the world. Since childhood, you have been assuming that everything is happening in reality, and that is why this has become entrenched in your mind. It has become a firmly established mental pattern. So, even when you are dreaming at night, you maintain the same attitude towards things, believing that everything is real.

But is everything really real? Right now, you are able to read this book, how? Light is colliding with this book, entering your eyes, where a reflection is forming on the retina, and this information is transmitted through the optic nerves to the brain. What exactly happens in the brain is not known to anyone. Even science does not have an accurate answer.

It is the mind that shows us things, not the eyes. The mind creates images. There are many blind spots in the eyes, but the mind fills in those blind spots. To illustrate, let's conduct an experiment.

In the illustration below, you will find two symbols: Sun and the moon. Cover your left eye with your left hand and focus on the sun with your right eye. Begin with the page approximately 2 feet away, then gradually bring it closer to your face. At a point about 6-7 inches from your face, you will notice that the moon has disappeared. The moon symbol is located at the blind spot of your eye, but your mind successfully fills it in because it creates those images.

This blind spot exists in your left eye as well. Now, covering your right eye, focus on the moon, and the sun will cease to appear.

There are numerous such defects in our eyes, but the mind fills them up. So, this is the mind. Some schizophrenic patients see people, talk to them, although there is no such person in reality—not in real life, not in front of them. A person on reddit shared his hallucination experience:

"After a summer holiday we had to drive back home in order for my dad to be back to work on time. This meant something like 30 hours of solid driving. I decided that instead of wasting this time sleeping, I would use our newly purchased portable DVD player to watch the original star wars trilogy, followed by every single episode of red dwarf and then a couple of other things. About 25 hours into this trip (and around 30 since I'd last been asleep) I began hallucinating. Firstly, every car we shared the road with transformed into horse drawn carriages, some drawn horses, others dogs and the occasional seahorse. The drivers of these carriages were men with pumpkins for heads wearing tophat and tails and I couldn't make out what the riders in these carriages were but they didn't quite look human. I then turned to look at my brother to find instead an octopus sitting next to me. It was at this point that I also realised I was not sitting in a car but sat on the back of a giant squirrel. I then closed my eyes and forced myself to sleep."

So, it's challenging to say what is real and what isn't. Could I, and this world, be just a dream? In this moment, you could be in a dream, who knows? Reading this book, how can you say that you are not dreaming? This book might not even exist in reality. There is no way now. Only after waking up do you realise that you were in a dream.

Nevertheless, we still consider the wakeful state as real because we have believed it to be reality since childhood. Hence, this has become a fixed attitude. So, attempting otherwise is like altering the flow of a river. When Śiva said that the world is an illusion, this is what he meant. He says that the entire world is a magic show, that it is all a dream. However, we are foolish beings. We interpret it incorrectly.

Once, I told my mother that this world is an illusion. She then questioned, "Why do you eat? Why do you make videos? What is the need to do anything if everything is just a dream?" But when did I tell her to alter the dream? There's no need to change anything; it's all about remembering that the world is a dream, and enjoying the dream. Because if we quit our jobs, stop eating, or make any changes, it implies that we are accepting everything as real.

Otherwise, why bother changing anything? Whether you eat or not, work or not, the dream will remain a dream. Starving won't awaken you. All that Śiva is saying is that whatever exists is a dream. All I am saying is just to remember things, not to try to change them; you don't need to do anything—you can't do anything about it either; you just need to consistently remember it.

Consistently try to remember that whatever you are doing is just a dream. In the beginning, this may seem very challenging. It will feel like pretence, like lying to oneself. *Brahma-satyam, jagan-mithyā*; consciousness is the sole reality, the world an illusion. But what a paradox—we perceive the world as real and consciousness as illusory.

It's akin to altering the flow of water. For ages, the course of water has been set in a particular direction, and now we are attempting to reverse it. Changing a mindset that has become entrenched is a formidable task. If you wish to alter a firmly established mental pattern, you must be ready to persist no matter what. You'll find yourself repeatedly falling into the old thought patterns without even realising it, and then, suddenly, you will remember, no, it's all just a dream. You need to stay consistently conscious.

The *tripuṇḍra*, three horizontal lines of ashes, I used to wear on my forehead, was a reminder that waking, dreaming, and deep sleep are all illusions. Whenever I applied it, and whenever I looked at myself in the mirror, it reminded me that I am in a dream and that I am the background of the three states of consciousness.

Almost a month had passed since I started doing this, and I began remaining wakeful even in my dreams—I was and I remain aware that it's all just a dream whenever I dream. Gradually, I began to stay aware even in deep sleep—only awareness remained. This technique is not entirely *śambhavopāya;* it lies between *śāktopāya* and *śambhavopāya*. However, I've shared it so that you can experience this truth. So, keep practising. If you can sustain this mindset for even a few months, one night, you will suddenly remember that it's a dream.

Then, the next morning, when you wake up, it won't feel like you are waking up from sleep; it will feel like you are passing from one dream to another. This conviction will then start to become a reality. If the twenty-four hours become a dream, if you can genuinely feel this throughout the day and remember that this is a dream, then you will truly be able to discern. You will become totally dis-identified with your states, and self-realisation will happen. ***Turiya* will manifest itself in all the states.**

Kṣemarāja interprets the Sūtra (*jāgratsvapnasuṣuptabhede turyābhogasambhavaḥ*) as follows: "Even during the three distinct states of consciousness—waking, dreaming, and profound sleep—persists the rapturous experience of the I-consciousness of the fourth state." According to his interpretation, this Sūtra delineates the nature of the enlightened state, elucidating what unfolds after attaining Bhairava. He suggests that great yogis remain detached from the three states at all times and enjoy them while rooted in the fourth state, their true self, consciousness. For them, *Turiya* manifests itself in all the states.

I believe that detailing the state following enlightenment is not as important as outlining a method for attaining it. Upon experiencing it, you will understand the nature of the enlightened state with a depth far surpassing the capacity of words to convey. Hence, I have not elaborated on this interpretation, but yes, both interpretations coexist harmoniously without contradicting each other. The judgement of which interpretation better aligns with this context is a choice I entrust to you, the readers, to discern.

This concludes our study of Sūtras Seven to Eleven.

CHAPTER 8

विस्मयो योगभूमिकाः ॥१२॥

|| VISMAYO YOGABHŪMIKĀH || 12 ||

The stages of yoga are wondrous.

Now, Śiva is expounding upon the nature of a yogi. He is revealing the distinguishing mark of the enlightened state. To compose this Sūtra, three words were used: *vismaya*, *yoga*, and *bhūmikā*. The term *bhūmikā* is derived from the word *bhūmi*, meaning ground, plane or realm. Here, the Sūtra elucidates the ground or plane of yoga, the state a yogi attains through yoga. This is referred to as the *bhūmi* of yoga. Now, what is yoga?

The meaning of yoga is union or oneness. This is the literal translation of the term yoga. Since we are trying to understand what yoga means in the context of Tantra, it would be appropriate to refer to Tantric scriptures.

योगं एकत्वम् इच्छन्ति वस्तुनोऽन्येन वस्तुना।

yogam ekatvam icchanti vastuno'nyena vastunā |

Yoga is said to be oneness of one entity with another.

(*Mālinīvijaya Tantra* IV.4)

The Goddess asked,

"Lord, how is yoga defined, and what is accomplished through yoga? Please enlighten me on all of this, Śamkara!"

Śiva replied,

"Yoga is defined as the unification of various pairs of opposites — the unification of inbreath and outbreath, of one's blood and semen, the unification of the sun and the moon, and of the individual Self with the supreme Self."

(*Yoga-bīja*, Gorakhnātha 88,90)

However, the question then arises in some people's minds: how can we become one with that which we already are? If Bhairava is everything, and everything is already one with him, then what is the basis of yoga in the philosophy of non-dualism? Abhinavagupta elucidates this in his commentary on the *Mālinīvijaya:*

Moreover this scripture teaches the yoga of Siva thoroughly. This yoga of Siva is said to be non-dualistic and beyond dichotomies. Instruction in this (yoga) is given in this way: if (something) is imagined to have a certain amount of division, it is explained by analysing it again and again.

For there is no method to practise for entering into and remaining in the all-pervading Bhairava who is without duality, as both entering and remaining are completely dependent on duality.

Therefore all the efforts made by teachers and disciples serve only to remove the inhibition caused by all the duality they imagine.

(*Mālinīvijaya Varttika* I.110-114)

And finally, when we are discussing the definition of yoga, it is unthinkable to ignore the definition given by Patañjali, the father of modern yoga, in his authored *Yoga Sūtras*. He has defined yoga as the state that occurs when the mind is completely silenced and thoughts come to a halt—*yogaścittavṛttinirodhaḥ*—yoga is the cessation of the fluctuations of the mind. This does not contradict the above-mentioned definitions because the cessation of mind liberates us from the confines of our individual identity, uniting us with the entirety of existence; with Bhairava.

In this state of oneness, when we have transcended the mind and attained the realm of yoga, what happens? Śiva says, *vismaya* happens. *Vismaya*—the third word of this Sūtra.

What is *Vismaya*? *Vismaya* literally translates to joy, wonder, surprise, astonishment, or amazement. *Vismaya* is synonymous with Śiva. One interpretation of the name Śiva that I experienced during meditation is *wonderous silence*. The word Śiva deconstructs into two sounds, *shh* and *vaah*. In my exploration of diverse languages, a fascinating pattern emerged.

In Hindi, we express awe by saying *vāh* (वाह) when something extraordinary occurs. This finds its echo in English with the ubiquitous *wow*, essentially a result of the English adapting and modifying sounds with a subtle *O* pronunciation. For instance, water is pronounced as *wotah* in British English. Across continents, this universal expression takes forms as *wow oh* in African or Nigerian languages, *vay* in Turkish, *wau* in Korean, *bay* in Russian, and so forth. This universal exclamation, *wāh*, appears to emanate from a collective human consciousness, transcending cultural and religious boundaries.

Interestingly, in Hindi, we classify such exclamatory words as *'vismaya bodhak'* (literally, the informer, or expressor of *vismaya*), acknowledging their role as an expression of the sense of wonder.

Shh...vaah.

The sound, *shh*, is an onomatopoeic representation of the sound people make to indicate silence or to hush someone. It is commonly used to request quietness or to signal that someone should stop talking or making noise. Regardless of language or culture, the sound *shh* seems to emanate from the depths of collective human consciousness as an expression of silence. When the first yogi experienced the state of yoga, there were no names for the absolute, no term for this oneness. It was then that the yogi bestowed upon it the name, the sound *shh...vaah.*

Memories and thoughts constitute the mind and create the illusion of our identity as humans, as someone's son or daughter.

When that first yogi transcended the mind, he realised he wasn't just a limited human; he was beyond, he was that state of oneness, the wondrous silence—*Shh...vaah*; he was Śiva.

It's the experience of *vāh*—the awe, the joy, the amazement when something feels magical, and we exclaim, *wow*! It's the feeling of that amazement, but there's also silence; the mind is not present to cause disturbance, to make noise. There is boundless peace; that's why *shh...shh...vaah.* This is the *vismaya* that this Sūtra is talking about.

I must caution that the basis of this interpretation is rooted in my personal experiences. It stands on the foundation of realisations bestowed upon me by Śiva. I do not have any scriptural references to claim authenticity.

Because other translators and scholars have used the term amazement in their translations of this Sūtra to convey *vismaya.* However, I hold the opinion that *vismaya* does not precisely align with the amazement commonly experienced. In this particular state of amazement, a profound silence prevails, and there is an absence of the mind. Normally, when one feels amazement, it is transitory, lasting only for a few moments. Then, the mind intervenes, raising doubts about the extraordinary occurrence, searching for logic, constructing theories, and connecting it to past events. This mental interference disrupts our presence in the moment. It buzzes incessantly, much like a mosquito, disturbing our quietude and preventing us from sustaining that state of wonder. Applying some useless logic, it makes it seem normal for us.

In years past, I immersed myself in the practice of magic—sleights of hand, misdirection, and all the techniques that conjure an illusion of the supernatural, instilling a sense of wonder in the minds of onlookers. One of the driving reasons was the profound effect it had on people: when inexplicable events unfolded before them, things they had never witnessed before and for which their minds held no answers, they fell silent, completely in the present, leaving behind all their guilt of the past and worries of the future.

In those moments, a genuine expression of amazement and joy adorned their faces, reminiscent of childlike wonder. Witnessing this brought me immense joy. Had I not chosen the path of a spiritual teacher, I might have gladly embraced a career as a magician. Because the goal remains the same—anchoring people in the present moment, quieting their minds, maintaining a constant feeling of amazement and joy. If magic tricks were capable of maintaining this *vismaya* forever, then I would be a magician.

During my days as a performer of magic, the true magic lay in witnessing the awe of the audience, only to see it dissipate upon the revelation of the trick's mechanics. I found it fascinating to observe how our supposed knowledge often robs us of happiness. Even when someone remained unaware of the trick's intricacies, their minds instinctively sought to rationalise the inexplicable and rob them of their sense of wonder. Like when I performed magic for my sister, she had no reaction. She would nonchalantly remark, "I don't know how you did it, but I'm sure there's some trick!"

Today, you may argue that we are in the twenty-first century, and almost everything has a scientific explanation. Nothing is extraordinary enough to evoke a sense of amazement. However, this is probably what people said a thousand years ago as well. They might not have possessed the correct knowledge about the scientific principles underlying physical phenomena, but they too had their own made-up theories that they believed in, robbing them of their joy and hindering them from truly living in the present.

Another point is that, as much as we trust in science, it doesn't have all the answers. Today, people hold the words of figures like Einstein in high regard, similar to how the teachings of Buddha, etc., were revered in the past. However, the truth remains that no scientist can accurately define even what matter is. If you ask ten scientists what matter is, you'll get eleven different answers. So, these theories and logics are just excuses of your mind to rob you of your sense of wonder.

Our minds rarely allow us to linger in awe for more than a fleeting moment. A film, once beloved, quickly loses its charm after a mere five or six viewings, and the fervour of a once-passionate relationship gradually wanes; we lose interest. It brings to mind the wisdom of Jesus of Nazareth, who said, "Truly, I say to you, unless you turn and become like children, you will never enter the kingdom of heaven."

The reason for this is that children mostly stay in awe. They keep questioning, playing, and their minds are not burdened because they don't have the delusion of knowledge. They will ask how butterflies fly, why they are so beautiful, and then they will go into awe, play, leap, and jump. However, we, as adults, live under the illusion that we know everything. In reality, you cannot precisely answer how a butterfly flies. You cannot explain why it has such diverse colours, why it is so attractive. When was the last time you asked yourself these questions? Our minds, veiled by the veneer of knowledge, convince us that these wonders are mundane—subject to scientific explanation, bereft of magic. It robs us of the joy of curiosity and steals the wonder that once fueled our souls.

Have you read the Harry Potter series? When Harry enters the magical world for the first time, he is filled with wonder; everything is brimming with amazement for him. However, for characters like Hermione and other wizards who have always lived in the world of magic, it's all mundane. It's ordinary. Similarly, our world is no less magical. Yet, our minds have stolen the magic and deceived us with the illusion of knowledge.

Whether that knowledge is right or wrong, it is enough to steal away our wonder. People fear staying ignorant. There is a line from a movie I cherished as a child that has stayed with me forever, *"people fear and despise what they don't understand."* Hence, in any way possible, people delude themselves into thinking, 'I know,' and the mind and ego cling to it, just like a drowning person clings to a straw. *Knowledge is bondage*, was the second Sūtra, if you remember.

The moment we attain the state of yoga, when our minds are silenced, and we become one with the entirety of existence, merging into the source of supreme bliss, in that moment, everything becomes joyful and amazing for us again. We become like children. In fact, the enlightened beings of the highest calibre, the *Paramahaṁsas*, are described in the *Upaniṣads* as behaving like children, or as someone possessed by demons, or lost in intoxication. That's how they wander in the world.

Through such an absorption, one gets the pure and secondless state, owing to the absence of difference then. This alone is the highest truth. He who knows this, will wander in the world like a naive child, a lunatic, or as if possessed by a demonic spirit.

(*Mandala Brahmana Upaniṣad* V)

That's how we become in the state of yoga. When we become one with the world, the mind ceases to exist, and only *vismaya* remains. Only such great souls can truly experience love because love never becomes boring for them. In this state, one doesn't feel boredom; one resides only in wonder, in that wondrous silence—that *shh...vaah.*

This concludes our study of Sūtra Twelve.

CHAPTER 9

इच्छा शक्तिरुमा कुमारी ॥ १३ ॥

|| ICCHĀ ŚAKTIR UMĀ KUMĀRI || 13 ||

The power of desire is Uma Kumāri

In elucidating this Sūtra, we commence with that fundamental aspect of the human condition which afflicts us all, and it is through its impact and the pursuit of its resolution that we have turned our gaze towards spirituality—we all have—suffering. What is suffering? Recall your most miserable moment. That incident, that moment when you experienced profound suffering. Recollect one or two more instances of sorrow that hold a position on the second and third rungs.

What is common in all these?

One or more incidents that occurred, and our desire, which was completely against that event.

Suffering is when you desire something and it's not coming to fruition, the sensation felt in that moment is suffering. Or perhaps something happens that you didn't wish for, that was undesired; that too is misery. My desire is to grant you all self-realisation with a simple touch, but it's not happening. What is happening is not what I desire, and what I desire is not happening—that's suffering, isn't it? The fundamental problem in everyone's life is that they desire one thing and get something else. We yearn for respect from everyone, yet behind our backs, they speak ill of us. We desire our parents to remain forever young, never to leave us, yet every day they age.

So, there are two factors at play here: the events unfolding and our desires. When these two don't align, the resultant feeling is termed suffering. However, we can't always control external events, can we? If you dislike your colleague, for example, you can't change jobs every time, etc.

And even with all this control, sorrow hasn't diminished. The human race has made significant progress and continues to do so. Today, you are here, reading this, because of technology; without the internet, you wouldn't know me or about the book, and we wouldn't be here. An ordinary person today enjoys as much comfort as was unimaginable for a king a few centuries ago. If you want to know something about any subject in the world, you can find out with just a click. With a click of your fingers, you can communicate with someone living on the other side of the world. Almost all diseases have become curable; medical advancement is at its peak. Earlier, it used to take months to travel from India to America; now, you can go and come back in just fifteen to twenty hours. In forty hours, you can travel around the world by aeroplane. You always stay in a comfortable room temperature, can listen to any singer or musician anytime, and there are thousands of entertainment options, something even the kings of the past didn't have.

We have democracy, a stable economy, and peace. Almost everything we need is available, and it's there when we need it. But has sorrow disappeared? On the contrary, it has increased. Since the recording of suicide rates began, it has only been on the rise. In this decade, the suicide rate is the highest in the last hundred years, and that too in a comfortable, developed, first-world nation like America. Even if things happen as we desire, suffering doesn't end; it just gets postponed.

What is the solution then?

The second factor of this equation, our desires, our yearnings.

DESIRES ARE THE ROOT OF ALL EVIL; RENOUNCE ALL DESIRES...**No!** Try renouncing all your desires. Just be where you are and do nothing; don't even breathe. If only for 2-3 minutes, close your nostrils. Renounce the desire to breathe. Can you do it? Can you renounce all desires? No, right? Life is inconceivable without desire. Everything requires desire.

There are three powers, as mentioned earlier in this book: the power of desire, the power of knowledge, and the power of action. The power of action arises from the power of knowledge, and the power of knowledge arises from the power of desire. Action, meaning doing anything, is not possible without knowledge. If I ask you to walk, you must first learn to walk; you cannot walk without knowing how to. And if you don't have the desire to walk, you will never learn. If you have no desire to learn, no matter what I do, I cannot teach you. Nothing can be forced upon anyone; only the desire in the mind can create a willingness to learn. Yes, fear can be induced, but even fear is a kind of desire—a desire to avoid something unwanted. Isn't that what fear is?

So, nothing can be forcibly taught; children are taught in schools through scolding and slapping, but even there, desire exists. Children do not desire to be slapped, so they learn the chapters. Do you understand? Many girls marry against their will; they have no desire to marry, but they desire to see their parents happy and to obey them. This desire compels them to act.

Therefore, nothing is possible without desire. This fact also has scientific evidence.

Psychologists Kent Berridge and Terry Robinson conducted an experiment on rats, where they blocked the dopamine receptors in their brains. Dopamine is often referred to as the 'neurotransmitter or molecule of desire'. The experiment revealed that even when food was placed in front of these rats, they did not eat because they had no (biochemical manifestation of) desire; Hence, they remained completely still, inert. They neither consumed food nor had any sexual intercourse, displaying a state of utter lethargy until eventually succumbing to death.

I must mention that dopamine itself does not create desires; it merely serves as a transmitter connecting desires and the body. It triggers the expression of desires biochemically within the body. This is analogous to the currents within a wire connecting a computer and a speaker. If you disconnect the wire, the sound ceases, but it doesn't imply that the sound is being produced by the wire itself. The currents within the wire are merely a medium to transmit the audio signals from the CPU to the speakers. Similarly, dopamine is a medium; that's why it is called a transmitter.

While desires cannot be blocked, the medium can be altered to observe the consequences of the absence of desires. The outcome is that one becomes lifeless, much like those rats.

Thus, desire is synonymous with life; it cannot be forsaken. So, what then is the solution?

Nārada, a figure in Hindu mythology, is both a sage and a demigod, serving as a messenger who conveys the messages of the divine to people. Despite possessing vast knowledge in all areas of study, there lingered a sense of sorrow within him. Seeking solace, he approached a sage, a teacher, and expressed, "I know; *ṛg vedam yajur vedam sāma vedam ātharvaṇam caturtham,* the *Ṛg Veda,* the *Yajur Veda,* the *Sāma Veda,* and the *fourth,* the *Atharva Veda; itihāsa purāṇam pañcamam,* history and the *Purāṇas,* as the fifth; I have acquired proficiency in *vedānām vedam,* grammar, *pitryam,* rites offered out of respect to the ancestors; *rāśim,* mathematics; *daivam,* the science of meteors and other natural phenomena and omens; *nidhim,* the science of underground resources; *vākovākyam,* logic; *ekāyanam,* moral science; *deva-vidyām,* astrology; *brahma-vidyām,* knowledge of the Vedas; *bhūta-vidyām,* geology; *kṣattra-vidyām,* archery; *nakṣatra-vidyām,* astronomy; *sarpa-vidyām,* snake-charming; *devajana-vidyām,* fine arts; I know all this. Yet, despite all this knowledge, my heart remains burdened with sorrow."

Even a demigod, possessing such vast knowledge, found himself laden with sorrow, contemplating a visit to an ordinary human teacher. It was then that the sage, the yogi, imparted to him:

यो वै भूमा तत्सुखं नाल्पे सुखमस्ति भूमैव सुखं ।

yo vai bhūmātat sukhaṁ nālpe sukhamasti bhūmaiva sukhaṁ |

That which is finite cannot bring joy; true joy arises only from the infinite.

Happiness can never be found in limitations or incompleteness. True joy is attained only in the unlimited, the complete. You must understand that your desires will never be satisfied with partial fulfilment; your desires crave everything. Until everything is obtained, desire remains, and as long as desire remains, there is sorrow.

We now possess sufficient context to understand this Sūtra. First, a dissection of its meaning, word by word.

Icchā śaktir umā kumāri ||

It contains four words—*icchā*, *śakti, umā,* and *kumāri. Icchā* translates to desire, will, or yearning; and *śakti* means energy, or power. This aphorism conveys that the energy of desire, the power of will is *Umā Kumāri. Umā* is an epithet of the supreme Goddess Pārvatī. And as we previously understood, Goddess Pārvatī is the Primordial Power, and the Freedom of Lord Śiva (*svātantrya-śakti*).

सा देवी सर्वदेवीनां नामरूपैश्च तिष्ठति ।
योगमायाप्रतिच्छन्ना कुमारी लोकभाविनी ॥

sā devī sarvadevīnāṁ nāmarūpaiśca tiṣṭhati |
yogamāyāpratichchannā kumārī lokabhāvinī ||

The Goddess of all Goddesses, the Highest Divine *Śakti*, known by various names, veils herself in the mystique of her illusionary powers. Among her appellations is *Kumāri*, and through her, the desires of all beings find fulfilment.

(*Svacchaṃda Tantra* X.727)

'सा ममेच्छा परा शक्तिरवियुक्ता स्वभावजा ।
वह्नेरूष्मेव विज्ञेया रश्मिरूपा रवेरिव ॥
सर्वस्य जगतो वापि सा शक्तिः कारणात्मिका ॥

That Highest *Śakti* is only my Will power (*Icchā*), inseparable from me. She should be considered as natural to me. She is to be known (in the same relation to me), as heat to the fire and rays to the sun. *Śakti* is the cause of the world.

(*Netra Tantra* I, 25-26)

Freedom is a central theme in this book. So, understand freedom. Common people, whatever they do, do compulsively, unconsciously; they lack freedom. However, what Śiva does is not driven by compulsion; it is the expression of his freedom. You may think you are free, but look closely, you are not. As I observe my parents right now, they are so tied down that taking a 10-day vacation is beyond their reach. They have taken so many responsibilities upon themselves. When there is time, and energy in the body, there is no money. When there is money, there is no time. And when both are there, there is no energy left in the body. You are bound in numerous ways; just observe yourself. If you choose even a slightly unconventional path, you have to endure the emotional blackmail of family and relatives. Society dictates your age for marriage, the age for working, and dictates nearly everything. You have to go to school and college; dropping out is not an option, even if you want to.

Ninety-nine percent of people are like zombies, living life mechanically, like robots. That's why they fear Artificial Intelligence because it can live a better mechanical life than them. What they are doing can be done more efficiently by AI. Otherwise, there is no competition between humans and AI. It is because we have become robots ourselves we fear that these new robots will defeat us. We have become robots programmed by *māyā* and society. We have no freedom. And even if you are free from society, you are bound by your mind and body. In 2008, a study by the Max Planck Institute used brain imaging technology called MRI to see how people decide which hand to use when pressing a computer button. Their brain activity clearly showed what their choices were going to be, up to seven seconds before they were consciously aware of it. This implies that our unconscious mind takes most of our decisions mechanically, even before we consciously realise it, and our conscious mind catches up a few seconds later only to justify the decision.

The goal of Tantra is to understand this bondage and break free from it. The deity in Tantra, the one we consider supreme, whom we aspire to attain, and whose qualities we want to embody, is simply free. Freedom is His power.

The essence of Tantra is freedom; Tantra means expansion. To spread out, to transcend all boundaries, to rise above all limitations—this is the heart of Tantra. The word Tantra itself is the root of the Sanskrit word for freedom (*svatantra*). Tantra begins with freedom and culminates in freedom.

So, what you desire is for everything; Desire cannot be satisfied with the finite, the incomplete. Any form of incompleteness is a form of confinement, no matter how much it may be—it is still limited. No matter how much you may acquire, it remains limited; somewhere is its boundary, and where there is a boundary, there is no freedom. Your desire wants you to be free, to transcend all your limitations; it wants you to be boundless, that you remain boundlessly expansive every moment. It wants you to recognize the true Self that is unconditionally liberated—the

Svacchaṃda Śiva, that is you. Hence, the power of desire is also called the power of freedom (*svātantrya-śakti*).

If I were to confine you to a small room for a month, let's say an eighty square feet room, for instance, and provide you only with simple rice and lentils for sustenance, you would undoubtedly experience suffering. Breaking through those four walls would become your utmost desire, and because that desire remains unfulfilled, you would find yourself miserable. After a month, I would move you into a larger room, let's say a one hundred sixty square feet room, doubling the space. There, along with rice and lentils, I would also provide you with paranthas (potato-stuffed flatbreads). This change would bring a temporary sense of joy and tranquillity within you since the desire to break free from limitations has been satisfied. However, in a short time, you will become aware of your new limitations, and the desire to surpass them will intensify, giving birth to suffering once more.

The sorrow will escalate to the same level as in the eighty square feet room, where you were being provided with only rice and lentils. Let's move beyond that and place you in a spacious hall, providing you with 4-5 different food options. For a day or two, or even a month, you may experience peace, happiness, and a sense of freedom. However, as soon as you begin to sense your limitations again, the desire to surpass them will become intense. This cycle will continue until you are completely liberated.

Desire is not an evil force; even if it is, you cannot do anything about it because desires cannot be renounced. Desire liberates you, and at the same time, it becomes your shackles.

After *umā*, the Sūtra adds *kumāri*. Sūtras don't contain any unnecessary words; Śiva has excluded any words that could be excluded. In this Sūtra, only *umā* could have been mentioned, but if *kumāri* has been included, it must be of significance. The word *kumāri* holds three essential meanings. Firstly, *kumāri* signifies an unmarried girl, someone who has not yet been wed, a virgin. This desire is without any specific content; it is pure energy of desire. It is not a desire for any particular thing; it is simply desire—virgin—not wedded to any particular object of desire.

However, she can lead you in both directions—towards the world and towards Śiva. The term *kumāri* holds another meaning: *kuṁ maryati iti kumāri*. She annihilates *kuṁ*, hence she is called *kumāri*. Here, the meaning of *kuṁ* is that illusory perception of differentiation—that I am different, you are different, and Śiva is different. In other words, it's the illusion of multiplicity. This illusion of multiplicity is what the world is. And She who annihilates this illusion is *kumāri*. As mentioned earlier, the energy of desire wants you to transcend all your limitations, and the limitations are transcended only when the limited identifications are transcended; when we become one with the entire universe, when there is no two—as Śiva reveals in the next Sūtra. Therefore, an interpretation of *kumāri* is this—*kuṁ maryati iti kumāri*—She puts an end to multiplicity for us and elevates us above all limitations; thus She is *kumāri*.

However, the term carries another meaning as well. *Kumāri* is the female counterpart of the word *kumār*, which translates to a young boy. For instance, *rājkumār* means the young son of a king. Now, the word *kumār* has its roots in the same origin as the word *krīḍā*, meaning play or sport. Children engage in play, which is why they are referred to as *kumāras* and *kumāris*—those who play. *Kumāri* is used for a girl who engages in play. Just like a child's play, the Goddess creates this world again for us. This world is, in fact, a playground, and its purpose is to play. It is just a divine play, a game, *krīḍā*. So, the maiden who plays also creates this multiplicity for the sake of playing. She can bring an end to this world for you, or keep you engaged in the game of this world. It depends entirely on you and what you desire.

Like fire; Fire is fire, neither good nor bad. When we warm ourselves by the fire during cold months and enjoy hot paranthas, the fire becomes good. However, when the same fire engulfs a house, devastates a forest, or burns your fingers, it becomes evil. But fire is still fire; its nature depends on how we utilise it.

Similarly, desire is desire. Jammu & Kashmir are popular tourist destinations, known for their scenic landscapes and beautiful valleys. In these places, you'll find crowds of young boys and girls. Many couples visit these destinations for their honeymoon, and the majestic mountains of Kashmir intensify their lustful feelings. It's not the fault of Kashmir; ancient scriptures and Tantras were written in these very valleys. The sages found spiritual enlightenment amidst these mountains. The *Śiva Sūtras* were discovered by Vasugupta in Kashmir. Whatever desire you pursue, you will find it. If you seek physical intimacy, your lust will intensify in the valleys, and if you seek spiritual knowledge, success in meditation will follow. Your destiny is shaped by your desires.

However, in the highest sense, desire is that force which wants you to be free, to transcend all your limitations; it wants you to be boundless, that you remain boundlessly expansive every moment. It wants you to recognize the Self that is unconditionally liberated—the *Svacchaṃda Śiva*, that is you. But how?

Śiva has revealed a practical method for this in the next Sūtra.

This concludes our study of Sūtra Thirteen.

CHAPTER 10

दृश्यं शरीरम् ॥१४॥

|| DRŚYAM ŚARĪRAM || 14 ||

Whatever is perceivable (this entirety of existence) **is verily your own body.**

OR

Even your own body is an object to perceive (in an unidentified, detached manner, as something separate from you).

In the preceding Sūtra, we explored what desires are. I clarified that desire is that force which wants you to be free, to transcend all your limitations; it wants you to be boundless, that you remain boundlessly expansive every moment. It wants you to recognize the Self that is unconditionally liberated—the *Svacchaṃda Śiva,* that is you.

The truth is that you strive relentlessly to free yourself from your constraints, yet your approach is misguided. You perceive your body as your true Self and attempt every possible means to free it. However, the nature of the body itself is bondage; it is subject to countless limitations. Our bodies are bound by genes—our height, hair colour, eye colour, size, shape, and skin colour are predetermined and unchangeable. Despite this, efforts persist; women wear heels to create an illusion of height, finding confidence in the deception. People dye their hair, wear coloured lenses, and resort to various measures. In India, numerous methods are employed to whiten the skin, including a plethora of creams, foundations, colours, and more.

Our bodies are also pre-determined by gender, hence limited. Yet, futile endeavours are being made to surpass these limitations. People undergo surgeries, take hormone injections, and engage in strange experiments in the Western world.

The movement of the body is also limited, and we can only walk through the use of legs, unable to fly. However, we have made numerous attempts to surpass this limitation, we have created motor vehicles, aeroplanes, helicopters, etc. Similarly, the body requires very specific conditions to survive. It cannot endure excessive heat or cold, function properly with either too much or too little oxygen, or thrive in extreme humidity conditions. It needs a delicate balance of temperature, sunlight, water, air, minerals, etc., for survival. There are countless other limitations on the body, yet we continuously strive to find solutions to overcome these limitations. However, our efforts seem to fall short, and our suffering persists. I am not suggesting that these efforts are useless—far from it. They make our worldly lives easier and more comfortable, pushing humanity forward. But the core issues of suffering and limitations remain unsolved. In fact, they seem to be increasing.

In this context, our solutions are not freeing us from our limitations but rather producing additional constraints. Heels were created to transcend the limitations of height, but now they have become a limitation themselves. One cannot go beyond that height, and another limitation has emerged—one has lost the ability to feel strong and confident without those heels, their confidence has become tied to them. They continue to wear heels despite the discomfort they cause. One solution has led to the emergence of 3-4 more problems. This pattern seems to apply to almost all the solutions we have devised to free our bodies.

These solutions are not working because our approach is misguided. So, what should be done?

Cease striving to free your body and strive to free yourself from the body. Because having identified oneself with the wrong entity, you have thereby accepted the limitations of that entity as your own limitations. And limitations mean bondage, the very root of desire and suffering. All of this has been elucidated earlier in this book. Allow me to quote my own words from the first chapter:

"Who is limited? Who is bound? One who is identified with a specific entity. Suppose you identify yourself with a certain position in a company. The limitations of that company's position become your limitations—limitations mean bondage. Understand this: limitations are the opposite of freedom. If your actions are confined, if you can only do so much and nothing more, then you are in bondage. If your thoughts are limited, if identifying with something sets a boundary on your thinking, then that is bondage. For example, if you identify yourself as religious, there are numerous things you are prohibited from thinking and doing—you cannot question the existence of God, cannot have physical relationships beyond your spouse, are forbidden from harbouring negative thoughts about others or causing harm. In such a scenario, you are not truly free; you are bound. Therefore, being limited is synonymous with being bound.

And where do these limitations come from? They stem from a particular identification. Identification is always connected to limitations. If you are a boy, you cannot cry; if you are a girl, you cannot laugh your heart out. If you are a spiritual leader, you are not supposed to amass great wealth, and so on.

And where does freedom come from? It comes from letting go of all identification. I am everything, and I can do anything and everything."

This is one approach—to identify with everything, to consider everything as your own body. Another approach is to not identify with anything; to look at even your own body and mind in a detached manner, as something separate from you.

Ādi Śaṅkarācārya had a devoted disciple who rendered years of service without receiving any formal instruction. One day, as Śaṅkara sensed footsteps approaching from behind, he inquired, "Who is there?" The disciple responded, "It is I." In response, the

Master remarked, "If this 'I' holds such importance for you, either expand it to the infinite or renounce it entirely."

And these are the two interpretations of this Sūtra. But first, a dissection of its meaning, word by word:

dṛśyam śarīram ||

This Sūtra contains only two words. In just two words, Śiva has revealed the truth and how to realise it. Let's understand.

Dṛśyam refers to what is visible, perceivable, things that we experience, and what we see around us. Every living being, creature, entity, plants, clouds, and rivers—everything in this universe—can be encompassed within this word—*dṛśyam*. The second word of the Sūtra is *śarīram*, meaning the body—your body—this entirety of existence is verily your own body.

Śiva elaborates on this more comprehensively in the *Vijñāna Bhairava Tantra*:

जलस्येवोर्मयो वह्नेर्ज्यालाभङ्गयः प्रभा रवेः । ममैव भैरवस्यैता विश्वभङ्ग्यो विभेदिताः ॥

jalasyevormayo vahnerjyālābhaṅgayaḥ prabhā raveḥ | *maiva bhairavasyaitā viśvabhaṅgyo vibheditāḥ* ||

As waves and tides are one with water, and the sparks of all flames are one with fire and as rays are one with the sun, in the same way. all the universal currents rise from me, this vast and infinite cosmic fields rise from me, me who is Bhairava.

सर्वत्र भैरवो भावः सामान्येष्वपि गोचरः । न च तद् व्यतिरेकेण परोऽस्तीत्यद्वया गतिः ॥

sarvatra bhairavo bhāvaḥ sāmānyeṣvapi gocaraḥ | *na ca tad vyatirekeṇa paro'stītyadvayā gatiḥ* ||

Bhairava is everywhere and everything; even the common folk are Bhairava Himself. He who knows that nothing exists apart from Him, attains the supreme state.

Interestingly, quantum mechanics also asserts the same—particles such as electrons do not have separate existences but are parts of a unified field—of a larger, cohesive whole—meaning that the notions of 'I am this' and 'I am not that' lose their significance. The distinction between you and me becomes blurred and ultimately ceases to exist.

In the above Sūtra, Śiva has employed the term *śarīram*, meaning body. He could have used *ātmā* (self), but why the body? The three reasons for this I will now explain to you. At this moment, you have a body. *Ātmā* is just a distinct concept for you, but this body is your actual self. Your identification is with this body. Perhaps you may not like hearing this, but this is the truth. If you were aware that you are not the body but the *ātmā*, you wouldn't be reading this book. Maybe you identify with the subtle body rather than the physical body. You identify with the mind and consider it the *ātmā*. But the mind is nothing but the subtle form of the physical body. Mind is your subtle body. Consciousness, the *ātmā*, is not yet your experience; it is not your reality. It is only what you have heard, what you have read, and what you have believed without experiencing. If it were your own experience, then just one aphorism would be enough to liberate you. There would be no need to read after the first Sūtra.

It's not that Śiva has written a lie; I have written a lie—No, for me, *ātmā* is the truth. For those who know, who have experienced the self, the Self is the truth. But for you, the body is the truth until the Self becomes your own experience.

I remember my past life; I was a Tantrik, a devotee of Śiva. Even in the final moments of my life, I worshipped Śiva. However, what happened after leaving the body is unknown to me. Whatever occurred between leaving the body and taking another birth was just like the moment between two dreams—unconscious. There was never a time I remember before my birth when I wasn't in a body. So how can I realise that I am something other than the body? When a person dies, they enter an unconscious state, the same state they were in before taking a breath. Your life is a dream, a series of dreams, and you are in a long and deep sleep. In this sleep, one dream ends, and for a few moments, you remain in deep unconscious slumber until the beginning of another dream.

Hence, you do not know of anything beyond the body, or how you will feel after death. Even if I ask you to imagine your death, you will still be in some kind of body, and through the eyes of that body, you will see another body that resembles yours. You cannot conceive of a state without a body because you have never experienced such a state. You have always known yourself only in the embodied form. That's why Śiva used the term *śarīram* here, not *ātmā*.

The second reason is that, in this world, everything is interconnected, much like the various organs of a body. Everything functions together as inseparable limbs of one universal being. I have explained this in the commentary of the fifth aphorism, illustrating how trees, soil, animals, and the sky are all connected, and there is no real ground to create distinctions between them. All of them function like organs of a singular cosmic body.

Allow me to quote my own words: "Consider your body with its many organs and the millions of cells that form them, and then think about the countless microorganisms that are a part of your body, necessary for its proper functioning. All these elements come together to form your body, and you recognize them as an inseparable part of yourself. Right now, you consider your body as yourself, and so these organs, limbs, and microorganisms constitute your identity. They are a part of yourself. So, why stop at the boundaries of our skin? Beyond our physical bodies, we are intimately connected to the trees, the earth, the sky, the sun, and everything in the universe. What prevents us from embracing oneness with the entire world? Why do we create divisions and boundaries?"

As I have mentioned earlier, in this thread, Śiva has concealed the secret truth and the method to realise it. So, one practical method hidden in this thread is to consider the entire universe as a part of your own vast body—include everything in your expansive identity; we have discussed it several times in the previous chapters. Now, let me explain another method briefly, a method that I instinctively followed or, you could say, that happened spontaneously.

Nestled on the outskirts of our town, my school found its haven just a stone's throw from the gentle embrace of the river Koshi in Bihar. Its murmurs served as a soothing symphony to my young mind. Along the river's bank, a patchwork of vibrant crops painted the landscape—wheat, maize, rice, each swaying in harmony with the breeze. Towering coconut and mango trees, along with a chorus of thick foliage, formed a natural boundary between the school and the flowing waters.

After the final bell tolled, I'd embark on a journey through that miniature jungle, a passage leading me to the tranquil riverbank. There, surrounded by nature's bounty, I'd find my sanctuary.

Every element around me—the rustling leaves, the swaying crops, the gentle currents of the Koshi—became the objects of my perception; *dr̥śyam*—that Śiva referred to. I would sit in their presence, feeling a sense of oneness. By the streaming river Koshi, I would merge with its current. I would fix my gaze upon the sky, becoming one with its boundless expanse.

I became that mango tree, feeling the pulse of my life coursing through it. There was a dialogue, a love that unified us. I was indeed the tree; it had become my body. Yet, the essence was within the heart of that tree. The centre remained within that tree.

This spontaneously happened; *dr̥śyam* became *śarīram*; as if my consciousness merged into the tree, into that river. Then, a profound tranquillity ensued. A boundless serenity, where all thoughts dissolved, and the very existence of all sorrows ceased.

Because identification no longer existed, and identification is indeed the root of all sufferings. If you can forget this false self, if you can let it go, then along with it, all misery also dissolves.

This false self, this identification with name and form, serves as a barrier to attaining the state of yoga. Yoga, in essence, means becoming one with the entirety of existence. Rise above embodiment and strive to see yourself in the bodies of others. See yourself in the tree, in the river, and in the sky. Start from the tree. Practise this for at least an hour every day.

Sit in the presence of a tree and experience that you have become the tree. When the wind blows and the entire tree starts swaying, dancing, sync with its movement, feel that dance within yourself. When the monsoon arrives, and the downpour of rain comes, the whole tree becomes alive and satisfied, a long thirst quenched, a long anticipation fulfilled—feel that satisfaction within. The tree becomes completely content and radiates with life. Feel that contentment, that fullness of life.

Then you will understand the tree; you will become aware of its subtle internal states. You may have looked at that tree for many years, but you do not know it from the inside. Once you get to know the tree from the inside, you start understanding its language, and the tree will share its thoughts with you. It will share its joy and sorrow. Then you will be able to grasp what it wants to teach you. This is a *śāmbhavopāya*. And such communion can happen with the entire cosmos.

The moment you discard this limited identity, you will feel that you are everywhere.

Now, there is another meaning to this Sūtra, and in that alternative interpretation, a different method of meditation is concealed by the divine, to free you from embodiment, to break your attachment with name and form. Allow me to elucidate.

The meaning of *drśyam*, as I have explained before, is that which is perceptible—something that can be seen, something that can be perceived. The existents we experience, the things we see; that are not us but that we observe. And *śarīram* translates to the body, our physical body. Not only our physical body but also the mind and the void body.

The second meaning of this Sūtra is to detach from your body and mind and observe them with a witnessing consciousness. Do not identify with them; just witness them in a detached manner. *Dṛśyam śarīram*—your body and mind are objects to witness.

In the *Vijñāna Bhairav Tantra*, Śiva has outlined certain practices that are an expansion of this Sūtra:

इन्द्रियद्वारकं सर्वं सुखदुःखादिसङ्गमम् । इतीन्द्रियाणि संत्यज्य स्वस्थः स्वात्मनि वर्तते ॥

indriyadvārakaṁ sarvaṁ sukha-duḥkhādi-saṅgamam | itīndriyāṇi saṁtyajya svasthaḥ svātmani vartate ||

All association with pleasure and pain occurs through the senses. Therefore detach yourself from the senses and abide within your own Self.

You must detach yourself from your body, and witness the body and all its sensations. Just as Shiva has instructed:

किञ्चिदङ्गं विभिद्यादौ तीक्ष्णसूच्यादिना ततः । तत्रैव चेतनां युक्त्वा भैरवे निर्मला गतिः ॥

kiñcid aṅgaṁ vibhidyādau tīkṣṇasūcyādinā tataḥ | tatraiva cetanāṁ yuktvā bhairave nirmalā gatiḥ ||

If a sharp needle pricks any part of the body causing pain, or if there is any kind of pain, or any other sensation in any part of the body, then by concentrating on that very point, becoming aware of it, one attains the pure state of Bhairava.

In a similar manner, detaching oneself from one's thoughts and observing them, or staying aware of one's breath, liberates an individual. In this interpretation, the term body extends beyond the physical entity. The body is fundamentally of three types: physical (*deha*), mental (*citta*), and void (*śūnya*). Śiva has explained this well in the scriptures.

Deha, meaning the physical body or the grossest form of consciousness, is the body made up of food. The hand with which I am writing belongs to the *deha*. The body that is composed of flesh, blood, and bones is *deha*. It is the body subject to birth, development, decay, and death, governed by the laws of nature, affected by injury, illness, and the extremes of temperature. This is the first type of body among the four.

The subtle form of *deha* is *citta*, also known as the mind. The physiological and psychological aspects are one. The physical body is the gross form of the mind, and the mind is the subtle form of the physical body. Therefore, the illnesses of the body also affect the mind. When the body indulges in intoxication, the mind is also affected. Similarly, when the mind is distressed or depressed, it affects the body. In modern science, this is referred to as Psychosoma, where psyche refers to the mind, and somatic refers to the body. Psychosoma means the oneness of mind and body.

When pure consciousness contracts itself into thoughts and emotions and begins to descend externally, that formation is referred to as citta. Thoughts and emotions are both pulsations of the same mind; in reality, they are two sides of the same coin. Without this connection, we could never express our emotions and thoughts in words or discuss them. Without them being vibrations of the same *citta*, we wouldn't be able to feel our thoughts, connect them with our emotions, or form coherent expressions in words.

Whenever we experience a strong emotion, it is always associated with a specific thought or memory, often buried deep in the recesses of the unconscious mind. For example, there was a beautiful devotional song of Lord Gaṇeśa. However, every time I listened to it, my heart would race, and anxiety would creep in. This reaction stemmed from a severe childhood illness episode. Amidst excruciating pain and fear, I experienced, my mother played that very song to distract me from my condition.

Unfortunately, the impression of that negative emotion got linked with the song. Now, the song evoked negativity, but that emotion isn't independent; it's linked to a specific memory buried in the unconscious. *Citta* is the second type of body among the four.

Somewhere between *citta* and *deha*, there exists something known as *prāna*, which translates to life energy or vital force. Traditionally, this is considered another distinct type of body. However, to simplify matters, we primarily consider only three types of bodies.

And then, there is the third: *śūnya*, the void. By *śūnya* I don't mean the nothingness that *Vijñāna Bhairava* describes as enlightenment or the ultimate state of Śiva.

For instance,

पृष्ठशून्यं मूलशून्यं युगपद् भावयेच्च यः । शरीरनिरपेक्षिण्या शक्त्या शून्यमना भवेत् ॥

pṛṣṭhaśūnyaṁ mūlaśūnyaṁ yugapad bhāvayeccha yaḥ ।
śarīra nirapekṣiṇyā śakyā śūnyamanā bhavet ।

Meditating simultaneously on the *śūnya* above and the *śūnya* at the base; by the power of the energy which does not depend on the body, one's mind attains the state of *śūnya.*

In this verse, in this method, Śiva has referred to the state of enlightenment as the *śūnya*-state However, the discussion of this *śūnya* is not taking place here. The term *śūnya-śarīra*, or void-body is being used here to denote *suṣupti*, a state of deep sleep, or deep unconsciousness. I would refer to it as unconscious + emptiness. Although the term *śūnya* is traditionally used, scholars like Abhinavagupta used this term to refer to the state of deep unconsciousness. This usage emerged during a time when Buddhism was flourishing, and its philosophy of emptiness was prominent. And they would confuse deep slumber with the state of emptiness. Having mastered the art of sleeping while maintaining a meditative posture, they considered it the ultimate truth.

They would say, "the Self does not exist, the supreme reality is nothingness!" It may appear like Buddhahood from the outside but is fundamentally different.

To critique these advocates of emptiness, scholars like Abhinavagupta used the term *śūnya* to refer to states of unconscious emptiness.

In reality, deep sleep is not true emptiness; it contains the existence of *tamas* (forgetfulness or inertia). If it is not empty of *tamas*, how can it be considered true emptiness? Our true Self is consciousness, as I thoroughly explained in the first chapter. Consciousness is the ultimate reality and the source of this world. It is the true emptiness. However, in states like deep sleep, *tamas* veils this consciousness. If *tamas* is subtracted, *true* emptiness will be attained. If deep sleep is transformed into *drśyam*, true emptiness will be attained. This has already been discussed in the previous chapters.

The same applies to these three bodies as well. If they are made *drśyam*. If, without identifying with them, we can make them the objects of perception and remain mindful towards them with a detached attitude, then the state of Bhairava will be attained. In the explanation of threads 7 to 11, I had clarified that we become the three states of waking, dreaming, and deep sleep; we start identifying with them—the witness consciousness is lost. I provided a meditation technique to reverse the process: you must be the witness, observe, experience, but do not identify yourself. Differentiate, stay aware in all states of existence. These three states and these three bodies are the same thing. In the waking state, identification occurs with the physical body, in dreams with the mind, and in deep sleep with the void body. What you need to do is disassociate from each of them one by one, disidentify from them, treat them like objects separate from yourself, just witness them, transform them into *drśyam*. The present method is different from the one explained in Chapter 7, but the boundaries are blurry and the goal remains the same.

The method is called *Vipaśyanā*—meaning to see, to be passively aware. Through its practice, Prince Siddhārtha attained enlightenment. You can initiate this by witnessing the objective world, starting with what is naturally *dṛśyam*. Just look, keep looking; there's no need to focus on anything specific, just witness, not only the form but also the sound, smell, touch, and taste. Appearance, sound, smell, touch, and taste together make up the objective, perceivable reality, so stay aware of these five. Simply watch with a dissociation from them. There should be only one feeling—that you are witnessing, a seer observing. This method is entirely different from the techniques discussed in previous chapters, so don't mix them. Just remain aware of form, taste, smell, sound, and touch. What's happening in the mind, what's happening in the body—these are not our concerns at this stage.

Even in this seemingly straightforward process, challenges will arise. Initially, you will maintain awareness for a brief moment, only to be swept away by thoughts about work, studies, business, or an array of future concerns. Even in the absence of worries, the mind has a knack for conjuring up imaginary problems. After a few minutes, the realisation dawns that you forgot the original intention, you were supposed to watch, to witness the form, taste, smell, sound, and touch. When this happens, return without any regret; there's no need for remorse. If you keep regretting it, beating yourself, getting angry, time will be wasted. Instead, acknowledge the wandering mind and gently redirect your focus to the present, resuming your awareness of the five subtle elements. As you make progress, gradually shift your awareness to the body and breath—the second stage in this practice. Pay attention to the sensations in your body and the rhythm of your breath—inhalation and exhalation. You don't need to think that the breath is going out; simply flow with it. As the breath goes out, let your consciousness follow; as it comes in, consciousness comes with it. Just stay mindful of the continuous cycle of breath without engaging in any mental commentary.

After engaging in this practice for one or two hours daily over the course of a month, start observing your thoughts—your mind. Your identification with the body would have significantly reduced at this point; now the primary identification will be with the mind, and its thoughts, memories, and feelings. This marks the third stage, and it will be the most challenging. Gradually, after four or five months, all your thoughts will vanish. But awareness must be maintained. Continue watching; if awareness fades, you will slip into deep sleep. This is not the state of *samādhi*; it's merely sleep. You have to keep observing, and even in that state of deep sleep, remain conscious to eventually attain the fourth state.

A doubt may have arisen in your mind: sometimes, it seems like I am advocating for you to identify with everything and become one with the entirety of existence, while elsewhere, I am suggesting becoming completely unidentified, merely observing everything like a distinct spectator. It appears as though I am contradicting myself. "If I am everything, why are you teaching me that I am not the body, not the mind, not the waking state, dream state, or deep sleep state? First, be sure for yourself whether I am everything or nothing at all!" Indeed, this is a valid question. I have answered this in the subsequent chapter, so here I quote it,

"Śiva alone is the path, the stairway that reaches to the highest peak, and He alone is the peak. *Śuddha-tattva* is the peak, which one must aim to attain. But to reach this summit, one must not be satisfied with the path or the stairs that lead to it. It is necessary to abandon the path altogether, for the path is not the destination. It is merely a means to reach it. But when one finally reaches the peak, they will see that the very material from which the peak is made is also the material from which the path was made. The soil and the stone are the same.

In like manner, when you are united with consciousness, you will realise that all things are constituted of that very essence of consciousness. All things have consciousness as their reality. All things are the expression thereof. It is this consciousness that has revealed itself in the guise of this world. And then, shall you perceive that consciousness pervading everything in this world.

As of now, we must reject this world, we must surpass this world, this body, mind, vital energy and ego. We must leave them behind, and rise above them all so that we may attain *śuddha-tattva*. But once we reach the destination, this world transforms into our playground. It becomes a supreme bliss for us to dwell in this world. Everything becomes joyful, for everything is perceived as being infused with consciousness."

This concludes our study of Sūtra Fourteen.

CHAPTER 11

From the innocence of childhood, we, Hindu children, were taught a sacred incantation by our elders. It is a verse of immense significance sourced from the Vedas:

ॐ कर्पूरगौरं करुणावतारं संसारसारम् भुजगेन्द्रहारम् ।
सदावसन्तं हृदयारविन्दे भवं भवानीसहितं नमामि ॥

oṃ karpūragauram karuṇāvatāram samsārasāram bhujagendrahāram |
sadāvasantam hṛdayāravinde bhavam bhavānīsahitam namāmi. ||

This incantation is an offering of surrender to Śiva and his consort, the Goddess Pārvatī, who are—*Karpūragauram*, of white, camphor-like complexion, an expression of their pure and unblemished nature. *Karuṇāvatāram*, the embodiment of compassion, as if kindness, benevolence, and love are incarnated within them. *Samsārasāram*, they are the heart of the world, the source, the essence, the very foundation upon which the cosmos stands. *Bhujagendrahāram*, the king of serpents' venomous beauty, adorns their necks.

However, it is the phrase *sadāvasantam hṛdayāravinde* that I want to emphasise. *Sadāvasantam hṛdayāravinde* means their permanent abode is in the lotus (*arvind*) of our hearts (*hṛdaya*), not in some far-off heavens or lofty mountaintops, but deep within our very being. They reside at the centre of our being, in the very heart of our existence.

Turn inwards, let the mind merge with the very heart of your being, and absolute truth shall be perceived. This is the message of Śiva in the fifteenth Sūtra:

हृदये चित्तसंघट्टाद् दृश्यस्वापदर्शनम् ॥१५॥

|| HṚDAYE CITTASAMGHATṬĀD DṚSYASVĀPADARŚANAM || 15 ||

(Turn inwards) **Merge the mind with the heart** (the source from where the mind originates) **and the perception of the underlying reality behind all that is perceivable will occur.**

I shall now expound upon this Sūtra, delving into its meaning word by word. The first word, *hṛdaya*, is translated into English as heart. To those who are ignorant, the heart may appear to be a mere mechanical organ, responsible for the propulsion of blood through the body via the contraction and expansion of its chambers.

During my days as a nonbeliever, I would console myself with the thought that it was foolish to assign such divine reverence to a mere pumping machine. Even though my understanding of the heart's workings was limited to my high school biology textbook, I remained convinced. Those who seek to disparage the teachings of *Sanātana Dharma* on the basis of 'science' often base their arguments solely on rudimentary knowledge gained through Google or textbooks from school and college. They are neither researchers nor true men of science, for if they were, they would have an idea of the intricacies of the universe. Even scientists themselves are not as confident in their theories as those who staunchly advocate science without truly comprehending the intricacies of the field. Doctors, too, may question the efficacy of their remedies or the accuracy of their diagnoses, while a pharmacist with no medical knowledge has unwavering faith in the effectiveness of his recommended medicine.

Werner Heisenberg, one of the pioneers of quantum mechanics, famously wrote—"What we observe is not nature itself, but nature exposed to our method of questioning. The observer and the observed are not independent of one another. In some strange sense, the very act of observation disturbs the system. We cannot observe the nature of things directly. If we try to observe nature, we find that it is not possible to do so without changing the nature of what we observe. What can be said at all can be said clearly, and what we cannot talk about, we must pass over in silence…The reality we can put into words is never reality itself."

Modern science is not based on knowledge derived from divine sources. It has yet to grasp even a tenth of the truth. Much of what is discovered amounts to surface-level understanding based on theories that are ever-changing with the passage of time. For example, medical science has long asserted that the heart is simply a mechanical organ, subservient to the brain like any other body part. However, recent discoveries have overturned this long-held belief.

Neurocardiology, an emerging interdisciplinary field of study, delves into the nervous system within the heart and its communication with the brain. This field of study was born in the early 1990s from the collaboration of cardiovascular researchers with neurophysiologists who shared a common interest. Researchers discovered that the heart has its own intrinsic nervous system, which is complex enough to be regarded as a miniature brain. This intricate network is composed of various types of neurons, neurotransmitters, proteins, and support cells that resemble the brain's components. The heart's nervous system can function independently, learn, remember, and even sense and feel. It includes around 40,000 neurons that detect heart rate, pressure, and circulating hormones. These neurons send neurological impulses to the brain through several pathways, including those that carry pain signals and other sensations.

Furthermore, these signals travel to the higher centres of the brain, where they can affect perception, decision-making, and other cognitive processes. They regulate many of the autonomic nervous system signals that flow from the brain to the heart, blood vessels, and other organs.

The heart's intrinsic nervous system plays a critical role in maintaining cardiovascular stability and efficiency, and it can operate independently of the cranial brain (in the skull). Its complex ganglia, which contain interneurons and transmitting neurons, are crucial components of this intrinsic cardiac nervous system.

Researchers at the HeartMath Institute, a non-profit research organisation, have found that the brain in the heart transmits more information to the cranial brain than the amount of information the cranial brain sends to the heart. This suggests that the heart has a greater influence on the brain than the brain has on the heart. One significant way that the heart-brain influences the cranial brain is when the heart is in a state of coherence, such as when experiencing joy, satisfaction, and love. In such a state, the body, including the brain, experiences a variety of benefits, including increased mental clarity and improved decision-making abilities. Contrary to popular belief, the heart is not merely a pumping machine but rather something mystical.

In recent years, the HeartMath Institute has conducted extensive research on the human heart. Their discoveries have been published in peer-reviewed journals, including the *Journal of Alternative and Complementary Medicine* and the *Journal of Scientific Exploration*, among others. In case of any doubt regarding the authenticity of the findings of these studies, I shall provide their sources in the footnotes.

Some years ago, scholars at the Institute of Noetic Sciences conducted a study in which it was discovered that the participants' nervous systems had foreknowledge of the kind of images that would be presented to them. These images were either negative or peaceful and positive, and the pictures shown to them were randomly selected from these two categories. Astonishingly, the participants' nervous systems predicted the emotional content of the picture that was to be presented, a few seconds before they were actually displayed. The HeartMath Institute recently replicated this study with a few modifications, such as the inclusion of devices that measure brain waves, ECG (heart's electrical activity), and HRV (heart rate variability).

Twenty-six adults participated, and a collection of forty-five images were used, which were divided into two categories. Fifteen images were selected to trigger strong emotional responses, such as a picture of a naked woman, or the fangs of a snake while the remaining thirty images aimed to trigger a peaceful state, like a picture of a cute rabbit or a calm seascape.

Initially, the participants were shown a blank screen for six seconds. After that, each of the forty-five images was randomly displayed on the screen, one at a time, for three seconds. After three seconds, the screen went blank for ten seconds before displaying the next image. To gain a comprehensive understanding of the participant's responses, the researchers recorded their physical data, including ECG and HRV, using specialised software.

The study's findings were remarkable. The data clearly indicated that before the computer had even selected and displayed the image, the participants' hearts and brains had already sensed the nature of the image and reacted accordingly. The participants' hearts and brains responded to the images about 4.8 seconds before the images were displayed on the screen.

The heart, however, was able to sense this information even before the brain. The director of research at the HeartMath Institute, Dr. Rollin McCraty *Ph.D.* explained, "It is first registered from the heart, then up to the brain (emotional and prefrontal cortex), where we can logically relate what we are intuiting, then finally down to the gut (or where something stirs)."[1]

Śiva, in the Tantras, has taught that the heart, which beats within our chest, is the throne of the living soul. It is the abode of

1 https://www.heartmath.org/articles-of-the-heart/a-deeper-view-of-intuition/

the individual self, the *jīva*. Within this heart, the mind, intellect, and ego find their dwelling place, and it is here that one's memories, identities, and personalities reside.

For example, the *Bhūtaśuddhi Tantra, Gautamīya Tantra, Tripurāsārasaṃucchasya, Tārārahasya*, and other Tantric texts have pronounced that the immortal abode of the soul, or *jīva*, is located within the heart. This same conviction is echoed in the *Upaniṣads*. However, this does not imply that the soul is restricted solely to the heart. Nay, the soul resides throughout the body and upon the demise of one body, it transmigrates into another. Yet, the heart serves as its throne, just as a king may inhabit any chamber within his palace but is often found on his throne. He is neither confined within the throne nor the palace.

This is no mere imagination. Dr. Paul Pearsall, an American neuropsychologist who conducted a decade-long study of transplant patients, made some truly astounding discoveries. He found that patients who had undergone a heart transplant received the donor's behaviour, personality, habits, and indeed, even memories.

In Nexus Magazine, Volume 12, Number 3 (April-May 2005), Dr. Paul Pearsall published an article that outlined 10 cases of heart transplant recipients and the observations made by their loved ones. Here, I shall recount three of those cases, using the exact words from the article without any paraphrasing.

The case of Timmy and Daryl.

The heart donor was a three-year-old boy Timmy who fell from an apartment window. The recipient was a five-year-old boy Daryl, with septal defect and cardiomyopathy.

The donor's mother reported:

"It was uncanny. When I met the family and Daryl (the recipient) at the transplant meeting, I broke into tears. Then we went up to the giving tree where you hand a token symbolising your donor. I was already crying when my husband told me to look at the table we were passing. It was the donor family with Daryl sitting there.

I knew it right away. Daryl smiled at me exactly like Timmy (the donor) did. After we talked for hours with Daryl's parents, we were comforted. It somehow just didn't seem strange at all after a while. When we heard that Daryl had made up the name Timmy and got his age right, we began to cry. But they were tears of relief because we knew that Timmy's spirit was alive."

The recipient reported:

"I gave the boy a name. He's younger than me and I call him 'Timmy'. He's just a little kid. He's a little brother like about half my age. He got hurt bad when he fell down. He likes Power Rangers a lot, I think, just like I used to. I don't like them anymore, though. I like Tim Allen on Tool Time, so I called him Tim. I wonder where my old heart went, too. I sort of miss it. It was broken, but it took care of me for a while."

The recipient's father reported:

"Daryl never knew the name of his donor or his age. We didn't know either until recently. We just learned that the boy who died had fallen from a window. We didn't even know his age until now. Daryl had it about right. Probably just a lucky guess or something, but he got it right. What is spooky, though, is that he not only got the age right and some idea of how he died, he got the name right. The boy's name was Thomas, but for some reason, his immediate family called him 'Tim'."

The recipient's mother reported:

"Are you going to tell him the real twilight zone thing? Timmy fell trying to reach a Power Ranger toy that had fallen on the ledge of the window. Daryl won't even touch his Power Rangers anymore..."

The case of a girl whose heart was filled with fear.

The heart donor was a three-year-old girl who drowned in the family pool. The recipient was a nine-year-old boy diagnosed with myocarditis and septal defect.

The recipient's mother said: "He (the recipient) doesn't know who his donor was or how she died. We do. She drowned at her mother's boyfriend's house. Her mother and her boyfriend left her with a teenage babysitter who was on the phone when it happened. I never met her father, but the mother said they had a very ugly divorce and that the father never saw his daughter. She said she worked a lot of hours and wished she had spent more time with her. I think she feels pretty guilty about it all... you know, the both of them sort of not appreciating their daughter until it was too late."

The recipient, who claimed not to know who the donor was, reported: "I talk to her sometimes. I can feel her in there. She seems very sad. She is very afraid. I tell her it's okay, but she is very afraid. She says she wishes that parents wouldn't throw away their children. I don't know why she would say that."

The recipient's mother said about the recipient: "Well, the one thing I notice most is that Jimmy is now deathly afraid of the water. He loved it before. We live on a lake and he won't go out in the backyard. He keeps closing and locking the back door. He says he's afraid of the water and doesn't know why. He won't talk about it."

The case of a police officer who was shot in the face.

The heart donor was a 34-year-old police officer Carl shot attempting to arrest a drug dealer. The recipient was a 56-year-old college professor Ben diagnosed with atherosclerosis and ischaemic heart disease.

The donor's wife reported:

"When I met Ben (the recipient) and Casey (Ben's wife), I almost collapsed. First, it was a remarkable feeling seeing the man with my husband's heart in his chest. I think I could almost see Carl (the donor) in Ben's eyes. When I asked how Ben felt, I think I was really trying to ask Carl how he was. I wouldn't say that to them, but I wish I could have touched Ben's chest and talked to my husband's heart.

"What really bothers me, though, is when Casey said offhandedly that the only real side-effect of Ben's surgery was flashes of light in his face. That's exactly how Carl died. The bastard shot him right in the face. The last thing he must have seen is a terrible flash. They never caught the guy, but they think they know who it is. I've seen the drawing of his face. The guy has long hair, deep eyes, a beard, and this real calm look. He looks sort of like some of the pictures of Jesus."

The recipient reported:

"If you promise you won't tell anyone my name, I'll tell you what I've not told any of my doctors. Only my wife knows. I only knew that my donor was a 34-year-old very healthy guy. A few weeks after I got my heart, I began to have dreams. I would see a flash of light right in my face and my face gets real, real hot. It actually burns. Just before that time, I would get a glimpse of Jesus. I've had these dreams and now daydreams ever since: Jesus and then a flash. That's the only thing I can say is something different, other than feeling really good for the first time in my life."[2]

Without a doubt, these inquiries and studies have lifted us at least a hair's breadth above the antiquated and orthodox views of the so-called modern science. Scientists are inching ever closer to the truth that Śiva spoke of, yet the destination remains light-years away. We have only skimmed the surface thus far. Given the pace at which science is advancing in the exploration of the inner dimensions, it may require at least a hundred years just to abandon the conventional understanding of human beings. And those cerebral simpletons who await someone else to prove the truth to them, who wait for these truths to be validated by the scientific community and inscribed in school and university

---

2 (https://www.paulpearsall.com/info/press/3.html)

science texts so that they can finally accept and commence practising meditation, are wasting their precious human birth.

No one shall prove the destination's existence to you. You must traverse the path yourself to discover it. To sit and await certainty is foolish. However, I fervently hope that someone among those who read these words shall undertake to prove these teachings of Śiva through the narrow lens of science, through objective research and experiments, which, I acknowledge, are incompetent for the vastness of these teachings.

Now let us redirect our focus to the heart. The heart is not only the abode of the being, the *jīva*, but also the seat of consciousness. It is the Kailāśa of Śiva. The Sanskrit word *hṛdaye*, and its English translation, heart, are derived from the same Sanskrit root *hṛd*. *Hṛd* translates to the center, the essence, the core, the crux. The heart lies at the core of your being. It is the crux of your existence, your identity and character, conduct, name and form, experience, knowledge, thoughts, and memories, likes and dislikes, delight and sorrow—it is the heart around which all of these revolve. The physical, anatomical heart merely symbolises this profound centre.
Hṛd refers to the pure element that serves as the foundation upon which this world stands. It can be likened to a blank canvas on which the world is painted. Abhinavagupta wrote:

भैरवात्मनो भगवतः शब्दराशेः विश्वशरीरस्य हृदयं सारभूतम्।

Bhairavātmāo bhagavataḥ śabdārāśeḥ viśvaśarīrasya hṛdayaṁ sārabhūtam |

If we view the universe as a body, then Śiva or Bhairava would be its heart, the very essence of the universe.

And the very essence that pervades the vast macrocosm is mirrored within the microcosm, and that which is outside is, in fact, inside. In the depths of our hearts lies the essence of Śiva. For, the heart not only serves as the seat of the individual soul, but also as the abode of consciousness.

Abhinava further defined,

yatrāntarakhilaṁ bhāti yacca sarvatra bhāsate | sphurattaiva hi sā hyekā hṛdayaṁ paramaṁ budhaḥ ||

That in which the whole universe shines and which shines (itself) everywhere, that scintillating Light is verily the One, Supreme Heart (say) the enlightened ones.

And,

dhyāyansmaranpravimṛśan kurvanvā yatra kutracit | viśrāntimeti yasmācca prollaseddhṛdayam tu tat ||

Whether meditating, remembering, reflecting, or acting in any way, that in which everything comes to rest and from where it arises, that is the Heart.

In the *Upaniṣads*, we find the same truth echoed time and again. Now I will expound upon a few verses from these sacred texts, that you may comprehend the significance of the heart. It is imperative to grasp the entirety of this Sūtra.

The *Kathā Upaniṣad* (II.3.17) says,

Puruṣo'ntarātmā sadā janānāṁ hṛdaye san-niviṣṭaḥ ||

The *puruṣa*, not larger than a thumb, the inner Self, always dwells in the hearts of men.

The *Brahma Upaniṣad* (2, 4)says,

hṛdyākāśe tadvijñānamākāśaṁ tatsuṣiramākāśaṁ tadvaidyaṁ hṛdyākāśaṁ yasminnidam* saṁcarati vicarati yasminnidam* sarvamotam*protam*| saṁ vibhoḥ prajā jñāyeran| na tatra devā ṛṣayaḥ pitara īśate pratibuddhaḥ sarvaviditi ||

Within the recess of the heart is that *ākāśa* (space) of consciousness-that with many openings, the aim of knowledge, within the space of the heart in which all this (universe outside) evolves and moves about, in which all this is warped and woofed (as it were). (Who knows this), knows fully all creation. There the *devas*, the *ṛṣis*, the *pitris* have no control, for being fully awakened, one becomes the knower of all truth.

padmakośapṛtīkāśaṁ suṣiraṁ cāpyadhomukham | hṛdayaṁ tadvijānīyādviśvasyā"yatanam mahat ||

The heart resembles the calyx of a lotus, full of cavities and also with its face turned downwards. Know that to be the great habitat of the whole universe.

The *Chāndogya Upaniṣad* (III.12.7-9, III.14.2-4, and VIII.3.3) says:

The Śiva or Brahman which has been thus described is the same as the (physical) *ākāśa* (space) outside a person. The *akaśa* which is outside a person is the same as that which is inside a person. The *ākāśa* which is inside a person is the *ākāśa* within the heart. The *ākāśa* which is within the heart is omnipresent and unchanging. He who knows this obtains full and unchanging prosperity.... He who consists of the mind, whose body is subtle, whose form is light, whose thoughts are true, whose nature is like the *ākāśa*, whose creation is this universe, who cherishes all (righteous) desires, who contains all (pleasant) odours, who is endowed with all tastes, who embraces all this, who never speaks, and who is without longing-He is my Self within the heart, smaller than a grain of rice, smaller than a grain of barley, smaller than a mustard seed, smaller than a grain of millet; He is my Self within the heart, greater than the earth, greater than the mid-region, greater than heaven, greater than all these worlds. He whose creation is this universe, who cherishes all desires, who contains all odours, who is endowed with all tastes, who embraces all this, who never speaks, and who is without longing-He is my Self within the heart, He is that Brahman. When I shall have departed hence I shall certainly reach Him; one who has this faith and has no doubt (will certainly attain to that Godhead).... That Self abides in the heart. The etymological explanation of heart is this: I am in the heart; therefore It is called the heart. He who knows this goes every day (in deep sleep) to Heaven (i.e. Brahman, dwelling in the heart).

The *Bṛhadāraṇyaka Upaniṣad* (II.5.10, IV.4.22) says,

ayamākāśaḥ sarveṣāṁ bhūtānāṁ madhvasyākāśasya sarvāṇi bhūtāni madhu yaścāyamasmīnākāśe tejomayo 'mṛtamayaḥ puruṣo yaścāyamadhyātma hṛdyākāśastejomayo 'mṛtamayaḥ puruṣo 'yameva sa yo 'yamātmedamamṛtamidaṁ brahmeda sarvam ||

This *ākāśh* is the honey (effect) of all beings and all beings are the honey (effect) of this *ākāśh*. Likewise, the bright, immortal being who is in this *ākāśh* and the bright, immortal being identified with the *ākāśh* in the heart of the body are both honey. These four are but this Self. The Knowledge of this Self is the means to Immortality; this underlying unity is Brahman; this Knowledge of Brahman is the means of becoming all.

sa vā eṣa mahānaja ātmā yo 'yaṁ vijñānamayaḥ prāṇeṣu ya eṣo 'ntarhṛdaya ākāśastasmiñche te sarvasya vaśī sarvasyeśānaḥ sarvasyādhipatiḥ sa na sādhunā karmaṇā bhūyānno evāsādhunā kaniyāneṣa sarveśvara eṣa bhūtādhipatireṣa bhūtapāla eṣa seturvidharaṇa eṣāṁ lokānāmasaṁbhedāya tametaṁ vedānuvacanena brāhmaṇā vividiṣanti yajñena dānena tapasā 'nāśakena etameva viditvā munirbhavati ||

That great, unborn Self, which is filled with consciousness and which dwells in the midst of the organs, lies in the *ākāśa* within the heart. It is the controller of all, the lord of all, the ruler of all. It does not become greater through good deeds or smaller through evil deeds. It is the lord of all, the ruler of all beings, the protector of all beings. It is the dam that serves as the boundary to keep the different worlds apart. The brahmins seek to realise It through the study of the Vedas, through sacrifices, through gifts and through austerity which does not lead to annihilation. Knowing It alone one becomes a sage.

The *Śvetāśvatara Upaniṣad* (III.20, IV.20) says,

aṇor aṇīyān mahato mahīyān ātmā guhāyāṁ nihito'sya jantoḥ |
tam akratuḥ paśyati vīta-śoko dhātuḥ prasādān mahimānam īśam ||

Subtler than even the subtlest and greater than the greatest, the (self) *ātmā* is concealed in the heart of the creature. By the grace of the Creator, one becomes free from sorrows and desires, and then realises Him as the God of Gods, Śiva (*īśam*).

na sandṛśe tiṣṭhati rūpam asya na cakṣuṣā paśyati kaścanainam |
hṛdā hṛdī sthaṁ manasā ya enam evaṁ vidur amṛtās te bhavanti ||

The form of Him, Śiva, stands not within the vision and none beholdeth Him by the eye; but by the mind (merged) in the heart, for in the heart is His abode; who thus know Him, they become immortal.

The *Mahānārāyaṇa Upaniṣad* (XII.1, 16, XIII.6-9) says,

The Infinite Self, more minute than the minute and greater than the great, is set in the heart of beings here. Through the grace of Śiva one realises Him who is free from desires based on values, who is supremely great and who is the highest ruler and master of all, and becomes free from sorrows.... In the citadel of the body there is the small sinless and pure lotus of the heart which is the residence of the Supreme. Further in the interior of this small area there is the sorrowless Ether. That is to be meditated upon continually.... One should meditate upon the Supreme, the limitless, unchanging, all-knowing cause of the happiness of the world, dwelling in the sea of one's own heart, as the goal of all striving. The place for His meditation is the ether in the heart. The heart which is comparable to an inverted lotus bud. It should be known that the heart, which is located just at the distance of a finger span (the distance between the tip of one's thumb and the tip of the little finger when the hand is fully extended) below the Adam's apple and above the navel, is the great abode of the universe. Like the bud of a lotus, suspended in an inverted position, is the heart, surrounded by arteries. In it there is a narrow space. In it everything is supported. In the middle of that remains the undecaying, all-knowing, omnifaced, great fire, which has flames on every side, which enjoys the food (objects of experience) presented before it, which remains assimilating the food consumed.

The *Maitri Upaniṣad* says (VII.5):

He, truly, indeed, is the Self (*ātmā*) within the heart, very subtle, kindled like fire, assuming all forms. This whole world is his food. On Him creatures here are woven. He is the Self, which is free from evil, ageless, deathless, sorrowless, free from uncertainty, free from fetters, whose conception is real, whose desire is real. He is the Supreme Lord. He is the ruler of beings. He is the protector of beings. This Self, assuredly, indeed, is Iśana, Śambhu, Bhava, Rudra (names of Lord Śiva).

Essentially, the heart is the resting place of everything. Every tangible entity, from trees and animals to mountains and the colour blue, as well as the entire spectrum of sensations, from anger to lust, and the intricate web of thoughts, all find their mainstay within the *citta*—the mind. And the mind, in turn, finds its resting place in the heart. This can be likened to the Russian doll analogy introduced in the preceding chapters.

Śiva says, *hṛdaye cittasaṃghaṭṭād dṛśyasvāpadarśanam. Saṃghaṭṭ* your *citta* and heart, *saṃghaṭṭ* your *citta* into the heart—your true self, your essence. Now, I will elaborate on these two words—*citta-samghatt*. I have expounded on the word *citta* in the previous chapter. Here, I am reiterating some of it again so that your momentum does not break, and your memory is refreshed.

Citta is mind. It is the manifestation of awareness that has been constrained into thoughts and emotions. Thoughts and emotions are impulses of the same mind, two sides of the same coin. If this were not true, expressing our feelings and emotions in words would not be possible. Talking or writing about something passionately would not be possible. If they were not the vibrations of the same *citta*, thoughts would be lifeless echoes without any emotional depth. The two spectrums of *citta* allow us to experience the intensity of emotions that arise from our thoughts.

One must exercise caution with two Sanskrit words: *cit* and *citta* (with two t's). *Citta* has just been elucidated. Now, *cit* or *citi* is the Sanskrit term for consciousness, elucidated in the first Sūtra. *Cit* is the foundation of reality and the crux, the heart of all existence. The term, *hṛdaye*, or heart in the Sūtra, *hṛdaye cittasaṃghaṭṭād dṛśyasvāpadarśanam* refers to *cit* alone. When *cit* is confined to thoughts and emotions, it becomes *citta*, the mind. The mind is the coarse manifestation of that one consciousness. In other words, when consciousness (*cit*) externalises into the confines of thoughts and emotions, it becomes the mind (*citta*).

The same idea echoes in the writings of Kṣemarāja:

चितिरेव चेतनपदादवरूढा चेत्यसंकोचिनी चित्तम् ॥

citiḥ eva cetanapadādavarūḍhā ceti saṅkocinī cittam ||

Consciousness (*citi*) itself, descending from its pure conscious state, becomes contracted by the object perceived: this (contracted state) is the mind.

तत्परिज्ञाने चित्तमेव अन्तर्मुखीभावेन चेतनपदाध्यारोहाच्चितिः ॥

tatparijñāne cittameva antarmukhībhāvena cetanapadādhyārōhāccitiḥ ||

On the full realization of that (the five-fold act of the Self) the mind (*citta*), by turning inwards, (or say through introversion) becomes pure consciousness (*citi*) and is revealed as nothing but consciousness.

(*Pratyabhijñāhṛdayam* 5, 13)

He elaborates it further:

cittaṁ saṅkocinīṁ bahirmukhatāṁ jahat antarmukhībhāvena cetanapadādhyārohāt grāhakabhūmikākramaṇakrameṇa saṅkocakalāyā api vigalanena svarūpāpattyā citir bhavati-swāṁ cinmayīṁ parāṁ bhūmimāviśati ityarthaḥ. |

The *citta* giving up the limiting tendency of extroversion, becoming introverted, rises to the status of the conscious Self, when by the dissolution of the aspect of limitation and attaining its real nature, it becomes pure consciousness. That is to say, it now enters its highest stage of *cit*.

I have already elaborated upon the heart being the seat of consciousness. Now, I will endeavour to unravel the meaning behind the word *hṛdaya* and demonstrate why it serves as a synonym for consciousness.

In the study of Vedic grammar, the term *hṛdaya* is composed of three Sanskrit letters— *hṛ*, *da*, and *ya*. Each of these letters has a distinct meaning. *Hṛ* indicates the sense of taking away or removing. Words such as *haraṇa* meaning seizing and *apahāra* meaning abduction are derived from this root *hṛ*.

Da means to give. The Sanskrit word *dān*, meaning donation or charity, originates from the same root *da*.

The root *ya* implies the sense of going or moving. The Sanskrit verbs *yāti* literally, to go, and *ayāti* meaning to come, and *utyāya* meaning to rise all share the same root *ya*.

In the *cit* or heart, there exists a ceaseless triad of actions. *Da* embodies the activity of creation. The power to produce, and give rise to existence. On the grand cosmic scale, *cit* is the source of all creation, the very cause of the universe's existence. And you are a miniature universe. The grand cosmic scale is mirrored within the microcosm. Your consciousness brings forth the world that surrounds you. Everything around you owes its existence to your own consciousness. This book you are reading, for example, appears to be an object external to you, separate and distinct from your being. But where do you truly experience it? It is only within your own consciousness, nowhere else but within you. The book is a mere projection of your own consciousness, resonating on a certain wavelength. This process of bringing things into existence, embodied in the root *da*, is ongoing, taking place every moment. It begins when consciousness manifests an object of perception, when it brings forth the object from within itself, and by limiting itself, becomes the perceived object. This object of consciousness can be anything, such as this printed book, the cerulean hue of the sky, reminiscences of a special one, the experience of joy, a flower, or a leaf, and so on. What's important, however, is that every object that you perceive is but a pattern of vibration that emerges from within your consciousness.

Hṛ embodies the activity of withdrawal. Just as consciousness brings forth this world, so too does it absorb it back into itself during what is often referred to as destruction, although this is not destruction or annihilation as understood in other cultures. In the philosophy of Śiva, it is recognized that there is nothing like destruction in the truest sense. At the end of the world, Lord Śiva withdraws this world back into himself. And as without, so within. We too withdraw our own surrounding world by becoming unaware of it, and we are constantly engaged in this act of creation and destruction. When we remove our focus from an object, emotion, or thought, it ceases to exist and merges back into consciousness, from where it originated. Its existence ends for us. However, our attention moves so quickly from one object or thought to another, this process of creation and destruction occurs so fast, that we do not realise when this withdrawal, this so-called destruction, occurs. But if we remain alert, we will notice that the process of creation and destruction is ongoing, always in motion.

The root word, *ya*, implies a sense of moving. It encapsulates the dynamic and transformative essence of consciousness, symbolising both its upward ascent and downward descent. The

Self, or *ātmā*, is consciousness, as Śiva has declared in the first Sūtra, *caitanyamātmā*. The consciousness that is being discussed is none other than the *ātmā*. Thus, the term *ātmā* is synonymous with consciousness. According to one interpretation from the Tantras, the word *ātmā* is derived from the root *at*, which means 'to move constantly.' Hence, one of the meanings of *ātmā* is *atati iti ātmā* — that which moves on constantly is the *ātmā*.

Consciousness, in a state of constant movement, is known as the *ātmā*. But what kind of movement is this? Consciousness moves between the triad of knowledge, knower, and known; or in other words, perception, perceived, and perceiver. Consciousness is the world, encompassing everything we perceive and become aware of. Consciousness is the perception, the awareness of this world; and it is consciousness which manifests itself as the limited individual perceiver who is aware of and perceives things. Consider this book that you are reading; it is an object of perception, something that you perceive. You, as the reader, are the perceiver, one who is aware of this book, and the third aspect is perception itself or awareness of this book. Consciousness is constantly moving between these three aspects. All three—knowledge, knower, and known—are forms of the same consciousness, just different wavelengths of its vibration.

When consciousness becomes an object of perception, such as this book or any other object, thought, feeling, or colour, it simultaneously gives rise to a separate individual perceiver who perceives and becomes aware of it. And this separate individual perceiver is called *citta*, the mind.

By this point, two things should have become clear—first, the oneness of consciousness and heart, and second, what *citta* is. The third word in this Sūtra is *saṃghaṭṭ*, which denotes the act of unification, combination, or bringing together. Its origin lies in the Sanskrit root *saṅgha*, which conveys the meaning of bringing together or unifying. In Hindi, the term *saṅgha* translates to an organisation, as in such an entity, diverse individuals come together to function as a singular body.

This Sūtra is a powerful method of meditation. Śiva instructs you to merge the mind with the heart, which is the pure essence from where the mind originates. Merge it back to its source, *hṛdaye cittasaṃghaṭṭād*, dissolve it from where it emerged, and the ultimate awakening will occur. Śiva describes this awakening as *dṛśyasvāpadarśanam*, meaning, *the perception of the underlying reality behind all that is perceivable (will occur).*

Dṛśyasvāpadarśanam; in order to obtain a clearer understanding of its meaning, I shall deconstruct this particular segment of the Sūtra into individual words.

As I had elucidated in the preceding Sūtra, *dṛśya* encompasses all objects of perception, from the tangible, like the printed book in your hands, the verdant mango tree, or the cerulean hue of the sky, to the intangible, like emotions, reminiscences of a special one, or sounds. Now, *svāpa* denotes the somnolent state of sleep, both the slumberous and the dreamy. Their combination, *dṛśya-svāpa*, encompasses the entirety of the perceivable objects and the domain of sleep.

When one attains the state of *dṛśya-svāpa-darśanam*, they are able to perceive the underlying reality of everything—all objects of perception, including sleep and dreams—as reverberations of consciousness, or rather, as the very embodiment of Śiva (the fundamental Self of everything). This perception of Śiva in everything is *darśan*. *Darśan* is to see things as they truly are, to perceive their underlying reality.

In this state of *dṛśya-svāpa-darśanam*, the disparate entity of the individual perceiver—the mind—dissolves in the heart, and the separation between the subject and the object vanishes. One begins to perceive everything in the form of consciousness, and the ultimate realisation of Śiva as the heart of everything that exists comes to be. Thus, the fifteenth Sūtra,

Hṛdaye cittasamghaṭṭād dṛsyasvāpadarśanam ||

Means, 'merge the mind with the heart, the pure essence from where the mind originates, and the perception of the underlying reality behind all that is perceivable will occur'.

Śiva elaborates on this further in the *Vijñāna Bhairava Tantra*:

हृद्याकाशे निलीनाक्षः पद्मसम्पुटमध्यगः । अनन्यचेताः सुभगे परं
सौभाग्यमाप्नुयात् ॥

hṛdyākāśe nilīnākṣaḥ padmasampuṭamadhyagaḥ | ananyacetāḥ subhage paraṁ saubhāgyamāpnuyāt ||

If one merges one's senses in the space of the heart, i.e. at the centre between the two halves of the heart-lotus with an undistracted mind, then, O Blessed One, one attains supreme blessedness.

(*Vijñāna Bhairava Tantra* 49)

Notice that this approach closely mirrors, if not entirely echoes, the earlier method of withdrawing energies. Essentially, our goal is to withdraw the objective world into the cognitive—the mind, and the cognitive world into the light of consciousness—the heart. When that happens, the underlying reality of everything is perceived. The mind creates a distorted perception of differentiation, of multiplicity, due to its own conditionings, preconceived beliefs, biases, and all of which it imposes on reality. Once the mind dissolves into the pure light of consciousness, everything is seen as it is, without any filters, without any sugar-coating.

You can initiate this by simply observing the mind, rooted in the witness consciousness, as mentioned in the previous chapter. In a year or two, it will dissolve into the witness consciousness, the heart. The perception of the underlying reality behind all that is perceivable will then occur.

This concludes our study of Sūtra Fifteen.

CHAPTER 12

Now, onto the sixteenth Sūtra. This Sūtra, much like the preceding one, contains a powerful method of meditation. In his commentary on the verse, Kṣemarāja inscribes it as "*śuddha-tattva-sandhānād vā apaśuśaktih*". However, I find myself in disagreement with him. In my view, *svapad-śaktiḥ* instead of *apaśuśaktih* fits more with the theme of the book. It is conceivable that I may be mistaken, but this is what Śiva revealed to me. This was my intuitive realisation as I meditated upon the Sūtra. Nevertheless, even if we were to follow Kṣemarāja's method in interpreting it, the essence of the Sūtra remains unchanged. I shall elaborate on this point later.
The sixteenth Sūtra:

शुद्धतत्त्वसंधानाद्वा स्वपद् शक्तिः ॥१६॥

|| ŚUDDHA-TATTVA-SANDHĀNĀD VĀ SVAPAD-ŚAKTIḤ || 16 ||

(With a steady aim, unwavering concentration) **By** (delving deep and) **becoming one with Śiva—the state free from any impurities or obscurities, śakti will return to its original state; Or...**(Continued in the next Sūtra...)

I shall now expound upon this Sūtra, delving into its meaning word by word. The first two words are *śuddha-tattva*. Śuddha means absolute purity, free from any contamination or adulteration. *Tattva* can be translated as element, reality, principle, or essence.

Śuddha-tattva is a state of being, a reality, a principle, that is entirely free from any impurities or obscuring layers. Śiva is *śuddha-tattva*, when He is naked and unencumbered by any veils, when He radiates in his full glory. More on this later.

As for the word *sandhān*, it literally means holding together, uniting, joining, tying, binding, or merging. It also refers to the act of aiming and focusing one's attention towards a specific target to such an extent that you become one with it. I shall regale you with a tale from the pages of the timeless epic, the *Mahābhārata*, that has been passed down through generations and echoed across time immemorial.

The scene was set in the midst of a forest, where the great warrior Dronāchārya stood before a group of eager disciples, each one determined to prove their worth. With a sense of purpose, the guru tied a wooden bird on a tree branch, its eyes glistening in the sunlight.

"Take aim (*sādha-yantu*) at the bird's eye," Dronāchārya instructed, his voice echoing through the forest. The disciples took their positions, readying their bows and arrows. But before they could release their weapons, the guru spoke again.

"Tell me, what do you see?" he asked, his piercing gaze sweeping over the group.

Most of the students replied that they could see the tree, the branches, the leaves, and the bird. But when it was Arjuna's turn, he gave a different answer.

"I can see only the bird's eye," he said, his voice steady and clear. "Nothing else exists for me except the eye."

Dronāchārya was impressed with the answer. It was clear that Arjuna had developed a deep understanding of concentration and focus, qualities that would be essential for a warrior.

"Very well," he said, nodding his approval. "You may shoot."

Arjuna pulled back his bowstring, his eyes fixed on the bird's eye. With a steady hand, he let go of the arrow, and it flew through the air, piercing the bird exactly in the eye.

Dronāchārya's face broke into a smile of satisfaction. "You have proven yourself, Arjuna," he said, patting the young warrior on the back. "You are the only one worthy of receiving further training. May your skills continue to grow and strengthen."

And so, Arjuna emerged as the greatest warrior of his time, a master of concentration and focus, and the friend of God. It was with Arjuna that God chose to keep company as a friend, and it was he who was bestowed with the enlightened knowledge of the *Gītā*. The story subtly revealed the reason behind this—Arjuna's unwavering ability of concentration and focus.

The word *sandhān* refers to the act of concentrating and focusing one's attention towards a specific target to such an extent that you become one with it. Dronacharya asked Arjuna to aim (*sādh*) at the eye of the wooden bird. The word aim (*sādh*) used here carries the same meaning as the word *sandhān* in this Sūtra. Both of these words, *sandhāne* and *sādh*, are derived from the same root.

Sandhān, in this case, requires delving deep into a certain aspect, examining it from every angle, and analysing it thoroughly, and to become one with it. In this case, the *sandhān*, is on *śuddha-tattva*, the state of pureness free from any impurities or obscurities.

The word was also used in the sixth Sūtra, *śakticakrasaṃdhāne viśvasaṃhāraḥ*. There, I translated *sandhān* as dissolve, merge, or become one—dissolve the host of śaktis into one another, make them one, and the world outside will disappear. The connotation is similar, and so is the aim. Also the method revealed in this chapter is more or less identical to the previous mention, with the only distinction being the identification of the *khecarī-śakti* as śuddha-*tattva*. However, this time we will interpret it differently, revealing another method. Keep reading.

The fourth word in the Sūtra is *svapad*; it translates to English as one's own position or one's original place. In Sanskrit, *sva* denotes one's own or self, while *pad* translates to position, place, or abode. *Svapad-śaktiḥ* means that the *śakti* will return to its original state. In other words, *gocarī, dīkcarī, and bhūcarī*, which had emerged from *khecarī-śakti* or consciousness like Russian dolls, will merge back into consciousness. Or we can say that the direction of the flow of śakti will turn inward, and it will merge with its original source. It is the merging of the host of powers that is being described here. Basically, it's another way of expressing the state of enlightenment.

Kṣemarāja reads it as *apaśuśaktih* instead of *svapad-śaktiḥ*; *apaśuśaktih* means the absence of binding power. Even if we adopt this reading, the essence of the Sūtra remains unchanged. It would translate to, "with a steady aim, unwavering concentration, by delving deep and becoming one with Śiva—the state free from any impurities or obscurities the practitioner becomes like one in whom the binding power existing in the limited Self is absent."

I adopted *svapad-śaktiḥ* from the *vārtikka* of Bhāskara because it fits more with the theme of the book.

And lastly, *vā*, which means *or*. This conjunctive word serves to connect the Sutra to the next one. Essentially, Śiva is saying that one can practise this, that, *or* the other (method of meditation).
Thus, the sixteenth Sūtra,

śuddha-tattva-sandhānāt vā svapad-śaktiḥ ||

Means, with a steady aim, unwavering concentration, by delving deep and becoming one with Śiva—the state free from any impurities or obscurities, *śakti* will return to its original state; Or…
(Continued in the next Sūtra...)
Śiva elaborates on this further in the *Vijñana Bhairava Tantra*:

सर्वज्ञः सर्वकर्त्ता च व्यापकः परमेश्वरः । स एवाहं शैवधर्मा इति दार्ढ्याद्भवेच्छिवः ॥

sarvajñaḥ sarvakarttā ca vyāpakaḥ parameśvaraḥ | *sa evāhaṁ śaivadharma iti dāḍhyādbhavecchivaḥ* ||

"The Supreme Lord is omniscient, omnipotent and all-pervading; I myself am He." By such a firm meditation, one becomes Śiva.

यदवेद्यं यदग्राह्यं यच्छून्यं यदभावगम् । तत्सर्वं भैरवं भाव्यं तदन्ते बोधसंभवः ॥

yad vedyam yad agrāhyam yacchūnyam yad abhāvagam | *tat sarvaṁ bhairavaṁ bhāvyaṁ tadante bodha-sambhavaḥ* ||

The unknowable, the ungraspable, the void, that which pervades even non-existence, contemplate on all this as Bhairava. At the end (of this contemplation) illumination will dawn.

नित्यो विभुर्निराधारो व्यापक श्चाखिलाधिपः । शब्दान् प्रतिक्षणं ध्यायन् कृतार्थोऽर्थानुरूपतः ॥

nityo vibhur nirādhāro vyāpaka ścākhilādhipaḥ | śabdān pratikṣhaṇaṁ dhyāyan kṛtārtho 'rthānurūpataḥ ||

"Eternal, omnipresent, without any support, all-pervading, Lord of all that is"—by meditating every moment on these words one attains fulfilment in accordance with their meaning.

सर्वं देहं चिन्मयं हि जगद्वा परिभावयेत् । युगपन्निर्विकल्पेन मनसा परमोदयः ॥

sarvaṁ dehaṁ cinmayaṁ hi jagadvā paribhāvayet | yugapannirvikalpena manasā paramodayaḥ ||

If one contemplates simultaneously that one's entire body and the universe consists of nothing but consciousness, then the mind becomes free from thoughts and the supreme awakening occurs.

(*Vijñana Bhairava Tantra* 109, 127, 132, 63)

The previously mentioned approach was essentially bottom-up, while the approach outlined in this Sūtra is top-down. So, how do you go about practising this?

As you go about your daily tasks, keep the awareness of being divine, "I am Śiva," alive within you. Whether you're on the metro, seated on a bus, or watering plants, let the conviction, "I am Śiva," flow incessantly. It's not a continuous stream of thoughts; it's a continuous state of Self awareness, an unwavering conviction in your divine nature. This state is *śāmbhavopāya.*

Here, it's not about actively thinking, "I am Śiva." It's about being fully aware. This is self-awareness, *ahaṁ vimarśa*. In our tradition, we don't categorise it as a thought or deliberation; self-awareness in Trika is not considered as thinking. It remains in the category of thoughtlessness, a state beyond thought.

Śaṅkarācārya describes this state of *śāmbhavopāya* as *nididhyāsana*—a state of self-awareness where there's no struggle to concentrate, no conscious effort. He writes,

यत्परं सकलवागगोचरं गोचरं विमलबोधचक्षुषः । शुद्धचिद्घनमनादि वस्तु यद् ब्रह्म तत्त्वमसि भावयात्मनि ॥

यद्विभाति सदनेकधा भ्रमान् नामरूपगुणविक्रियात्मना ।
हेमवत्स्वयमविक्रियं सदा ब्रह्म तत्त्वमसि भावयात्मनि ॥

यच्चकास्त्यनपरं परात्परं प्रत्यगेकरसमात्मलक्षणम् ।
सत्यचित्सुखमनन्तमव्ययं ब्रह्म तत्त्वमसि भावयात्मनि ॥

yatparam sakalavāgagocaraṁ gocaraṁ vimalabodhacakṣuṣaḥ |
śuddhacidghanamanādi vastu yad brahma tattvamasi bhāvayātmani ||

yadvibhāti sadanekadhā bhramān nāmarūpaguṇavikriyātmanā |
hemavatsvayamavikriyaṁ sadā brahma tattvamasi bhāvayātmani ||

yaccākāsty anaparaṁ parātparaṁ pratyagekara-samātmalakṣaṇam | *satyacitsukhamanantamavyayaṁ brahma tattvamasi bhāvayātmani* ||

That Supreme Brahman which is beyond the range of all speech, but accessible to the eye of pure illumination; which is pure, the Embodiment of Knowledge, the beginningless entity—you are that Brahman, meditate on this in your mind.

That Reality which (though One) appears variously owing to delusion, taking on names and forms, attributes and changes, Itself always unchanged, like gold in its modifications—you are that Brahman, meditate on this in your mind.

That beyond which there is nothing; which shines even above *māyā*, which again is superior to its effect, the universe; the inmost Self of all, free from differentiation; the Real Self, the Existence-Knowledge-Bliss Absolute; infinite and immutable—you are that Brahman, meditate on this in your mind.

(*Vivekacūḍāmaṇi* 255, 262, 263)

Now, don't expect to maintain this self-awareness constantly right away. It may slip from your grasp, as when you walk from one room to another, and your little toe meets the table, momentarily shattering your self-awareness. Instead of saying, "I am Śiva," you might hurl abuses! That's why you should set aside an hour or two during the day to practise maintaining this awareness. Find a quiet place, sit down, close your eyes, and maintain the awareness that you are Him.

I will share another way to meditate on your oneness with Śiva. *Śuddha tattva* is the pure form of Śiva—radiant in all His glory. Although Śiva has become the world, the world itself is not His pure form. We will delve deeper into this in the forthcoming chapter.

Traditionally, He is depicted with five heads or faces, each representing a distinct aspect of His identity. Our own head or face holds significant reverence, as it is closely linked to our sense of Self and identity. When we accomplish something praiseworthy, we naturally hold our head high; conversely, in moments of embarrassment, we tend to conceal or cover our face. The head is tightly linked to our identity.

And so the five heads of Śiva are an especially Hindu way to represent His five identities. All five identities are assigned a particular duty, an activity. Thus, a pair of hands is associated with each identity. Hands are linked with work, tasks, or activities. In other words, Śiva has five aspects, five activities (*Pañcakṛtya*) in which He is involved, and thus He appears with five heads and ten hands. Each head represents a distinct identity, while each pair of hands symbolises a particular activity performed by Him.

The five identities are Brahmā, Viṣhṇu, Rudra, Maheśhvara and Sadāśiva. The five activities consist of creation, maintenance, annihilation, concealment, and revelation.

In the Śiva Purāna, Brahmā and Viṣhṇu asks Śiva—

"O Lord, please tell us the characteristic features of the five-fold duties beginning with creation."

Śiva said—

"I shall tell you the great secret of the five-fold duties, out of compassion for you.

O Brahmā and Vișhṇu, the permanent cycle of the five-fold duties consists of creation, maintenance, annihilation, concealment, and revelation.

Sarga is the creation of the world; *Sthiti* is its maintenance; *Saṃhāra* is the annihilation; *Tirobhāva* is the removal and concealment;

Liberation (from ignorance) is my grace. These five are my activities but are carried on by others silently as in the case of the statue at the Portal.

The first four activities concern the evolution of the world and the fifth one is the cause of salvation. All of these come under my authority.

To look after these five-fold activities, I have five faces, four in the four quarters and the fifth in the middle.

O sons, because of your austerities you two have received the first two activities—creation and maintenance. You have gratified me and are blessed, therefore."

Now, If I am Śiva, why am I incapable of performing these five activities? Why am I incapable of creation and destruction? The answer is simple: you are already engaged in these activities, but you don't realise it; you are not aware of it. And your not being aware is itself the fourth activity. Unbeknownst to you, you are constantly creating, sustaining, and dissolving. You only conceal your true self, keeping your own eyes closed, yet you have the ability to uncover your eyes and to know your own nature. Let me elucidate.

As you read this book now, do you feel the sensations in your feet? The contact of your feet upon the floor? You do now, but those sensations didn't exist until your attention was drawn to them. The touch of your hands and the book remained unnoticed, non-existent, until you focused on them. The remaining pages of this book don't exist until you become aware of them. In this world, only what you pay attention to, what you're aware of, truly exists. The sensations in your feet that you weren't feeling before are now alive, vibrant, because your consciousness is there, your awareness is there. And this is maintenance—the second activity. Your awareness preserves that sensation. Your touch on this book or any sensation experienced, exists in reality because you're conscious of it, and thus, it is preserved. This is the second activity you're performing. By maintaining your awareness of its existence, you perform the act of preservation.

To aid your comprehension, let me narrate a tale. Read attentively.

Picture a scenic ancient Chinese school courtyard with books and scrolls scattered around. A pavilion stands prominently in the centre.

Enter Zhu Yingtai, a young maiden, disguised as a male scholar, wandering through the school courtyard.

Zhu Yingtai: (whispers) My heart yearns for knowledge, and I will not let societal norms hold me back. I shall disguise myself as a man and pursue my dreams.

Enter Liang Shanbo, another scholar studying at the school.

Liang Shanbo: (to himself) What an exciting place to learn and grow.

Zhu Yingtai and Liang Shanbo cross paths and soon become close friends, studying and discussing various subjects together. Time passes, and Zhu's feelings for Liang deepen.

Zhu Yingtai: (nervously) Liang, I've been meaning to say something…I am in love with you…

Liang Shanbo: (surprised) I share the same sentiment, my dear friend and brother. We've sworn an oath of brotherhood.

Zhu is heartbroken that Liang does not see her as a woman.

Enter Zhu's parents, who announce her arranged marriage.

Zhu's Father: (firmly) Zhu Yingtai, you are to marry Ma Wencai, a wealthy young man from a prominent family.

Zhu Yingtai: (pleadingly) Father, I cannot marry another. My heart belongs to Liang Shanbo.

Zhu's Mother: (disapprovingly) You've gone too far with this charade. Marry Ma Wencai and forget this foolishness.

Distraught, Zhu tries to reveal her feelings to Liang once more but fails.

Zhu's wedding procession day arrives. She writes a letter to Liang

Zhu Yingtai: (crying) With tears streaming down my cheeks, I must confess, Liang, I cannot bear to go through with this arranged marriage my parents have imposed. Before it's too late, you need to know the truth that has been hidden within me—I love you. I am not the man you believed me to be, but Zhu Yingtai, who disguised herself as a male to pursue knowledge and education.

Liang reads the letter and is struck with shock. He succumbs to a severe illness.

Zhu Yingtai: (determined) I must see Liang before it's too late.

As Zhu rushes to Liang's side, a fierce storm arises, blocking her path.

Zhu returns home heartbroken, unable to reach Liang in time.

Zhu Yingtai: (weeping) I should have been by his side when he needed me the most.

Liang passes away without knowing that Zhu had come to see him one last time.

Zhu Yingtai: (sorrowful) Liang, forgive me for not being able to say goodbye.

Zhu is forced into her wedding, but she refuses to enter the groom's sedan chair.

Zhu Yingtai: (defiant) I cannot marry when my heart belongs to another.

In her grief, Zhu runs away from the wedding hall, reaches the cremation ground, and throws herself onto Liang's burning body. Two butterflies emerge, dancing together in the air, symbolising the eternal union of their souls.

This story had no connection to the chapter. I narrated it purposefully, to steal your attention away from your feet. In that moment, you unknowingly enacted the act of withdrawal or destruction. And now, as you return your awareness to your feet, you have once again performed the act of creation!

As you wander through the garden, your attention is drawn to a yellow object below. Until this moment, the object remained indistinct, a shape yet undefined, open to any possibility. But as your awareness deepens, the object reveals itself as a sunflower. The act of creation has happened. You take a moment to bask in its beauty, savouring its presence. Your awareness remains fixed, preserving this moment. The act of preservation is in play. Then, your awareness shifts to a nearby red rose. In this process, two acts unfold: the sunflower dissolves as you withdraw your awareness, and the rose comes to life as your awareness embraces it.

Unaware of this transition, you remain engaged in an unceasing cycle of creation and destruction. One thought emerges, followed by another. In the fleeting space between the dissolution of one thought and the birth of the next, lies a space, the key. Hold on to that space, the fifth act—the act of revelation, shall unfold. Yet, you never hold on to this interval, nor are you conscious of this transition, therein lies the fourth act—the act of concealment.

You may wonder, "How can withdrawing my awareness cause their dissolution when the rose and sunflower exist outside of me?" Consider this book—it appears external, outside but where do you experience it? Within yourself. The world appears separate, external, but in truth, you experience it from within. You experience it inside, but you project it outside. The world exists because you experience it. This act of experiencing divides you into three: the one experiencing, the object being experienced, and the act of experiencing.

In reality, all three are one—they are simply different facets of consciousness. Everything is consciousness. Realise this, and be free.

तत्परिज्ञाने चित्तमेव अन्तर्मुखीभावेन चेतनपदाध्यारोहाच्चितिः ॥

tatparijñāne cittameva antarmukhībhāvena cetanapadādhyārōhāccitiḥ ||

On the full realisation of that five-fold act of the Self (creation, maintenance, dissolution, vieling and revelations) the mind (*citta*), by turning inwards, (or say through introversion) becomes pure consciousness (*citi*) and is revealed as nothing but consciousness.

(*Pratyabhijñāhṛdayam* 13)

Another way to practise this Sūtra might be:

समः शत्रौ च मित्रे च समो मानावमानयोः । ब्रह्मणः परिपूर्णत्वादिति ज्ञात्वा सुखी भवेत् ॥

samaḥ śatrau *ca mitre ca samo mānāvamānayoḥ* | *brahmaṇaḥ paripūrṇatvād iti jñātvā sukhī bhavet* ||

To those who harbour equal feelings for both friend and foe, who remain the same in both honour and dishonour, Brahman (Śiva) unveils Himself. In this revelation, they attain completeness and remain happy.

(*Vijñana Bhairava Tantra* 125)

Śuddha translates to pure. But what is purity? Purity is that which is constant throughout, not subject to change. In chemistry, for example, a pure substance is often defined as one that is not mixed with any other substance, and its composition remains constant. *Śuddha-tattva*, the pure essence, is that which is not subject to change; it is permanent. Consider, if you will, the human body. This vessel that we inhabit cannot be considered pure. It is a composition of cells, DNA, proteins, fats, and carbohydrates. Upon further inspection, one will discover that these cellular components are themselves not pure; they are in fact a structure of hydrogen, oxygen, carbon, and nitrogen molecules. Hence, the body which they combine to form is ever-changing, inevitably subject to constant flux.

Every day, fifty to seventy billion cells in our bodies die and are replaced. A staggering fifteen million cells are replenished every second. It is a constant cycle of growth and decay. Our bodies were once mere embryos, nestled within our mother's womb. And now, they have grown, or even surpassed the size of our mother's body. This transformational process is incessant and will eventually culminate in the moment when it is consumed by the decay of death and is decomposed.

From the moment the last breath is taken, the body, once a vessel for the living, begins its descent, through various stages. In the beginning, the body enters a stage of freshness, where the muscles stiffen and the temperature drops, as if awaiting some arcane metamorphosis. Then comes the stage of bloating, where the body swells and discolours, blistering in grotesque ways. In the following stages, the body rapidly breaks down, consumed by the insatiable appetites of bacteria and fungi, as putrid odours and gases fill the air. Eventually, only the skeleton remains, with dry skin and hair clinging to it like memories of a distant past. And in the final stage of this journey, the body dries out completely, leaving only the bones and some hair or nails, a stark reminder of the fleeting nature of our mortal existence.

As the years pass, the constituent atoms of this mortal form—hydrogen, oxygen, carbon, and nitrogen—gradually return to their pure state. Though they may not be entirely pure, for they are susceptible to change. But these transformations differ vastly from those that occur within the body. Even if left undisturbed for a thousand years, these atoms may still be returned to their original form. But the body, alas, cannot be restored.

These atoms, though purer than compounds, do not exist in their purest, most subtle form. For their subtler form is energy, and the subtlest form of energy is consciousness.

Seek the eternal, unchanging, everlasting.

Heraclitus, the Greek philosopher, once said, "No man ever steps in the same river twice, for it's not the same river and he's not the same man." We are all subject to the impermanence of life, and our very lives are in a state of flux. Therefore, we must seek that which is not subject to change, find that, and become one with that which is constant and unchanging.

It happened. As the sun rose over the verdant fields of the Japanese countryside, a farmer of bygone times stood silently, his gaze fixed on the horizon. His name was lost to the winds of time, but his tale of woe and fortune would be recounted for generations to come.

In those days, a horse was the ultimate symbol of wealth and prosperity. When the farmer acquired his first horse, the villagers were full of admiration and envy. They fawned over him, showering him with praises and lauding his good fortune. But the farmer remained equanimous, with a faint smile on his face, as if he knew something they did not.

Days passed, and one morning the farmer woke up to find his horse had broken free from the paddock and fled into the countryside. The villagers were quick to offer their condolences and expressed their sympathy, calling it a terrible tragedy. But the farmer remained calm, his smile unwavering, as if he knew something they did not.

Yet, just as quickly as the horse had vanished, it returned, accompanied by two wild horses. The villagers were surprised, exclaiming in disbelief at the farmer's good fortune. But the farmer remained unflappable, his smile unchanged, as if he knew something they did not.

As fate would have it, the farmer's son attempted to domesticate the new horses, but was thrown from one and broke his leg. It was harvest time, and the son was a great help in the field. The farmer now faced a great challenge in collecting his crops. The villagers clamoured in despair, "What a misery! What bad luck!" But the farmer remained composed, his smile still in place, as if he knew something they did not.

A few days later, the Emperor declared war, and the Imperial Army began conscripting young men to fight. The farmer's son was excused from service due to his broken leg. And so it was that the farmer, his son, and their land were spared from the horrors of war.

Life is a constant flux, forever in motion, sometimes in your favour and sometimes not. Amidst the ever-changing landscape of life, you should become one with that which remains constant and unchanging.

Utpaldeva (was the grandmaster and inspiration of Abhinavagupta, and the disciple of the disciple of the revealer of this book. In a boat, amidst the enchanting surroundings of Dal Lake in Kashmir, he found himself overwhelmed with inspiration and composed verses, which he passionately sang. In one of these verses, he) sung:

जयन्तोऽपि हसन्त्येते जिता अपि हसन्ति च। भवद्भक्तिसुधापान मत्ताः
केऽप्येव ये प्रभोः ॥

jayanto 'pi hasantyete jitá api hasanti ca | bhavad-bhakti-sudhāpāna mattāḥ ke'pyeva ye prabhoḥ ||

If they get victory, they laugh, if they are defeated, they laugh.
Those who are intoxicated with the wine of your devotion O Śiva,
laugh whether they are defeated or victorious.

Some practitioners think they've achieved *sthita-prajña*—equanimity, because they've suppressed their emotions. Even when they receive something they desired, they stifle their happiness and cling to the delusion of unchanging equanimity in all circumstances. It's total foolishness, utter ignorance.

Neutrality is not the nature of Self, *ātmā*; it is a state of mind. Patanjali distinguishes the states of mind as either *klișța*—agitated with pain, anger, or frustration, or *aklișțaḥ*—neutral, emotionless. He deliberately avoids using *ānanda* (bliss) or *harşa* (joy). He uses the precise term, *aklișțaḥ*. For bliss, joy, and happiness are the essence of Self, your essence. The *ātmā* is fully alive, aware, conscious, and ecstatic like the madmen. If you cannot taste this delight, you're distant from the *ātmā*, estranged.

Even if the dreary, disheartened, neutral and unresponsive practitioners were to reach heaven, *Śiva-loka*, Śiva would abandon that realm and descend to earth!

Spiritual beings resemble children; they lack seriousness. Life is their playground. As you progress spiritually, you'll incessantly experience this ecstatic madness, regardless of others' praise or blows.

My advice to practitioners is to live like humble servants in their homes, labouring ardently, exhausting themselves, collapsing into bed at night, totally spent. And yet, even in that weariness, if they're still blissful, revelling in it, they're close to the Self. When ten people hurl abuses at you, and you remain unruffled, joyous, then you are indeed close to the Self.

Witness everything joyfully, just as the sky witnesses clouds, remaining unaffected, firmly established in its own nature. For the unchanging, pure essence within you, the *śuddha-tattva*, is bliss and the witness to all. It is the seer of everything, the core of your being, and the very heart of your existence—it is you. This is the point where the lines between the observer and the observed dissolve into nothingness.

In this moment, there is only you. A point of singular existence that cannot be further witnessed. It is a place where the division of Self into subject and object becomes impossible. All that remains is pure and undiluted subjectivity, a witness consciousness that simply is.

Remain steadfast, serene in motion's flow,
Unwavering midst the ebb and the throw,
Amidst change's dance, unchanging be,
The divine lies therein to see.

This concludes our study of Sūtra Sixteen.

CHAPTER 13

The next Sūtra.

वितर्क आत्मज्ञानम् ॥१७॥

|| VITARKA ĀTMAJÑĀNAM || 17 ||

Analyse, unravel, and behold the revelation of your true Self.

This Sūtra is once again the continuation of the previous one, where Śiva revealed methods to establish Śakti in her original state. The previous Sūtra ended with the conjunction *or*. Now, moving forward…first, a dissection of its meaning, word by word.

The Sanskrit word *tarka* can be translated into English as reasoning, analysis, examination, or logic. It refers to a method of logical analysis used to establish the truth or falsity of a statement or belief, in this case, falsity of the lower identifications. The term has been extensively used in the Nyāya school of Indian philosophy. In Nyāya, *tarka* is defined as the use of inferential knowledge to establish the validity of a proposition. It involves a systematic examination of the premises and the conclusion of an argument to arrive at a rational and logical conclusion.

Now, the prefix *vi-*, means a special application. It is used to modify the meaning of a word, often in a way that intensifies or clarifies its meaning. For example, in the word vitarka, *vi-* modifies the root *tarka* (analysis) to indicate a more refined and discriminating form of analysis or contemplation. Similarly, in the word *vijñāna*, *vi-* modifies the root *jñāna* (knowledge) to indicate a higher or more profound level of knowledge or understanding. *Vijñāna* usually refers to spiritual or transcending knowledge.

When the prefix *vi-* is joined to a word, it refines its meaning, making it more special and more subtle to be used in spiritual contexts. For example, the word *vitarka* implies a more transcending analysis, a more meditative, a more intuitive examination of something.

The words *vitarka* and *sandhān* carry similar connotations to some extent. Both of these words embody the acts of analysis, examination, or concentration, but there is also a significant difference between them. *Vitarka* is negative in its approach. Its meaning lies in analysing something, examining it, and then moving beyond, leaving it behind. It involves analysing and transcending it, negating it, breaking something down into its component parts to examine it in order to gain a deeper understanding of its nature, and then moving beyond it, proving its falsity, and ascending ahead.

On the other hand, the word *sandhān* refers to the act of concentrating and focusing one's attention towards a specific target, to such an extent that you become one with it. In *sandhān*, we delve into the depths of the object and become one with it. We don't negate it, we don't transcend it, we become one with it. *Sandhān* is positive in its approach.

Again, one can transcend their limitations in two ways—either become identified with everything, encompassing the entire world within one's identity, or by negating everything and abandoning all identifications. This Sūtra deals with the latter method. Here, we rely on *vitarka* to disidentify from everything. We logically negate everything. This ultimately leads to self-realisation.

If through analysis we get rid of all our identifications what would come to fruition? *Ātmajñānam*. Self-revelation. The dawn of enlightenment would happen, shedding light on the knowledge of your very Self. A newfound consciousness would engulf you, and you would be awakened to a state of illumination. The enshrouding veil of forgetfulness would be lifted, and you would come to know your true self, the one that has been concealed for so long.

The preceding Sūtra outlines a direct approach, while the aphorism at hand delineates a more indirect approach. In the former, meditation centres directly on the form of Śiva, the true self, fostering a firm conviction: "I am Śiva", "I am consciousness." However, this method entails negating all that is not the self—transcending identifications with the body, mind, or vital energy. Continuously negate the superficial until you reach the core, the heart. Keep on negating the steps until the summit is reached. Do not linger on the steps; instead, continue ascending beyond them.

vitarka ātmajñānam ||

Analyse, unravel, and behold the revelation of your true Self.

There is another interpretation of the prefix *vi-*. This prefix carries a dual meaning. Firstly, it refines and amplifies the meaning of a word. Secondly, it can act as a negation or opposition marker, conveying the idea of separation, reversal, or negation, depending on the context. For example, *yoga* means union or joining; when the prefix *vi-* is added to *yoga*, it becomes *viyoga*, meaning separation. Similarly, *deśa* means my own country, and with the addition of the *vi-* prefix, it becomes *videśa*, meaning a foreign country. Thus, *vi-* carries dual meaning. This is the beauty of Sūtras.

Thus, in this context, *vitarka* would mean 'without any reasoning,' a sort of *reasoning-less reasoning*. This kind of reasoning leads to the realisation of Self. It implies that analysis or reasoning based solely on thoughts cannot and will not lead to self-realisation. It represents a special kind of logic, a refined and subtle analysis, almost opposite to the normal analysis based on thoughts. It is a transcendental and intuitive analysis, which lies on a plane above the typical analytical process.

The rationale behind this assertion lies in the inherent limitations of logic, which always lead to confusion. The mind lacks the capability to discern the truth; it is incapable of certainty about anything, let alone the discernment of Self. In such discernment, the mind, even with its intellect, is transcended. Overwhelmed by a deluge of thoughts, the mind flounders in indecision, thus incapable of clarity. Its tumultuous nature resembles a troupe of monkeys, incessantly bickering and leaping from one thought to another, causing chaos, unable to make sound judgments. However, with the arrival of Rāma—the consciousness—the cacophony subsides, and the entire mind falls into silence. In this state of transcendence, consciousness assumes control. Only when the mind is silent, once there is a state of transcendence of mind, consciousness is very sharp and clear. There is no question of either/or, there is no question of choosing; whatever the consciousness does is choiceless. It simply does that which the clarity allows it to do. It is always right. Just as the mind is always wrong, the consciousness is always right.

No breakthrough scientific discoveries had been made through the use of mental reasoning. The mind has basically two states—10% waking, and 90% sleep. After these states, the domain of consciousness begins. The deeper layers of the sleepy, unconscious, mind marks the point where the realms of the mind and consciousness intersect. Therefore, even those who are not yogis can connect with their consciousness to some extent during sleep. Thus, they come to know in their dreams the answers that the mind, no matter how much it thinks, will never be able to give. Many scientists have experienced breakthrough discoveries through ideas that came to them in their dreams.

A journalist once asked the renowned physicist Albert Einstein about the secret of his creative process. Einstein replied that there comes a point in the state of sleep when the intellect takes a long leap and reaches the highest level of consciousness. Most scientific breakthroughs in the world have occurred in this state.

The famous scientist James Watt discovered a simple method for making spherical balls for a steam engine through the medium of dreams. Whether one believes it or not, it's a fact that solutions to many complex mathematical problems in the field of mathematics have also emerged from the world of dreams. The renowned French mathematician Henri Poincaré, for example, once asked his collaborators around the world whether their inspiration for solving complex mathematical problems came from contemplation or discussion with colleagues. Seventy-nine percent responded that it came through dreams.

Dr. Otto Loewi, a German-American pharmacologist awarded the Nobel Prize in 1921 for the discovery of the hormone acetylcholine, acknowledged that the idea came to him in a dream.

These are just a few examples.

The enlightened man is nothing but the man who is rooted in his consciousness functions through his consciousness. One might question then how a yogi, who has dropped his mind, who remains in the state of no-mind, decides what is right and what is wrong. To this, the enlightened one responds: One has to decide what is wrong and right if he lives under the impact of the mind—and none of his decisions is going to prove right. Whatever he chooses he will suffer, and he will always look back: "Perhaps the other alternative was better?" The enlightened man never chooses, he lives in a choiceless awareness. In the light of his awareness he knows what is right; it is not a question of decision. And the moment you know what is right, with your total being, you never repent.

This kind of analysis, reasoning, or discrimination, this kind of tarka leads to the realisation of the Self. This is *śāmbhavopāya*. But to reach there, you must begin with *śāktopāya*. So, the method I am going to reveal now is mostly *śāktopāya*, but it leads you to *śāmbhavopāya*.

All that you presently regard as your Self must be transcended. Transcend them; shed them aside. How? By negating them one by one. Begin with the tangible: the earth, your occupation, family, nation, home—those objective existences you identify with. Ascend further, refuting each with analysis and direct experience.

Transcend them. To transcend is not to deny. Transcending them doesn't entirely negate my identification with them; rather, it implies a broader perspective, an understanding that I am more than just them—I am something subtler, more transcendental. Neither my job nor my family can define me. There was a time when neither existed, and there will come a time when both cease to be. Hence, they can't be absolute truths, being subject to change. Secondly, if I identify myself with them, I live in constant fear of their loss; losing them feels like losing the anchor that keeps you grounded in your sense of self, leaving you adrift and unsure of who you are. This also manifests as fear of death. Thirdly, if I identify myself with them, I become limited, as their limited nature becomes my own limitation. Transcendence means moving beyond the constraints imposed by any identity. *Vitarka* isn't mere analysis; it's transcendent analysis.

I am my body, that's one aspect of truth, not the complete truth, because I am not confined to it; I am more than just my body. Its limitations are not my limitations. Reject the belief that you are just your physical form and transcend it. Similarly, I am the cosmic elements, they are an aspect of my identity, but not entirely. I am more than just the cosmic elements.

Ādi Śaṅkarācārya, when he was a child, unconsciously adhered to orthodox religious beliefs such as untouchability. During that phase, he experienced a sense of separation and lacked complete faith in the notion that everything in the world is Śiva.

One saffron-tinged morning, as he emerged from the sacred waters of the Ganges after his purifying bath, he encountered an untouchable outcast accompanied by his four dogs. Unintentionally, the outcast's hand brushed against Śaṅkarācārya's body, eliciting an indignant outburst from him: "How dare you lay your defiled touch upon me?"

The outcast turned towards him, maintaining a steady gaze, and calmly uttered these words, "I remain untouched by you, and you remain untouched by me. I am not the body, or the elements of air, water, fire, earth, and space. None of the thirty-five cosmic elements define me either."

These words to Śaṅkara were like a bolt of lightning in the darkness. Moved by this happening, his poetic soul surged within him, urging him to weave his newfound understanding into verse and rhythm. Thus, he commenced a spontaneous composition, breathing life into the *Manīṣā Pañcakam*. The composition begins with a poignant refrain:

"If a person has attained the firm knowledge that he is not an object of perception, or the (thirty-five) cosmic elements, but is that pure consciousness which shines clearly in the states of waking, dream and deep sleep, and which, as the witness of the whole universe, dwells in all bodies from that of Śiva to that of the ant, then he is my guru, irrespective of whether he is an outcaste or a sage. This is my conviction."

I will elucidate this method of meditation through a verse from the *Vijñāna Bhairava*:

मानसं चेतना शक्तिरात्मा चेति चतुष्टयम् । यदा प्रिये परिक्षीणं तदा तद्भैरवं वपुः ॥

mānasaṁ cetanā śaktirātmā ceti catuṣṭayam | yadā priye parikṣīṇaṁ tadā tadbhairavaṁ vapuḥ ||

O Dear One, when the mind, the (individual) consciousness, the vital energy and the limited self, these four have disappeared, then the nature of Bhairava appears.

(*Vijñāna Bhairava Tantra* 138)

In the tradition of Vedānta, this method is called '*neti-neti*'. It means 'not this, not this.'

There is a story, sourced from the revered *Taittirīya Upaniṣad*, which illuminates how Ṛiṣi Bhṛgu attained self-realisation through the practice elucidated in the Sūtra.

The morning air was crisp and invigorating as Varuṇa, the venerable sage, stood amidst the verdant forest. His deep and perceptive eyes gazed upon his son, Bhṛgu, who approached him with a fervent yearning for enlightenment. The young man's eyes shone with an intense thirst for knowledge, a passion to unravel the ultimate nature of existence, and comprehend the essence of Śiva.

Varuṇa's penetrative gaze, honed by years of meticulous study and profound reflection, perceived the burning curiosity that ignited his son's heart. He recognized that Bhṛgu was ready to embark on a journey of self-discovery. His voice, resolute and authoritative, filled the tranquil air, "Bhṛgu," he spoke, "the entirety of nature lies before you, and you possess the means, the organs of sense perception, mind, and intellect to comprehend it. However, it is not enough to simply possess these faculties. You must refine them, integrate and harmonise them, attaining seamless coordination of mind and body. Only then can you direct these perfected faculties towards the unwavering consciousness of the ultimate Truth and abide in that awareness. This is what we call austerity."

Varun continued, his words carrying the weight of ancient wisdom. "Bhṛgu, Śiva is the source of all life, the very essence from which all living beings are born, exist, and merge at the time of dissolution. Meditate on this truth, contemplate it deeply, practice *vitarka*, and return to me with your discoveries. I shall dispel any doubts that linger."

Bhṛgu heeded his father's words, embarking on a quest to uncover the truth of Śiva. He delved deep into prolonged contemplation, his mind unyielding to distractions. In the end, he arrived at the conclusion that Śiva, that from which all things are created, nourished, and merge at the time of dissolution, must be food. It has to be food.

He realised that the body is created from food, sustained by it, and ultimately dissolved back into it. Bhṛgu felt what every man before him had felt—that the body was his reality. "When the body comes into existence," he pondered, "I come into existence. If the body lives, I am alive. And when the body perishes, so do I.

Therefore, all living beings are born from food. For, if a mother does not eat after conceiving, the delicate threads of life that weave together to form a child's body will not be spun. And even before the child's existence, the mother's own body would not have been possible without food. Without food, we cannot survive, and when our bodies die, we become food for maggots. We return to the earth and become food once again." He saw that food was the common thread that tied everything together.

When Bhṛgu presented his findings to Varun, his father was not pleased. "The body is not reality," Varun spoke, "and food is merely a substance—a beginning and an end, much like anything else. It could not be the cause of the universe because it too had a cause." Varun was not disappointed either, for he saw the young man's unwavering commitment to the search for truth. And so, with a knowing smile, he encouraged Bhṛgu to continue his search for Śiva, through *tapas*, through *vitarka*, through the endless pursuit of truth. For Varun knew that the journey was every bit as important as the destination.

Bhṛgu delved deeper into his inquiry. He sought to understand something much more subtle and fundamental than food, and the physical. His concentration and contemplation took him beyond the material plane of existence and into the realm of the life force, *prāṇa*.

Through his deep concentration, Bhṛgu began to perceive the intricate web of life that was woven together by the flow of *prāṇa*. He realised that it was this life force that separated the living from the dead and the animate from the inanimate. "*Prāṇa* is the source of all life," he mused, "the very essence from which all living beings are born. It controls the breath and organs that keep us alive. And it is *prāṇa* in which we merge at the time of dissolution. When *prāṇa* leaves the body, one is considered dead."

Despite this realisation, Bhṛgu remained unsatisfied. He knew that *prāṇa* was not conscious, but rather a force that could be controlled by the mind. It was not the fundamental Self that he sought. Thus, he turned to his father for guidance and was advised to continue his search for Śiva, through *tapas*, through *vitarka*. And so, the journey of inquiry continued for Bhṛgu, as he delved ever deeper into the mysteries of the Self and the universe.

After much contemplation, he arrived at a new understanding—the mind is Śiva. Through the mind, living beings come into existence, and without it, they would be lifeless and inert. It is through the mind that they live and into which they dissolve during dissolution. However, as he delved deeper into this notion, he began to question its veracity.

His contemplation led him to a new conclusion."The mind is merely a tool or instrument, much like the eye or the ear," he pondered. "It can be observed. I am observing it, so there is something else more subtle that witnesses it. And it does not transcend; it loses its existence in the state of deep sleep. Therefore, the mind could not be the most subtle, the purest essence."

Despite his newfound knowledge, Bhṛgu remained unsatisfied, and so he sought the counsel of his father. However, his father gave him the same answer as before—to know Śiva, one must meditate. And so Bhṛgu continued to meditate.

Bhṛgu delved even deeper into his inquiry. Bhṛgu's *vitarka* had brought forth an understanding subtler than ever—that the very essence of Śiva is intelligence, science, the knowledge obtained through observation, witnessing, through contemplation. For it is this intelligence, this knowledge that brings forth life, sustains it, and ultimately merges everything into itself during dissolution.

Everything that existed, from the tiniest particle to the grandest of cosmic structures, was imbued with knowledge. He marvelled at the intelligence inherent in the creation of a child within a mother's womb, at the intricate workings of the seed that *knows* how to become a tree, and at the vastness of the knowledge that surrounded him.

But as he delved deeper into this realisation, he found himself faced with a paradox. How could knowledge be the most subtle, the root cause of all? It, too, does not transcend; it loses its existence in the state of deep sleep. Was there something even more fundamental, more subtle than knowledge?

With each passing moment, Bhṛgu's mind became more focused, and his thoughts clearer. He searched for answers and pondered the very essence of existence. And finally enlightenment dawned upon him.

Śiva is bliss itself, the very essence of being. It is the blissful self, the source of all knowledge, all existence. Bliss transcends all the state, for are we not blissful in the state of deep sleep? Don't we feel relaxed and happy after waking from a deep sleep?

आनन्दो ब्रह्मेति व्यजानात् ।
आनन्दाध्येव खल्विमानि भूतानि जायन्ते।
आनन्देन जातानि जीवन्ति ।
आनन्दं प्रयन्त्यभिसंविशन्तीति ॥

ānando brahmeti vyajānāt |
ānandādhyeva khalvimāni bhūtāni jāyante |
ānandena jātāni jīvanti |
ānandaṃ prayantyabhisaṃviśantīti ||

That Joy was Brahman, he realised.
From Joy, indeed, are these beings verily born;
By Joy, when born, do they live;
Into Joy do they, when departing, enter.

(*Taittirīya Upaniṣad* III.2.6.1)

Bhṛgu's heart was overflowing with gratitude and awe. He had finally arrived at the ultimate truth. It was a truth that had always been present, but now he had glimpsed it with such clarity that he was transformed. As he walked towards his father's presence, the beauty of the world around him shone with new radiance. Every particle and every being seemed to be infused with the same bliss that he had just realised. His heart was filled with wonder and reverence for this sublime mystery.

His father could see the light in Bhṛgu's eyes, and he knew that his son had discovered the deepest truth of existence. Varun said, "My Son, you now hold all the knowledge. Embed this truth deep in your heart."

Bhṛgu bowed deeply before his father, his heart overflowing with gratitude and humility. He knew that his life had been forever changed by this realisation, and that he would never be the same again.

All these methods are similar to each other; the aim, once again, is to merge the external reality into the senses, the senses into cognition, and finally, cognition into consciousness. The only difference lies in the approach. In this particular method, the body, composed of food, is initially merged into *prāṇa* (in this approach, *prāṇa* encompasses the senses). Then, *prāṇa* is merged into cognition. Here, cognition consists of two divisions: mind and intellect. Finally, cognition is merged into consciousness. Consciousness, or Śiva, is realised here in the form of bliss. Consciousness equals freedom equals bliss. There is no difference between these three. We will understand consciousness in the form of bliss in the next Sūtra.

Śiva is present in everything. Nay, He *is* everything. To merely say that Śiva is present in everything would be an understatement. Śiva alone is everything. He has become this world we inhabit, and everything within it. Śiva is the potter who moulds the clay, and simultaneously, Śiva is the pot and also the clay.

Śiva alone is the path, the stairway that reaches to the highest peak, and He alone is the peak. *Śuddha-tattva* is the peak, which one must aim to attain. But to reach this summit, one must not be satisfied with the path or the stairs that lead to it. It is necessary to abandon the path altogether, for the path is not the destination. It is merely a means to reach it. But when one finally reaches the peak, they will see that the very material from which the peak is made is also the material from which the path was made. The soil and the stone are the same.

In like manner, when you are united with *śuddha-tattva*, you will realise that all things are constituted of that very essence of purity. All things bear the form of *śuddha-tattva*. All things are the expression thereof. It is this *śuddha-tattva* that has revealed itself in the guise of this world. And then, shall you perceive that *śuddha-tattva* pervading everything in this world.

As of now, we must reject this world, we must surpass this world, this body, mind, vital energy and ego. We must leave them behind, and rise above them all so that we may attain *śuddha-tattva*. But once we reach the destination, this world transforms into our playground. It becomes a supreme bliss for us to dwell in this world. Everything becomes joyful, for everything is perceived as being infused with consciousness and bliss. This is what Śiva shall unveil to us in the next Sūtra—*lokānandah samādhisukham.*

This concludes our study of Sūtra Seventeen.

ཨོཾ

CHAPTER 14

लोकानन्दः समाधिसुखम् ॥१८॥

|| LOKĀNANDAḤ SAMĀDHI-SUKHAM || 18 ||

The joy of *samādhi* resonates throughout the entire world.

OR

The bliss experienced by ordinary people is not different from the joy of *samādhi*.

OR

Ordinary joy can lead you towards the realisation of *samādhi*.

In the preceding Sūtra, we explored Bhṛgu's journey of self-realisation through *vitarka*, where he discovered that truth is bliss—his true Self. The current Sūtra is a continuation of this. Let's understand, but first, dissect its meaning, word by word.

The term *loka* generally translates to mundane or ordinary; aspects of day-to-day life or anything related to the ordinary populace. It also conveys the notion of an ordinary person. On the other hand, *ānanda* translates to bliss, particularly the pleasantness attained through enlightenment—the bliss of the realisation of one's true Self. The supreme reality in the East is often referred to as *chit-ānanda*—consciousness-bliss.

However, Śiva employs *ānanda* in conjunction with the mundane and ordinary, emphasising the absence of any fundamental distinction whatsoever between the joy found in ordinary experiences in the world and the bliss attained through enlightenment. *Samādhi-sukham*; *samādhi* translates to the transcendental state of enlightenment, and *sukham* means ordinary joy, the sensual pleasures derived from activities such as relishing tasty food or engaging in sexual relationships. These pleasures are often shunned and looked down upon by certain traditions—yet Śiva equates them with the bliss of *samādhi* sought by the same traditions.

The first meaning is clear. There is no fundamental difference between the pleasures you commonly experience and the bliss of meditative states; we'll delve into this further.

In the preceding Sūtra I elucidated that once we reach the destination, this world transforms into our playground. It becomes a supreme bliss for us to dwell in this world. Everything becomes joyful, for everything is perceived as being infused with consciousness and bliss.

Every experience transforms into the same bliss. It's not as if this joy only comes when you close your eyes and remain still like a dead starfish; no, this joy is experienced in whatever you do, in every situation. As Utpaladeva sings:

duḥkhāny api sukhāyante viṣam apy amṛtāyate | *mokṣāyate ca saṁsāro yatra mārgaḥ sa śāṅkaraḥ* ||

Where even suffering is transformed into joy, where even poison becomes nectar, where the world itself is a way of liberation: there is the way of Śiva.

The Buddha said over two and a half millennia ago that this existence is suffering, and that only suffering truly exists in this world. No one is truly happy; everyone is in agony. This sentiment is echoed in almost every school of Eastern philosophy. However, the path of Śiva is such that the world, whose inherent nature is misery, overflows with joy. Suffering transforms into exuberance. For a Śaiva yogi, everything begins to appear as an expression of one's own bliss. In reality, this world is like a mirror. Whatever you are, that's what you'll see.

You must have heard the story of Duryodhana and Yudhiṣṭhira. Yudhiṣṭhira was truly righteous; he never even spoke a lie in his life, and Duryodhana played the role of the villain in this tale. Both of them had the same teacher in their childhood. The teacher said to Duryodhana, "I give you some time. Bring me a genuinely good person, someone with a pure heart." To Yudhiṣṭhira, he said, "Find me a wicked person."

When both returned after some time, they appeared distressed. Yet, their responses were the same—they hadn't found anyone. Duryodhana lamented, "I couldn't find a good person. I encountered plenty of wicked ones. It was so much easier for Yudhiṣṭhira. He got off lightly, assigning me such a difficult task. I searched the entire kingdom, but I couldn't find a single good soul!"

Yudhiṣṭhira, on the other hand, humbly replied, "I couldn't find a wicked person master. Everyone has their place in this world. Some are a bit misguided, but no one is truly evil. Please forgive me.

Such is the nature of our world: when inner happiness blossoms, the entire world seems to radiate with joy. Every person appears kind, birdsongs become melodies of romance, clouds shower love, and sunlight appears as a delightful sunny day. Conversely, when you are sad inside, the birds' chirping pierces your ears, the rain dampens your mood, and the sunlight feels like it's sucking your blood.

Haven't you felt that when you're frustrated, everything starts going wrong, as if the world is conspiring against you to exacerbate your frustration? Your little toe hits the table leg, or things that always worked perfectly start malfunctioning, and so on. Everything seems to frustrate you even more. But when you are happy inside, this world plots to keep you happier. Every little thing will bring you joy. That tiny flower on the roadside will make you jump with joy like a child. Whatever you need will come to you instantly, and in the least expected way.

Reflecting on past experiences, I recall a time when my ageing laptop struggled with video editing, often crashing and erasing hours of my work. I didn't have the money to buy a new laptop because I hadn't monetized my YouTube channel, and I never charged anyone for consulting me either. Despite all this, I remained happy. Then, unexpectedly, one of my students gifted me a top-of-the-line laptop perfectly suited to my needs. It is on this very laptop that I now share this story.

Similarly, when I visited Kedāranātha (a revered and remote pilgrimage site dedicated to Lord Śiva, located in the Himalayas at about 11,755 feet above sea level), there was a line of pilgrims almost a kilometre long right from the checkpoint, even before the trek had begun. If you stood in that line, you would have to spend about ten hours waiting, and by evening, trekking wasn't allowed anymore; it would resume the next day. Even if it were allowed, how could one trek in below-zero temperatures at night? However, what happened was that where I had pitched my tent, next to it was another person's tent, and he was an engineer. He had come to Kedāranātha on behalf of the government to install washrooms for the pilgrims at various locations. Neither did he know me nor did I know him. I am a bit of an introvert; I didn't even approach him. He himself approached me, and we talked. Then out of nowhere, he told me that I wouldn't be able to stand in the line, but not to worry, he'd do something. The next morning, he handed me a weird-looking machine used by engineers and put my trekking bag in one of the sacks of his team, signalling me to come with him. If the guards asked where we were going, he instructed me to tell them that I was an engineer there to inspect the washrooms. And that's how I bypassed that long line in five to ten minutes. Many such incidents have happened to me. So when you stay happy, this world fills with joy. Śiva himself takes charge of protecting your happiness.

Janaka was an enlightened and virtuous king. Legend has it that once the gods decided to test him by sending him to hell. In this fiery realm, souls writhed in agony amidst scorching flames, engulfed in torment. Lava flowed, smoke billowed, and red flames illuminated the landscape. However, upon Janaka's arrival, a transformation occurred. Within a radius of ten metres around him, a cool breeze seemed to envelop the area. The tormented souls found solace, and the floor, resembling burning coal, cooled to the touch and became like ice. With each step Janaka took, the coolness and serenity grew, bringing relief to those in suffering. This is the nature of a person who has attained inner joy. When you are brimming with happiness, even amidst hellish conditions, you will remain joyful and content. This is one of the central themes of Śiva's teachings—to cultivate inner joy, to radiate happiness—and upon reaching this state, you will embrace every situation that life throws at you with joy.

As expressed in the verses of Utpaldeva, upon attaining this state, suffering transforms into joy, poison turns into nectar, and the ties of the world become pathways to liberation.

The entirety of existence starts to be seen as a manifestation of Śiva Himself, and thus it all becomes filled with joy. Consciousness and bliss are one and the same. Remember, I told you what sorrow is — sorrow means limitations. When we feel limited, desires arise, the force that wants us to transcend our limitations. And until these desires remain unfulfilled, until we do not transcend our confinements, the state we remain in is sorrow.

And consciousness is completely free, without any confines, as we understood in the first chapter. That's why consciousness is pure blissfulness. There is no trace of suffering there. Thus, consciousness equals freedom equals joyfulness. If any of these three is without the others, then it is not complete; they cannot exist without each other—because all three are, in a way, different names for the same existence.

So when it is understood that everything is consciousness, and within consciousness—then everything feels like an expression of our own freedom, an expression of our own joy. What we are resonates throughout the entire world.

Thus, the first interpretation has been clarified: The joy of *samādhi* resonates throughout the entire world.

The second message conveyed in this Sūtra, as we touched upon earlier, is that there exists no fundamental distinction between the pleasures commonly experienced and the profound bliss of *samādhi*. This is important. Over time, a misconception has pervaded Indian society that renouncing pleasures and happiness is an act of holiness. This notion, however, is deeply flawed—it is *viśuddha* foolishness, nothing else. Such a belief system essentially promotes the denial of life. When people witness a spiritual figure indulging in worldly pleasures, they are often met with disdain, their saintliness questioned, and accusations of hypocrisy follow suit. However, the Śaivas hold a different perspective. Śiva explicitly elucidates that whether pleasure arises from intimacy, a delicious meal, or gazing into the eyes of beloved, it holds no fundamental distinction from the ultimate bliss of spiritual enlightenment. The difference lies only in quantity, not quality. The former are akin to a handful of water from the Ganges, whereas the latter resemble the mighty stream of the Ganges itself. Both are in essence the same, yet one is limited while the other is infinite.

Now, if lifelong bliss were to be attained through, let's say, sex, I would then teach you to abandon all spiritual practices and just indulge in sex, preaching it to be the greatest meditation. However, this isn't the case. Only a momentary pleasure is experienced, and for that fleeting pleasure, we develop cravings for more and more. Similarly, if taking drugs were to provide you with a lifelong high, then I wouldn't have any problem with drugs. Instead, I would preach indulgence in drugs and abandonment of all spiritual practices. There would be no need left for spirituality. Unfortunately, these worldly ways are incapable of providing permanent joy. Only that which was always yours will remain yours forever. And that which was always yours can only be found within. Yes, but that state of pleasure is the same. Joy is like the light of the sun, and the mind is like clouds. Sometimes, the mind completely covers that light, and then darkness of sorrow prevails. Sometimes, the mind partially covers it—half light, half darkness—and then a neutral state is felt. And when the mind completely disappears, then bliss shines in its full radiance. As I mentioned earlier—

"Neutrality is not the nature of Self, *ātmā*; it is a state of mind. Patañjali distinguishes the states of mind as either *kliṣṭa*—agitated with pain, anger, or frustration, or *akliṣṭaḥ*—neutral, emotionless. He deliberately avoids using *ānanda* (bliss) or *harṣa* (joy). He uses the precise term, *akliṣṭaḥ*. For bliss, joy, and happiness are the essence of Self, your essence. The *ātmā* is fully alive, aware, conscious, and ecstatic like the madmen. If you cannot taste this delight, you're distant from the *ātmā,* estranged."

Fundamentally, all states of pleasantness are the same; it's all about how much of the mind is involved. You'll notice that when joy is abundant, thoughts are scarce. The greater the joy, the fewer the thoughts. And the lesser the joy, the more the thoughts. When you're in misery, the mind never stays in the present—never. It's always either imagining fake scenarios of what might happen if things continue as they are, or dwelling in the past, recalling the good old days or similar moments of sorrow to feel more miserable. Because if you remain thoughtless, if you remain in the present moment, then there will never be any suffering.

Even in the third-degree torture employed to mentally break down the accused, so that they confess their crime or reveal the needed information, the crux lies in convincing the accused to believe that this torture is never going to end and it will keep on increasing if they don't comply. This doesn't allow their mind to remain in the present. The mind keeps dreading the future, anticipating how it will endure this torture, etc. And, of course, the mind remains in the past, reminiscing about the days before this torture, the comfortable days at home with family, which immensely exacerbates the torture. If the mind remains in the present, then there will only be physical pain, not suffering or misery. There is a difference between suffering and pain. Pain is inevitable, but suffering is a choice. Pain is physical, but suffering is a mental creation.

Dissolve the mind back into consciousness, remain in the present, and that will end all the suffering.

Have you ever pondered why jokes and humour elicit such joy within us? The reason lies in their unpredictability. A joke's punchline is always unexpected; if it becomes predictable, if you foresee what's coming, the humour falls flat. It's the element of surprise that triggers our laughter, for instance:

Sherlock Holmes and Dr Watson were going camping. They pitched their tent under the stars and went to sleep. Sometime in the middle of the night Holmes woke Watson up and said: "Watson, look up at the sky, and tell me what you see." Watson replied: "I see millions and millions of stars." Holmes said: "And what do you deduce from that?" Watson pondered for a minute, "Astronomically, it tells me that there are millions of galaxies and potentially billions of planets. Astrologically, I observe that Saturn is in Leo. Horologically, I deduce that the time is approximately a quarter past three. Theologically, I can see that God is all powerful and that we are small and insignificant. Meteorologically, I suspect that we will have a beautiful day tomorrow. Why, what does it tell you?" And Holmes replied: "Watson, you idiot, it means that somebody stole our tent."

Laughter is triggered when something catches us off guard, and the greater the surprise, the heartier the laughter. In that moment of unexpectedness, our minds are momentarily stunned, bringing us fully into the present moment. The realm of the mind thrives on the known and the expected, thus the mind is at best boring. On the contrary, the unknown, the novel, the unexpected lie beyond the mind; they startle and momentarily suspend its activity, creating a sense of wonder and joy. This state of being fully present, free from the constant chatter of the mind, is where happiness blossoms forth.

There was a recent study where it was found that people are happiest during sex, and they are also most present and aware during sex. So these two things are not only correlated but also causative.

Pleasantness always remains the same; it's just the influence of the mind that varies. Therefore, in the *Vijñāna Bhairava Tantra*, Śiva has revealed certain meditations wherein one can attain *samādhi* by meditating on the pleasure derived from sex, etc.

शक्तिसङ्गमसंक्षुब्ध-शक्त्या वेशावसानिकम् । यत्सुखं ब्रह्मतत्त्वस्य तत्सुखं स्वाक्यमुच्यते ॥

śaktisaṅgamasaṁkṣubdha-śaktyā veśāvasānikam | yat sukhaṁ brahmatattvasya tat sukhaṁ svākyamucyate ||

The joy experienced at the time of sexual union when the female energy is excited and when the absorption into her is completed, is similar to the bliss of enlightenment (lit. the bliss of Brahman) and that bliss is said to be that of the Self.

लेहनामन्थनाकोटैः स्त्रीसुखस्य भरात्स्मृतेः । शक्त्यभावेऽपि देवेशि भवेदानन्दसंप्लवः ॥

lehanāmanthanākoṭaiḥ strīsukhasya bharātsmṛteḥ | śaktyabhāve›pi deveśi bhavedānandasamplavaḥ ||

O Goddess, even in the absence of a woman there is a flood of delight by merely remembering the sexual joy experienced while kissing, embracing, pressing etc.

आनन्दे महति प्राप्ते दृष्टे वा बान्धवे चिरात् । आनन्दमुद्गतं ध्यात्वा तल्लयस्तन्मना भवेत् ॥

ānande mahati prāpte dṛṣṭe vā bāndhave cirāt | ānandamudgataṁ dhyātvā tallyastanmanā bhavet ||

At the time of experiencing such great bliss, or the joy of seeing a friend or relative after a long time, one should meditate on the rising of this bliss and, while merging with it, one's mind will become one with it.

जग्धिपानकृतोल्लास रसानन्दविजृम्भणात् । भावयेद्भरितावस्थां महानन्दस्ततो भवेत् ॥

jagdhipānakṛtollāsa rasānandavijṛmbhaṇāt |
bhāvayedbharitāvasthāṁ mahānandastato bhavet ||

When one is filled with joy arising from the pleasure of eating and drinking, one should meditate on the state of fullness. Then the great bliss (of enlightenment) will arise.

(*Vijñāna Bhairava Tantra* 69-72)

From all these verses, it is evident that the pleasure experienced by ordinary people is not qualitatively different from the bliss of *samādhi*; the difference lies only in intensity. Śiva is suggesting that if one meditates on these pleasures, focuses on this pleasantness, and maintains it for some time, the mind will dissolve, and one will merge with the source of that pleasantness. This constitutes a meditation practice falling under the category of *śāmbhavopāya.*

You simply try to sustain those feelings you enjoy the most. If you relish eating noodles, try to preserve the pleasant sensation derived from consuming them for a certain duration, let's say three hours. For three hours, try to maintain that state of pleasantness, that sensation. It could be any sensation you savour, anything that brings you pleasure. Whether it's the enjoyment derived from indulging in sexual thoughts or experiencing an orgasm, that's acceptable—all I ask is that you maintain that sense of pleasure with the same intensity; albeit without any external support—you cannot continuously indulge in eating noodles, for instance, because even if you do, it won't be of any help. Instead, it will harm you. If you keep eating noodles, gradually, with each subsequent bite, that feeling will diminish. In fact, there is a certain law in economics—the law of diminishing marginal utility—that suggests that as a person consumes more units of a good or service, the satisfaction, pleasure, or utility derived from each additional unit tends to decrease. So, with each bite, that feeling of pleasantness will decrease. Therefore, as soon as you feel that pleasure, simply close your eyes and meditate on it, aim to maintain it. Discard the means through which that sensation was triggered. If you can somehow sustain this state, with the same intensity, for three hours, you will attain the ultimate bliss of enlightenment.

However, the human condition is so pitiful that even the feelings they relish the most become unattainable to sustain for more than a few moments, let alone other objects of meditation. They engage in sex, but they can't maintain that state of pleasure for even half an hour, unable to sustain that orgasm. This is their enslavement. Even though that state exists within them, they still have to rely on external means every time. And even after that, the state doesn't last for more than a few moments; instead, it intensifies their craving for more.

I am not suggesting that one shouldn't enjoy delicious food or indulge in sexual pleasure, etc. I say, by all means, do it, but at least try to maintain that state for a minimum of three hours if you enjoy it so much. But yes, don't forfeit your independence in this process by becoming addicted to that thing. Other than this, in the path of Śiva, there is no prohibition.

Thus, the third interpretation has been clarified: Ordinary joy can lead you towards the realisation of *samādhi*. Meditate on it, maintain it at the same intensity for at least three hours, and your mind will merge with the source; *samādhi* will occur.

Among the wealth of knowledge within this book, if there's one practical lesson to take to heart and implement immediately, let it be this: always remain joyful. Remain unconditionally joyful, independent of external factors. I want you to recognize that genuine happiness doesn't hinge upon achievements, indulgent food, surroundings, sexual pleasures, or relationships—they merely serve as fleeting triggers that momentarily settle down the mind, and happiness blossoms forth. Dependence on them leads to addiction. You will crave them more and more. It erodes your innate ability for unconditional happiness, leaving you accustomed to sorrow.

A beggar had just passed away in the city, and his father was also a beggar who begged for a living. He had instructed his son in the art of begging from a young age, and the boy had been begging since childhood. Whatever little he managed to receive from people, he survived on. When he died, a foul smell emanated from his body. People discussed among themselves that his body should be removed from the area, thrown into a river, or a drain. So, the body was removed. Someone suggested that the place where he used to sit and beg every day should also be cleaned by removing some of the dirt from there so that the place could be purified. When they removed the dirt, they discovered that beneath the spot where he begged every day, there were ten pots filled with gold coins. He had been begging there every day, spending his entire life seeking alms, yet he never made an effort to explore what was within him, what was within the spot he sat on every day; he never realised that he could be the owner of immense wealth.

I want your fate not to be like that beggar's. Within you lies the wellspring of your happiness—the treasure trove of joy resides within—but you remain expecting to find happiness outside, much like the beggar. You remain begging for happiness from the outside world. You never try to look within yourself. You beg to be treated well, to be loved, to be given a job, to find a good life partner. But no more. From this moment forward, I implore you to be unconditionally happy, even if only for a month. No matter what happens outside. Whether your house catches fire, whether you lose your job, whether your boyfriend or girlfriend leaves you, whether your loved ones hurl abuses at you—whatever happens will be dealt with later, for now, just be happy.

It's possible that society has indoctrinated you with the belief that happiness is reserved for the future, that you should be grinding now, that you should endure suffering now to find happiness later, that happiness will come tomorrow, that happiness will come after death...tell those people to go to hell. There is no place for such thoughts here. Be happy now and leave the worry of tomorrow for tomorrow. Give it a try. Just for a month; if you don't like the outcome, come to my doorstep and vent your frustrations, but give it a chance. Be unconditionally happy. Without any conditions, without any triggers, whether you get little or much to eat, whether you get anything at all, whatever the circumstances, wherever you find yourself—simply be happy.

Should you achieve this, you'll notice a cessation of misery altogether after the month concludes. You'll come to realise that the wellspring of your happiness resides within, not without. External occurrences need not impact your inner state even in the slightest. You'll hold the reins of your emotions firmly in hand. Once you master this, you'll have traversed half the path—only the remaining half towards self-realisation will remain.

This concludes our study of Sūtra Eighteen.

CHAPTER 15

शक्तिसन्धाने शरीरोत्पत्तिः ॥१९॥

|| ŚAKTISANDHĀNE ŚARĪROTPATTIḤ || 19 ||

When the energies unite, anything can be materialised.

भूतसंधानभूतपृथक्त्वविश्वसङ्घट्टाः ॥२०॥

|| BHŪTASANDHĀNABHŪTAPṚTHAKTVAVIŚ VASAṄGHAṬṬĀḤ || 20 ||

Things can be united, separated, and all that exists in the entire world can be brought together (transcending the boundaries of space and time).

शुद्धविद्योदयाच्चक्रेशत्वसिद्धिः ॥२१॥

|| ŚUDDHAVIDYODAYĀCCAKREŚATVASIDDHIḤ || 21 ||

Due to the arising of pure knowledge, Lordship over śakti-***cakra*** **is attained.**

The nineteenth Sūtra also comprises four words: *śakti*, meaning the power of consciousness and absolute freedom, the primordial power or the foremost energy; *sandhān*, meaning to unite, aim, or combine; *śaktisandhāne*, meaning when we merge all the fragments of energy. The stream of consciousness transforms into cognition, then into the senses, and eventually into objective existents—when this stream begins to flow in the opposite direction and all these unite, as elucidated in the sixth Sūtra—that state is known as *śakti-sandhān.* And what happens when this state is attained? *Śarīrotpattiḥ*—manifestation becomes possible. *Śarīrotpattiḥ* translates to manifestation or materialisation (lit. materialisation of body). This Sūtra unveils that when one turns inward, merging with the power of consciousness and freedom, which is also the power of will, the ability of manifestation emerges within them; they can materialise whatever they desire.

It happened. Ādi Śaṅkara travelled extensively across India, engaging in philosophical debates with proponents of various beliefs. On one occasion, he arrived in Kerala, where his wisdom and debating prowess were renowned. Even the king of the region had become his disciple. In order to propagate the nondual Vedānta, Śaṅkara challenged the scholars of another belief in Kerala to a debate. The scholars were afraid, knowing that defeating him in a debate is impossible. Therefore, they deliberated among themselves and devised a strategy.

In Kerala, two gatherings were organised on the same day, fifty miles apart. Representatives from both assemblies informed the king that they had invited Śaṅkara for a philosophical debate. They declared that if he didn't attend, he must accept defeat and acknowledge their beliefs as truth. Despite the king's pleas for separate sessions on different days, both parties remained adamant. Disheartened, the king recounted everything to Śaṅkarācārya. Deep in meditation, Śaṅkara listened attentively and solemnly responded, "They wish to test my yogic prowess. So be it. I accept their challenge. I shall be present in both assemblies simultaneously." Hearing this, the king was bewildered.

Two grand assemblies were held that day. In the first assembly, Ādi Śaṅkara answered thousands of questions from the scholars with logical and in-depth explanations, rendering them silent. Though they tried to prolong the session, they were left speechless, their minds blank. Hearing the quotations of countless scriptures from Śaṅkara›s mouth, they were amazed, yet inwardly content that they had outwitted Śaṅkara by leaving him no time for the second assembly. Unbeknownst to them, Ādi Śaṅkara had materialised a second body, identical to him, which engaged in debate in the other assembly. He was present at both places simultaneously and emerged victorious in both debates.

Here we encounter a remarkable instance where literally the human body (*śarīra*) was formed through *śaktisandhān*. Within the tradition of Tantra, numerous similar accounts abound, such as the narrative I shared in the third chapter, illustrating the transmission of this tradition in the Kali Yuga.

"Long ago, when the Kali Yuga began, Śiva manifested himself on Mount Kailāśa, amidst the sacred peaks that kissed the heavens. He sought to restore the teachings of the Tantras, lost amidst the ravages of the Kali Yuga. To the sage Durvāsā, he imparted this long-forgotten, ancient science. At Kailāśa, during initiation, Śiva entrusted Durvāsā with the task of spreading the Tantrik wisdom throughout the vast universe, to anyone who was worthy. Having completed his teachings, Śiva vanished from sight.

Durvāsā, consumed by his yearning for a deserving disciple, embarked upon a quest to find one who could bear the weight of initiation, but his efforts were in vain. It was no ordinary initiation; it was practical, wherein the teachings were made clear through direct realisation. The disciples underwent spiritual experiences, transcending mind and intellect, and achieving instantaneous enlightenment. Disheartened by his fruitless search, Durvāsā turned inward (*śakti-sandhāna,* introversion) and, by becoming one with the world, he brought forth three sons and a daughter, created from his own thoughts… Having created them, Durvāsā fully initiated them into the enigmatic secrets of the Tantras.

Following in their father's footsteps, Durvāsā's sons, too, created mind-born offspring and guided them into the realm of the Tantras. Thus, fifteen siddhas were brought forth through the power of the mind. However, when the fifteenth siddha attempted to create a mind-born son, he faced failure. He had not fully turned inward, remaining entangled in the illusion that the world existed separate from himself (extroversion). Bound by the chains of *āṇava mala*, he failed to realise that everything existed within himself, that he was whole and complete. Consequently, his endeavour of creating a mind-born heir met with disappointment. Driven by an ardent desire, he sought solace in this world, discovering a radiant woman who possessed every virtue. Love blossomed, and he sought her father's blessing for their union. Together, they bore a son named Saṁgamāditya, and from that point forward, sons who were initiated into the Tantras were born biologically.

Incidentally, Saṁgamāditya's great-great-grandson became the disciple of Vasugupta, the mystical luminary who discovered the scripture that currently lies open before you."

Some yogis have chosen to completely renounce their physical bodies and reside in their etheric bodies (*prāṇa-śarīra*). This choice might stem from the recognition of the inherent challenges of the physical form. It requires food, water, sunlight, and oxygen, etc. to stay alive. One-third of your life must also be dedicated to sleep. If these necessities are not met on time, it fills us with pain, constantly distracting us in our pursuit. Regular exercise is also necessary, or else some parts of the body will cease to function, and you will fall prey to diseases. It also cannot endure extreme cold or excessive heat, and even with all its requirements fulfilled, it is subject to the inevitabilities of sexual needs and ageing. In other words, this body is a heavy burden.

Therefore, some yogis renounce their physical bodies. They practise their spiritual practices while residing in their etheric bodies. And when the situation demands—such as when they need to appear before someone—they, turning inward, materialise a new body through their power of will. The body and mind are one. The body is the outward expression of the mind, and the mind is the inner essence of the body. When the body indulges in intoxicants or suffers from ailments, it affects the mind as well, resulting in depression, a dampened mood, or impaired functioning. Similarly, when the mind is sad or depressed, it manifests in various physical ways such as headaches, loss of appetite, and weakened immune system. In modern science, this oneness is termed psychosomatic; psyche, meaning the mind and soma the body—psychosomatic, meaning the oneness of mind and body. So, just the existence of the mind is sufficient to manifest the gross body. Mahāvatāra Bābājī, and many other yogis throughout history, have demonstrated this by manifesting bodies through the power of their will, through the process of *śarīrotpattiḥ,* materialisation. Abhinavagupta's *Tantrāloka* also references similar phenomena, noting how various gurus roam in the etheric plane with their wives and materialise various physical forms to dispel doubts and elucidate truths for others.

However, as I have mentioned earlier, the concept of *śarīrotpattiḥ* extends beyond the mere materialisation of our physical bodies. This entire universe is our body. Therefore, *śarīrotpattiḥ* refers to the materialisation of literally anything, even an entirely new universe.

There is a tale in the ancient scriptures about King Triśaṅku, who wished to ascend to heaven in his mortal body. Seeking a solution, he approached sage Viśvāmitra, whom he endeavoured to please, hoping for assistance. Viśvāmitra, moved by Triśaṅku's earnestness, consented to help him. Initially, a fire ritual was conducted to appease Indra, the celestial ruler, but it was deemed invalid by the deity. This angered Viśvāmitra, and he declared, "Arise, Triśaṅku, I shall elevate you to heaven by my own power." As soon as he said this, Trishanku began to rise and reached the gates of heaven. The gods stopped him and said, "You cannot enter heaven. Go back to Earth." As Triśaṅku plummeted, Viśvāmitra intervened, halting his descent midway between heaven and Earth. Resolute in his commitment, Viśvāmitra declared, "Should Indra obstruct your path to heaven, I shall fashion an alternate celestial realm for you."

Then, using his willpower, he created another universe and constructed another heavenly realm. He was about to create another Indra when the gods intervened and stopped him.

Such is the power of a yogi's will. They can manifest whatever they desire. Not only can they manifest, but they can also accomplish anything. Śiva reveals further:

bhūtasandhānabhūtapṛthaktvaviśvasaṅghaṭṭāḥ ||

Bhūta can be translated as things, existents or that which exists. Śiva explains that a yogi has the ability to unite (*sandhāna*) things, to separate them—*pṛthaktva* means separate—and *viśvasaṅghaṭṭāḥ*, he can bring together all that exists in the entire world, transcending the boundaries of space and time.
The same idea echoes in the *Spanda-Kārikās* (III.4-5):

यथा ह्यर्थोऽस्फुटो दृष्टः सावधानेऽपि चेतसि । भूयः स्फुटतरो भाति स्वबलोद्योगभावितः ॥
तथा यत्परमार्थेन येन यत्र यथा स्थितम् । तत्तथा बलमाक्रम्य न चिरात्सम्प्रवर्तते ॥

yathā hyarthaḥ sphuṭo dṛṣṭaḥ sāvadhāne'pi cetasī | *bhūyaḥ sphuṭataraḥ bhāti svabalodyogabhāvitaḥ* ||
tathā yatparamārthena yena yatra yathā sthitam | *tattathā balamākramya na cirātsampravartate* ||

For instance, sometimes, we experience the peculiar situation of searching for an object within our room, yet despite scouring every inch, it eludes our sight. It is in the room, hidden in plain sight, right before our eyes, evading detection. Despite our exhaustive search spanning the entire room or even the entire house, our efforts remain fruitless. Anger sets in, prompting a renewed search; this time we put all our energy, intensity, and focus into searching for that thing. Eventually, the missing object is found.

Similarly, this verse illustrates that when a yogi unites their host of energies, turns inward, immerses themselves in meditation, and becomes one with Śiva, any object—regardless of its nature (*yat*), form (*yen*), or location (*yatra*)—whether it be a hundred miles away or a hundred years in the past, whether living or deceased, in any state (*yathā*)—manifests immediately in the presence of that yogi (*tat*), without delay (*na cirāt*).

Viśvasaṅghaṭṭāḥ, he eliminates the distance between himself and the object, whether that distance spans a hundred miles or a hundred years.

In this context, I will now explain *bhūtapṛthaktva*. Just as when we consume tea or caffeine, it temporarily separates us from sleepiness and fatigue, allowing us to work energetically, free from drowsiness. However, the deferred sleep eventually catches up with us, often with even greater force, and we end up sleeping throughout the day.

Similarly, a yogi can detach himself from his fatigue, hunger, thirst, and even his illnesses for the time being, so that without concern for bodily needs, he can focus on his pursuits. However, illnesses, etc., are determined by our past *karmas*. Therefore, they can be postponed for a while but cannot be avoided. Just as caffeine consumption cannot compensate for lack of sleep.

Now, just as we can separate or detach diseases, fatigue, hunger, and thirst from ourselves through the unification of the host of energies, similarly, when necessary, we can connect ourselves with the source of infinite energy. This is also possible through the unification of *śakti-cakra*. There is an incident I read in the news about Lauren Kornacki, a twenty-two-year-old ordinary girl whose father was a car mechanic. One day, while he was repairing a car brake outside, the car suddenly fell on him. When Lauren found her father unconscious under the car, she reacted with sheer panic. Rushing towards him, she feared losing him. In an instant and effortlessly, she lifted the heavy BMW car with both her hands and threw it aside. Yes, she indeed threw it. Then, she pulled her father out, performed CPR on him, and saved his life.

There are many real incidents like this, where people suddenly acquire supernatural power when they are very scared or in extreme anger, etc. These moments are meditative. Śiva elaborates on this in the *Vijñāna Bhairava*.

kṣutādyante bhaye śoke gahvare vāraṇa-drute | kutūhale kṣhudhādyante brahmasattā samīpagā ||

At the beginning and end of sneezing, in a state of fear or sorrow, (standing) on top of an abyss or while fleeing from a battlefield, at the moment of intense curiosity, at the beginning or end of hunger; such a state comes close to the reality of Brahman.

In other words, when we are gripped by deep fear, when we find ourselves fleeing for our lives, or when we're driven by an urgent need to protect someone dear to us—someone whose loss we couldn't fathom, someone we'd move mountains to save—these moments are profoundly meditative. In such instances, we become one with the infinite source of energy, because the mind ceases to exist. Indeed, the mind is the barrier; the cessation of its fluctuations is yoga. Thus, when a severe crisis looms, the mind halts, thoughts recede, and that state draws near.

If, during such moments, we redirect all our awareness, all our attention inward, we can attain Śiva. This was elaborated upon in the sixth chapter. Patañjali wrote that when the mind becomes free of thoughts and stands supportless, the seer—the self—is in its true state—*tadā draṣṭuḥ svarūpe 'vasthānam.*

In the state of meditation, we unite with the source of energy, for what separates us from it but our own minds? It is we who have put our hands before our eyes and cry that it is dark. We are Śiva, who has bound himself. Thus, when we enter samadhi, when we merge with our true selves, we become capable of everything.

The world is a dream, a projection of our own consciousness. Despite being the creators of our dreams, we feel completely at the mercy of them. For example, recall when you had a nightmare. You were terrified to the core. You felt completely powerless; even though it was your own dream, the terror you felt was your own creation, yet in the moment, you had no recognition of this truth. Otherwise, you would have been capable of shaping it however you wished.

I recall a particularly terrifying dream where a demon seemed to be choking me. The fear was so intense that it jolted me awake, though my eyes remained closed. It was then that I realised I had conjured this nightmare myself. With this newfound awareness, I transformed the dream: now, I was the one choking the demon, and it was scared. This shift was possible because I had awakened to the reality that I was the creator of the dream, with the ability to shape it as I wished.

In a similar vein, our waking world is also a dream, and upon awakening to this truth, we realise our innate capability to influence and shape our reality. There's a verse in the *Spanda-Kārikās* (III.1); understanding it in this context would be appropriate.

यथेच्छाभ्यार्थितो धाता जाग्रतोऽर्थान् हृदि स्थितान् । सोमसूर्योदयं कृत्वा सम्पादयति देहिनः ॥

yathechchābhyārthito dhātā jāgrato'rthān hṛdi sthitān |
somasūryodayaṁ kṛtvā sampādayati dehinaḥ ||

Dhātā, meaning the one in whom the entire universe resides, who encompasses everything within himself. *Dhātā* is another name for Śiva, our true Self. He fulfils all the desires of the *dehinaḥ*, the embodied yogi. Who is a yogi? A *jāgrataḥ*, an awakened one, who has risen from the dream and realised that this dream is his own projection. And how does he awaken? Through *somasūryodayaṁ*, the rise of the moon and the sun together. It is symbolic. When the sun rises in the morning, we wake up. And when the moon appears, we sleep. *Somasūryodayaṁ* means the moment when the moon and the sun rise together. It is when we have awakened to the dream, yet remain within it, still asleep. It is when we have realised our true selves, yet remain in the physical body and the world. Despite this awakening that we are not the body, that we are dreaming, the desire to continue the bodily existence, to continue the dream persists. Whatever desires remain in the heart of such a yogi, *Dhātā* fulfils them. Kṣemarāja writes:

parameśvaro hi cidātmā yadyantarmukhocitasevākrameṇārthate tattatsampādayata eva ||

The supreme Lord, whose nature is consciousness, unquestionably fulfils all the desires for which one prays with real inner sincerity.

This reminds me of a time before I began writing this book when I did not believe in the concept of a personal god. I didn't believe there was a god who accepted our worship, interfered in the matters of our personal lives, and fulfilled our heartfelt desires. I was a non-dualist, believing only in the formless, impersonal consciousness that doesn't concern itself with accepting prayers or caring about our personal lives or desires. So, there had been an error in my identification document that couldn't be rectified. I had been trying to fix it for almost three years, and until it was corrected, all my official work came to a halt, including travelling and bank-related tasks. I even visited various cities where official government centres were present to get it fixed, but to no avail. So, this was a significant problem in my material life, but I never asked Śiva to fix it because I neither believed in this theory nor did it seem right to me to ask for such trivial worldly things. I was trying to solve it on my own.

One night, before going to sleep, something happened. I don't know why but I prayed, "Lord Śiva, if your personal form also exists, if you really accept my prayer, then please solve this problem of mine. I will accept that you exist, that you listen to prayers, that you help us in our day-to-day lives, that you fulfil desires…" And with that, I fell asleep. I forgot about it in the morning, went about my work, and when I checked the government website, the problem with my identity document was miraculously resolved. What couldn't be fixed for years, just asking God once made it happen, in a single night. So, there definitely is the personal form of Śiva; He does accept your prayers, and what Kṣemarāja writes is true.

The supreme Lord, whose nature is consciousness, unquestionably fulfils all the desires for which one prays with real inner sincerity.

Śiva reveals further:

śuddhavidyodayāccakreśatvasiddhiḥ ||

First, a dissection of its meaning, word by word: It comprises six words. The first two are *śuddha-vidyā,* meaning pure knowledge—that knowledge which is free from all filters, and impurities. It is defined in the *Kulārṇava Tantra* and the *Upaniṣads* as, *sā vidyā yā vimuktaye*, that knowledge which liberates. Pure knowledge is that which is absolute, impartial. It enlightens us about this dream-like nature of the world. It is the realisation of the Self. Śiva eloquently describes in the *Svacchaṃda Tantra.*

तस्मात्सा तु परा विद्या यस्मादन्या न विद्यते । विन्दते ह्यत्र युगपत्सार्वज्ञयादिगुणान्परान् ॥
वेदनानादिधर्मस्य परमात्मत्वबोधना । वर्जनापरमात्मत्वे तस्माद्विद्येति सोच्यते ॥
तत्त्रस्थो व्यञ्जयेत्तेजः परं परमकारणम् । परस्मिस्तेजसि व्यक्ते तत्त्रस्थः शिवतां व्रजेत् ॥

tasmātsā tu parā vidyā yasmādanyā na vidyate | *vindate hyatra yugapat sārvajñyādigunānparān* ||
vedanānādidharmasya paramātmatvabodhanā |
varjanāparamātmatve tasmād vidyeti sochyate ||
tattrastho vyañjayettejaḥ param paramakāraṇam |
parasmistejasi vyakte tattrasthaḥ śivatāṁ vrajet ||

Therefore, as there is no other *vidyā* (knowledge) like her, she is the highest *vidyā.* In this (i.e. on the appearance of this *vidyā*) the yogi acquires the greatest qualities like omniscience, etc. all at once.

She is designated *Vidyā*, because she brings about investigation of the supreme characteristic of Siva, viz; *Svātantrya Sakti* (the power of absolute freedom), because she brings about the knowledge of the Highest Self and because she dispels all that is not that Highest Self. Established in that (i.e. the *Unmanā* state), one can manifest the highest lights, the highest cause. Established in that state one attains Siva.

(*Svacchaṃda Tantra* IV.396, 397)

History, Geography, Economics, and other sciences are *aśuddha-vidyā* (contaminated knowledge) — relative and contextual, as their existence is only within the realm of this world. After dissolution, these sciences will also become meaningless. Their meaning and purpose are grounded in this illusory world of dreams. However, true knowledge is to realise that this universe is an expansion of myself, and there is no independent existence beyond me. Pure knowledge is to abide in the constant state of *Śivoham* (I am Śiva).

The mind contaminates knowledge, and all thoughts of the mind are relative, limited to this world alone. The mind distorts knowledge into thoughts and uses it to survive. It cannot survive without thoughts, and all thoughts of the mind are garbage, whether they pertain to God or anything else, as they do not allow you to remain in the present. Thoughts persist incessantly, echoing the past. The mind itself is the past. What is the basis of these thoughts? Memories—impressions of past experiences. Remove memories, and thoughts will cease to exist; nay, the mind will cease to exist. The existence of impure knowledge lies in the past, but pure knowledge is in the present. Impure knowledge is heard, read, obtained from scriptures, but it lacks the ability to liberate. Pure knowledge is lived, experienced every moment. Impure knowledge affirms arrogance, claiming 'look, I know all the scriptures'. Pure knowledge destroys arrogance, acknowledging 'I do not know even a drop of the ocean of infinite knowledge named Śiva'.

In the *Kulārṇava Tantra*, Śiva eloquently expresses:

paramārthaṁ na jānanti paśupāśaniyantritāḥ ||
vedaśāstrārṇave ghore tāḍyamānā itastataḥ |
kālormigrāhagrastāśca tiṣṭhanti hi kutārkikāḥ ||

Those who have plunged into the deep well of the philosophies, yet remain ensnared by the shackles of animal bondage, are incapable of reaching the ultimate zenith—Śiva. As they struggle within the depths of the ocean of Vedas and scriptures, they become entangled in the fierce currents and lurking crocodiles of fallacious reasoning and philosophical arguments.

kathayantyunmanībhāvaṁ svayaṁ nānubhavanti hi |
ahaṅkārahataḥ kecidupadeśavivarjitāḥ ||
paṭhanti vedaśāstrāṇi vivadanti parasparam | *na jānanti paraṁ tattvaṁ dava pākarasaṁ yathā* ||

They speak of egoless consciousness (*unmānī-avasthā*) but do not experience this state. Some are the victims of Egoism, and some remain deprived of instructions. They chant the Vedas and dispute among themselves but like the spoon that does not know the taste of the honey it holds, they know not the Truth.

(*Kulārṇava Tantra* 91-94)

So, that is *śuddha-vidyā,* obtained through direct experience. The third word of the Sūtra is *udaya*, meaning rise or emergence, as in sunrise (*sūryodaya*). *Śuddhavidyodayā (śuddha-vidyā-udaya)* signifies the rise of this pure knowledge, the emergence and experience of truth, that this world is a dream. It is the awakening from this dream. *Śuddhavidyodayā* is the sunrise of knowledge, which dispels the night of ignorance and awakens us from this dream-like world. What happens with the emergence of this pure knowledge? *Cakreśatvasiddhiḥ*—a certain attainment is achieved. *Siddhi* means attainment or perfection. What kind of attainment? *Cakreśatva*; *cakra* + *iśatva*.

Chakra means *śakti-cakra*—the collective cycle of energies. We discussed *śakti-cakra* in the commentary on the sixth Sūtra. *śakti-cakra* means the host of śaktis, or the collective cycle of śaktis. It is a collection of four śaktis—*khecarī, gocarī, dikcarī, and bhūcarī*. In other words, it represents consciousness, cognition, senses, and objective existents. It is a recurring cycle; the expansion of khecarī as bhūcarī signifies the process of creation, while the retraction of bhūcarī into khecarī represents dissolution. This perpetual cycle of creation and dissolution is why it is referred to as the *śakti-cakra*.

If we simplify it, chakra means *saṁsāra cakra*—the wheel of *saṁsāra* (world, life). The world is a cycle. The cycle of expansion of consciousness as the universe and the contraction of the universe into consciousness, and it is also the cycle of cause and effect. Every event is the result of some cause, and every result is the cause of some event. Just as a tree grows from a seed, bears fruit, and fruit contains seed, similarly, this world is happening. The world is not the name of any object; it is a verb, an action. The world is this cycle that is constantly in motion. Just as running is not an object but the name of an action, similarly, this cycle of *khecarī* and *bhūcarī*, the cycle of cause and effect, the cycle of life and death, the cycle of action and its consequences, which is constantly in motion, is what we call the world. The world exists as long as this cycle is in motion; if it stops, there is no world.

Iśatva can have two meanings. Firstly, *iśa* translates to one who is capable of doing everything, or omnipotent; *-tva* is a suffix that, when added to any adjective or verb, turns them into abstract nouns. In English, the equivalent of *-tva* can be *-ness* or *-hood*. For example, if *iśa* is God, then *iśatva* would be Godhood. *Iśatva* means the state of being God, the state of omnipotence. So, *cakreśatva,* thus, means being capable of ruling over the worldly cycle, being capable of everything.

Secondly, *cakreśatva* refers to the power to limit oneself according to one's own will. It means enjoying the illusion of duality (*bhūcarī*) according to one's own will, and then, when one desires, merging back into non-dual consciousness (*khecarī*). The common man is limited; he lives in the illusion of duality but has no other power besides this. He is not free enough to establish himself in non-duality whenever he wills. He has descended down to *bhūcarī* but cannot go back up to *khecarī* because he has forgotten that he also has the power to ascend. *Cakreśatva* means complete awareness of this power.

The greatest example of this state is Lord Kṛṣṇa. His universal form was proof of this principle. He was at the highest stage of yoga.

Śuddhavidyodayāccakreśatvasiddhiḥ, means, when the dawn of pure knowledge arises, we become capable of everything in this world. Just as when we wake up within a dream, when the dawn of this awareness arises that I am in a dream, and it is my own dream, then we gain complete control over that dream. We can do whatever we want in that dream. We can wake up from it whenever we want, and we can return to that same dream whenever we wish. When I found a dream interesting, and due to lack of time, I had to wake up in the morning, I continued that same dream from where I left off the next night. This becomes possible when the emergence of this knowledge within us occurs that I am in a dream, and I am the creator of this dream.

So, possessing these purported supernatural powers within us isn't as extraordinary as it may seem; we just lack awareness. I may have mentioned that I learned the art of magic at one point in my life. The sleight of hand, misdirection, and all the methods by which the illusion of supernatural powers can be created in a person's mind. Ninety-nine percent of the supernatural powers we see and hear about are merely imitations. But behind every imitation, there is a reality that is being imitated. And amidst these ninety-nine imitations, lies that one truth that is usually overlooked as an imitation.

I've read somewhere that in the 1920s, a competition was organised in California to see who could do the best imitation of Charlie Chaplin. Nearly forty contestants participated in that competition. When the real Charlie Chaplin found out about the competition, he decided to participate, albeit in a light-hearted manner. He portrayed his own famous character, which he himself had created. However, no one recognized the original Charlie Chaplin, and he ended up in twenty-seventh place in his own competition!

Science often overlooks the genuine Charlie Chaplin—the genuine supernatural occurrences. In science, there exists an analogy, a metaphor, to understand how scientists work: imagine Śiva and Śakti engaged in a cosmic game of chess. We remain oblivious to the rules governing this game, merely spectators trying to figure out its intricacies. Gradually, we discern a recurring pattern: the pieces move according to specific rules. We meticulously document our observations; for instance, noting that the bishop exclusively advances diagonally, never in a straight or sideways manner. This knowledge is inscribed in our 'rule book'. Later, we notice that the bishop consistently remains on the same colour squares, reinforcing our previous observations and deepening our understanding of its movements.

All appears to progress smoothly until an unexpected occurrence transpires in one corner: the king moves two squares sideways, and the rook adjacent to it shifts to the square next to the king. Two moves executed simultaneously—this catches us off guard; it violates the rules we had established. Thus, begins a thorough examination to ascertain whether these rules were indeed breached or if it was merely an illusion. We wait for it to happen again. Following a thorough investigation, adjustments are made to the rules outlined in the rule book. A new rule emerges: castling.

But the problem here lies in our inability to discern whether a new move has been made in this game of chess or if we have been deceived. Have the rules we have noted so far truly been broken, or are we simply being misled? Because 99.9% of it is mere deception, we often make the mistake of ignoring the genuine occurrences as well. Also, because these occurrences are exceedingly rare and challenge most of the rules and beliefs we hold.

The theory of relativity, put forth by Albert Einstein, was rejected by scientists for decades simply because accepting relativity would invalidate Newton's renowned classical mechanics, necessitating numerous modifications. Consequently, thousands of scientists opposed this new theory. In fact, in 1931, a booklet titled "Hundert Autoren Gegen Einstein—100 Authors Against Einstein" was published, featuring articles by 121 authors and scientists arguing against relativity.

Somewhere in this resistance, there's also the factor of confirmation bias at play. Confirmation bias refers to our tendency to see only what we already believe. If we encounter something that contradicts our assumptions or fails to confirm our preconceived beliefs, we tend to ignore it or attempt to refute it through reasoning or debate, as those authors did with Einstein.

All these factors contribute to why modern science and most people do not believe in supernatural powers. Belief holds significant power. Our beliefs construct our reality.

In the 1950s, a man named Mr. Wright was diagnosed with a deadly disease called *lymphosarcoma*, one of the most lethal forms of cancer. His body was riddled with tumours as large as oranges, and his condition was pitiable, marked by dwindling strength and vitality at every step.

Doctors had given up hope, stating that he only had a few days left to live. However, fate had something else in store for him. One day, a physician informed Wright about a new drug, *Krebiozen*, which had been discovered to be highly effective in curing cancer. Though it was a lie, it acted as a straw for a drowning man. Wright found himself buoyed by waves of hope.

He pleaded with the doctors to administer the drug to him.

The doctor filled his syringe with water, pure water, and injected it into Mr. Wright's arms. Yet, just as placing snowballs on a hot stove causes them to melt away, Mr. Wright's tumours began to disappear one by one. And he was discharged from the hospital completely unscathed. It was his unwavering belief in the medicine's efficacy, his conviction that it would cure him, that saved him from the clutches of death.

We all possess extraordinary abilities within us, but we have forgotten them, erecting various barriers upon them, fueled by our preconceived beliefs. And our belief in something makes it true for us. As spoken by Jesus the Christ:

> Truly I tell you, if you have faith as small as a mustard seed, you can say to this mountain, 'Move from here to there,' and it will move. Nothing will be impossible for you

So, if you firmly believe that these supernatural powers do not exist, then that will become your truth; they will cease to be a part of your reality.

But yes, there is another aspect. An enlightened being who is completely liberated may hardly ever feel the need to use such powers. Rāmakṛṣṇa Paramahaṁsa suffered from throat cancer in his final days. He used to be in extreme pain; even eating was painful for him. He had taken upon himself all the bad *karmas* of his devotees.

One day, a devotee asked him why he didn't use his power of meditation to cure his illness. Initially silent, upon insistence, he responded, 'I have merged my mind into the divine consciousness, and you want me to bring it back to the level of the body?'

However, once, Swāmi Vivekānanda and other young disciples of Rāmakṛṣṇa wanted to pick some fruits from a tree, unaware that a deadly snake lurked beneath its branches. At that time, Rāmakṛṣṇa lay on his deathbed, his condition so severe that he relied on others even to turn him from side to side.

So, on that day, his wife witnessed him descending the stairs of his room 'like an arrow' and then climbing back up, which surprised her greatly. Later, Rāmakṛṣṇa explained that their children's lives were in danger, so he chased away the snake.

He also expressed that his illness would serve to distinguish true devotees from those who seek him merely to fulfil their desires. Behind the visits of the latter group lies the hidden motive of having their desires fulfilled and problems solved through supernatural means. When such people see Rāmakṛṣṇa lying on his deathbed, they will not come to him again thinking him to be a charlatan, and only those who genuinely love him will remain close to him.

Rāmakṛṣṇa once mentioned that Lord Kṛṣṇa had told Arjuna, 'Friend, if you want to experience my supreme reality, you must renounce all your supernatural power. Either you can attain me or the powers.'

So those who have attained these powers have reached a level where they do not feel the need to use these powers.

A person came to meet a Tantrik, an enlightened mystic, travelling from afar. Alone, he met the Tantrik and said, "Great soul, I seek mastery of *vaśīkaraṇa vidyā* (the occult of hypnotism), grant me the mantra. I love this girl, but she loves someone else. I want to marry her. Please bestow upon me the power of vaśīkaraṇa so that she may forever be mine." The Tantrik explained to him, "Do not chase after occult powers. Seek to gain control over your own mind and thoughts rather than attempting to control the minds of others and the world. If you want spiritual practices to gain control over yourself, I can guide you, not otherwise." Saying this, the mystic departed.

However, the person did not give up. Wherever he went, he pursued the mystic, incessantly requesting for supernatural powers. One day, frustrated, the mystic said, "I have bound all my powers into the broom used for cleaning toilets. If you want them so much, go, take it." Such is the insignificance of those powers in the eyes of an enlightened being. This is the value these *siddhis* hold in the perspective of a truly wise person.

This concludes our study of Sūtra Nineteen to Twenty-One.

CHAPTER 16

महाह्रदानुसंधानान्मन्त्रवीर्यानुभवः ॥२२॥

|| mahāhradānusaṃdhānān mantravīryānubhavaḥ || 22 ||

Due to concentrating & merging with the Great Lake, one experiences that which invigorates mantras.

We have now reached the final thread of this volume, which in a way, concludes all the preceding Sūtras. Let's understand, but first, dissect its meaning, word by word.

Mahāhrada; *Hrada* translates to a deep lake, a large or deep body of water. It generally means a lake but can be used to refer to a river, etc. As per Monier-Williams Sanskrit-English Dictionary:

Hrada (ह्रद):— a large or deep piece of water, lake, pool (rarely applied to the sea; with Gāṅga, 'the water of the Ganges'), [Ṛg-veda] etc. etc.

Mahā is an adjective that translates to great, or supreme. *Mahāhrada*—the Great Lake or River. Here it symbolically refers to the reservoir of consciousness. More on that later.

Ānusaṃdhān, reiterated several times previously, refers to the act of concentrating and focusing one's attention towards a specific target, to such an extent that you become one with it.

Due to concentrating & merging with the Great Lake…what happens? *Mantravīryānubhavaḥ*; one experiences—*anubhavaḥ* literally translates to experience—that which invigorates mantras. *Vīrya* translates to that which gives power, strength, virality, energy to something; that which invigorates something. In medicine, *vīrya* refers to the 'potency of drugs'. In this context, the potency of mantras, that which gives strength and life to mantras—that is being discussed.

mahāhradānusaṃdhānān mantravīryānubhavaḥ ||

Due to concentrating & merging with the Great Lake, one experiences that which invigorates mantras.

This, in a way, serves as a concluding Sūtra that encapsulates the essence of the entire volume. It reiterates what has been stated before, albeit in different words. Śiva's expressions are poetic, often repeating and rephrasing the same concept in various ways to ensure clarity and prevent misinterpretation. The core message throughout the book remains consistent: to turn inward, recognize one's true self, and regain freedom. This Sūtra speaks of becoming one with the great reservoir of consciousness. Śiva likens consciousness to a vast body of water from which the waves of *gocarī, dikcarī*, and *bhūcari* arise—or let's say, the waves of mind, senses, and objective existences. One has to become one with this ocean.

In the ancient epics, consciousness is symbolised by the ocean—*kṣīra sāgara.* This ocean belonged to Lord Śiva. The deities requested Śiva's permission to churn this ocean, and from this churning, numerous siddhis emerged: health, wealth, and ultimately, the nectar of immortality. Consuming this nectar rendered the deities immortal. Churning the *kṣīra sāgara* is a metaphor for meditation on consciousness. By meditating on consciousness, one can attain all kinds of siddhis, as revealed in the previous chapter, and ultimately achieve immortality. Immortality not of the body, but from the body. Immortality here implies liberation from the cycle of birth and death. It is the realisation of one's true Self and the annihilation of all *malas*, impurities—those that create the illusion of limitation within us.

The ocean or a lake serves as a fitting comparison to understand the nature of consciousness. Just as currents and waves rise in the ocean, similarly, they do within consciousness, and those waves are the world and all worldly objects. Then, this world dissolves back into that same ocean. Understand this, like when you dream, and in the dream, there is the whole world, people, animals, etc., that dream rises from within you, from consciousness, like currents from within the ocean. And after dreaming, it merges back into that same consciousness. Just as in a dream, so is the world; in fact, dreams exist for a precise purpose. We dream to understand the reality of the world so that we can understand that within us, too, there is the capability to create a world. Dreams and hallucinations are, in fact, eye-openers. If there were no dreams and hallucinations, we would never believe that this world is merely an appearance that emerges from within us—we would think everything is real and separate from us. Just as waves rise in the ocean, similarly, they rise in consciousness, and those waves are the world. Water can take any form; all forms are inherent in water. Isn't it? All the forms of water are inherent in water. Similarly, consciousness can also take and does take many forms, all of which are inherent in consciousness. Currently, consciousness manifests in the form of this book and the form of your body and the world around you; later, all these forms will dissolve back into formless consciousness.

In Tibet, there was a monk who aspired to attain the state of the rainbow body. The rainbow body is a profound state in spirituality where it becomes experientially evident that this body, the world, and everything else are mere formations of consciousness, culminating in the merging of the body back into that formless consciousness. Gradually, colourful lights start to emanate from one's body, and then one completely disappears, merging with consciousness. So, this monk meditated for many days, and other monks would come to watch him every day, noticing that his body kept shrinking, with colourful lights resembling the colours of the rainbow emanating from it. Finally, after some time, the monk completely disappeared. There are many such examples. Abhinavagupta also entered a cave during his final days and closed the entrance with a large stone. Then he vanished inside. This demonstrates that the body is a solidification, a concretization of consciousness. This body and the world, as I explained, exist in consciousness just like all forms of water in water—or let's say they are like the waves of the ocean. Just as waves rise in the ocean, similarly, this world rises in consciousness. That's why consciousness is referred to as the *Mahāhrada* here.

We can categorise these waves into three categories: *gocarī, dikcarī,* and *bhūcarī,* rising in the ocean of *khecarī.* I have explained these terms multiple times in earlier chapters. There, we utilised the analogy of a river or a flowing stream to understand them—the outward flow of the stream of consciousness. The river of consciousness flows outward, thus creating the world, and between consciousness and the world, there are two intermediate sub-stages: cognition and senses. So, if you wish to proceed using the same analogy, it's perfectly acceptable, since the term *hrada* can also refer to a river—the source of the river of consciousness. Śiva has specifically used the word *hrada* for consciousness; interestingly, this word sounds similar to the word *hṛdaya* which means heart. Śiva had earlier instructed to merge the mind with the heart. Essentially, he was conveying the same message—merge the mind, which is the initial wave of consciousness from which emerge the senses and the world, back into consciousness.

Throughout this entire book, directly or indirectly, all the methods mentioned aim to merge with this consciousness, to become one with the source of the world, to turn inward. Withdraw the waves that have risen in the ocean of consciousness in the form of the world; dissolve them back into the ocean. Redirecting the outward-flowing stream inward—however you may do it—is the aim. Before concluding this volume, Śiva has reiterated this aim once again.

And what will be its outcome? You will experience what gives life to all mantras. In the fourth Sūtra, we learned that the impurities which enslave us, those three malas—*āṇava-mala, māyīya-mala, and karma-mala*—have *mātṛkā* as their substratum, their breeding ground where the seed of ignorance sprouts and becomes the tree, whose shoots are the illusion of multiplicity, and where grow the branches of karmic entanglements.

And who is *mātṛkā*? I had elucidated earlier—

"*Mātṛkā* is the energy that pervades within the letters. She is the source, the heart of everything made of words, every book, and mantras. In a literal sense, *mātṛkā* can also be translated as 'she who gave rise to all mantras and Tantras.' The depiction of the Goddess in Tantra often shows her adorned with a garland of half a hundred skulls—these fifty skulls symbolise the fifty alphabets of the Sanskrit language. The use of skulls is intentional as they represent the pronunciation of these letters, emanating from the head, as the sounds are articulated through moving the tongue and lips in certain ways."

Now, in this Sūtra, the same *mātṛkā* is being referred to when Śiva speaks of the *mantravīrya*. She who energises these mantras, invigorates these mantras—those mantras made of syllables—she is the *mantravīrya*, and she is *mātṛkā*.

We learned in the fourth chapter that *mātṛkā* is unknown, unfamiliar; we do not know her. That's why we are in bondage. The moment we recognize her, she becomes our power of absolute freedom. Then there remains no bondage; we become totally free, free from all impurities, all wrong notions. In this Sūtra, Śiva is asserting that when you turn inward, merging with the source, at that moment you experience this *mātṛkā*— you understand her completely; you recognize her as your very own power of freedom.

Roughly, all that was required to understand this Sūtra has been elucidated by me. Now, I want to conclude this book by discussing mantras, which are related to this Sūtra because the subject matter here also pertains to the power that enlivens the mantra. Mantras are sacred formulas, various in existence, chanted for various purposes. Generally, all Tantric practitioners today give the utmost importance to mantras. For them, the mantra is everything, and in the entire philosophy of Tantra, there is nothing greater than the mantra. Their philosophy begins with the mantra and ends with the mantra. That's why an orthodox Tantric practitioner reading this book might be a little surprised that I have discussed Tantra but haven't mentioned mantra practice at all. They might think I lack knowledge of Tantra, but this is a misunderstanding on their part. The first thing is that this entire volume is based on *śāmbhavopāya*, meaning the highest and most direct method of attaining truth—and in this approach, there is no place for mechanical chanting. That concern is predominantly addressed in the third volume, and to some extent in the second volume.

In this particular approach, we are striving to directly connect with that consciousness which enlivens all mantras. It is said in the *Spanda-Kārikās*—

तदाक्रम्य बलं मन्त्राः सर्वज्ञबलशालिनः । प्रवर्तन्तेऽधिकाराय करणानीव देहिनाम् ॥

tadākramya balaṃ mantrāḥ sarvajñabalaśālinaḥ |
pravartante'dhikārāya karaṇānīva dehinām ||

Resorting to that power of consciousness (*spanda*), the divinities, Mantra etc. together with the sacred formulae (their mantras) which serve as their indicators, being endowed with the power of omniscience proceed to carry out their assigned functions towards the embodied ones just as the senses of the embodied ones by resorting to the power of consciousness proceed to carry out their (specific) functions.

(*Spanda-Kārikās* II.1)

So, the deities, the divinities worshipped, who are invoked through these mantras, themselves, along with these mantras—their sacred formulae, to which so much importance is being attributed—all derive their power and life from this consciousness. The subsequent verse states that ultimately, all these mantras and divinities return, merge back into consciousness after fulfilling their roles.

Therefore, I have emphasised on that source itself. Once you turn inward, once you establish yourself within, experience the *mantravīrya*, then these mantras, for which one has to perform 3-4 million repetitions for them to work, will become effective with just 3-4 recitations.

What are those deities you worship through the mantra? They are nothing but manifestations of your own consciousness. Abhinavagupta says that they are *chid'ghana*, the solid form of consciousness. Consider water; water is formless consciousness, but when it takes the form of ice, it assumes a specific shape. Similarly, when we invoke deities through their mantras and *yantras*, we are giving our consciousness a tangible form and certain other attributes through our devotion. It's like jelly, solid and liquid at the same time. And the sacred formulae acts as the trigger, initiating this transformation.

In this manner, the mantra itself is the deity, as it imparts that particular formation to consciousness. Śiva says, *"śriṇu devi pravakṣyāmi bījānāṃ deva-rūpatām mantroccāraṇamātreṇa deva-rūpaṃ prajāyate"*, "Listen, Devi, I will tell you the divine nature of the mantras. Simply by, *mantroccāraṇa*, pronouncing the mantra, it takes the form of the deity." So, the mantra itself is the deity. Just as the whole Bodhi tree is contained within a small seed, similarly, within the mantra, the complete deity resides. Its recitation manifests the form of that deity, which is your own consciousness.

And this mantra derives its energy from the *mātṛkā*. In the *Tantrasadbhāva*, Śiva reveals,

सर्वे वर्णात्मका मन्त्रास्ते च शक्त्यात्मकाः प्रिये । शक्तिस्तु मातृका ज्ञेया सा च ज्ञेया शिवात्मिका ॥

sarve varṇātmakā mantrāste ca śaktyātmakāḥ priye | śaktistu mātṛkā jñeyā sā ca jñeyā śivātmikā ||

Dear one, all mantras are composed of letters. Letters are forms of Śakti. That Śakti should be known as mātṛkā. And this mātṛkā is the heart of Śiva, the Self of Śiva.

And you experience that *mātṛkā śakti* when you turn inwards, when you merge with your consciousness, and attain the knowledge of your real Self. Indeed, without this knowledge, chanting mantras will never be fruitful. It has also been said:

पृथङ्मन्त्रः पृथङ्मन्त्री न सिद्ध्यति कदाचन । ज्ञानमूलमिदं सर्वमन्यथा नैव सिद्ध्यति ॥

pṛthaṅmantraḥ pṛthaṅmantrī na siddhyati kadācana | jñānamūlamidaṃ sarvamanyathā naiva siddhyati ||

If the one chanting the mantra perceives themselves as *pṛthak* from that mantra, different, separate, then the mantra will never be realised. It will never attain fruition. *Jñānamūlamidaṃ*, knowledge is the root of attainment; which knowledge? The knowledge that 'I am that deity', 'I am consciousness'; *naiva siddhyati,* otherwise, the mantra will never be realised.

Hence, I have ventured directly into the centre, the fundamental essence of Tantric tradition—turning inwards and regaining your freedom. Rituals like deity worship, mantra recitation, breathing exercises, and magic, while significant, only scratch the surface of this profound philosophy. Its heart lies in the profound exploration of consciousness and the recognition of oneself as Śiva.

With this, we draw to a close the first volume. I offer reverence to the consciousness dwelling within you.

Oṁ Namaḥ Śivāyaḥ

This concludes our study of Sūtra Twenty-Two.

THE TWENTY TWO SŪTRAS

Below are the twenty-two sutras presented separately. Take time to meditate on each one, allowing their echoes to reverberate within you. Follow the echoes, and you may discover yourself transported to the same wordless space from which I penned this commentary.

चैतन्यमात्मा ॥१॥

|| **CAITANYAMĀTMĀ** || **1** ||

Consciousness is the Self, the reality (of all that is).

ज्ञानं बंधः ॥२॥

|| **JÑĀNAṀ BANDHAḤ** ||**2**||

Knowledge is bondage.

योनिवर्गः कलाशरीरम ॥३॥

|| **YONIVARGAḤ KALĀŚARĪRAM** ||**3**||

(and also) **The illusion of multiplicity and embodiments of action.**

ज्ञानाधिष्ठानं मातृका ॥४॥

|| **jñānādhiṣṭhānam mātṛkā** || **4** ||

Mātṛkā **serves as the base, the breeding ground of** (incomplete) **knowledge.**

उद्यमो भैरवः ॥५॥

|| **Udyamo Bhairavaḥ** || **5** ||

(Active) **Effort is *Bhairava.***

शक्तिचक्रसंधाने विश्वसंहारः ॥६॥

|| ŚAKTICAKRASAṂDHĀNE VIŚVASAṂHĀRAḤ || 6 ||

Dissolve the host of *śaktis* into one another, make them one, and the world outside will disappear.

जाग्रत्स्वप्नसुषुप्तभेदे तुर्याभोगसम्भवः ॥७॥

|| JĀGRATSVAPNASUṢUPTABHEDE TURYĀBHOGASAMBHAVAḤ || 7 ||

If one can discern (between the Self and nonself) **in the states of waking, dreaming, and deep sleep, the experience, the enjoyment of *Turiya* becomes possible.**

ज्ञानं जाग्रत् ॥८॥

|| JÑĀNAM JĀGRAT || 8 ||

The waking state is external knowledge, based on cognitive activities.

स्वप्नो विकल्पाः ॥९॥

|| SVAPNO VIKALPĀḤ || 9 ||

Dreaming is a state of mental constructs.

अविवेको माया सौषुप्तम् ॥१०॥

|| AVIVEKO MĀYĀ SAUṢUPTAM || 10 ||

Deep sleep is a state of non-discernment and self-concealment.

त्रितयभोक्ता वीरेशः ॥११॥

|| TRITAYABHOKTĀ VĪREŚAḤ || 11 ||

***Vīreśha* is the experiencer of the three states.**

विस्मयो योगभूमिकाः ॥१२॥

|| VISMAYO YOGABHŪMIKĀḤ || 12 ||

The stages of yoga are wondrous.

इच्छा शक्तिरुमा कुमारी ॥ १३ ॥

|| ICCHĀ ŚAKTIR UMĀ KUMĀRI || 13 ||

The power of desire is Uma Kumāri

दृश्यं शरीरम् ॥१४॥

|| DRŚYAM ŚARĪRAM || 14 ||

Whatever is perceivable (this entirety of existence) **is verily your own body.**

OR

Even your own body is an object to perceive (in an unidentified, detached manner, as something separate from you).

हृदये चित्तसंघट्टाद् दृश्यस्वापदर्शनम् ॥१५॥

|| HṚDAYE CITTASAMGHATṬĀD DṚSYASVĀPADARŚANAM || 15 ||

(Turn inwards) **Merge the mind with the heart** (the source from where the mind originates) **and the perception of the underlying reality behind all that is perceivable will occur.**

शुद्धतत्त्वसंधानाद्वा स्वपद् शक्तिः ॥१६॥

|| ŚUDDHA-TATTVA-SANDHĀNĀD VĀ SVAPAD-ŚAKTIḤ || 16 ||

(With a steady aim, unwavering concentration) **By** (delving deep and) **becoming one with Śiva—the state free from any impurities or obscurities,** śakti **will return to its original state; Or…**(Continued in the next Sūtra...)

वितर्क आत्मज्ञानम् ॥१७॥

|| VITARKA ĀTMAJÑĀNAM || 17 ||

Analyse, unravel, and behold the revelation of your true Self.

लोकानन्दः समाधिसुखम् ॥१८॥

|| LOKĀNANDAḤ SAMĀDHI-SUKHAM || 18 ||

The joy of *samādhi* resonates throughout the entire world.

OR

The bliss experienced by ordinary people is not different from the joy of *samādhi*.

OR

Ordinary joy can lead you towards the realisation of *samādhi*.

शक्तिसन्धाने शरीरोत्पत्तिः ॥१९॥

|| ŚAKTISANDHĀNE ŚARĪROTPATTIḤ || 19 ||

When the energies unite, anything can be materialised.

भूतसंधानभूतपृथक्त्वविश्वसङ्घट्टाः ॥२०॥

|| BHŪTASANDHĀNABHŪTAPṚTHAKTVAVIŚ VASAṄGHAṬṬĀḤ || 20 ||

Things can be united, separated, and all that exists in the entire world can be brought together (transcending the boundaries of space and time).

शुद्धविद्योदयाच्चक्रेशत्वसिद्धिः ॥२१॥

|| ŚUDDHAVIDYODAYĀCCAKREŚATVASIDDHIḤ || 21 ||

Due to the arising of pure knowledge, Lordship over *śakti-cakra* is attained.

महाह्रदानुसंधानान्मन्त्रवीर्यानुभवः॥२२॥

|| mahāhradānusaṃdhānān mantravīryānubhavaḥ || 22 ||

Due to concentrating & merging with the Great Lake, one experiences that which invigorates mantras.

इति श्रीमनस्वच्छन्दनाथशिवपादपद्मोपजीवि-श्रीसुयशराज-विरचितायां शिवसूत्रविर्माशिन्यां शाम्भवोपायप्रकाशनं नाम प्रथम उन्मेषः ॥

iti śrīmanasvacchandanāthaśivapādpadmo'pajīvi-śrīsuyaśarāja-viracitāyāṃ śivasūtravirmāśanyāṃ śāmbhavopāyaprakāśanaṃ nāma prathama unmēṣaḥ ||

And thus ends the first volume of the commentary on the Śiva *Sūtras* pertaining to *śāmbhavopāya* by Suyaś Rāja, dependent on the lotus feet of Lord Svacchandanāth Śiva.

Oh Śiva! Witnessing the decline of your teachings due to inconsistencies and contradictory interpretations of the Vedas and other scriptures, I have endeavoured to clarify the intricate and esoteric meanings of your teachings. For any errors in this endeavour, I seek your forgiveness. Oh Śiva! I have disclosed even the hidden secrets of the Tantric tradition, driven by my deluded compassion for humanity. Oh Dayānidhi! I seek your forgiveness for any transgressions committed, for it is not fitting to harbour anger towards deluded beings.

॥ इति शिवम् ॥

www.ingramcontent.com/pod-product-compliance
Lightning Source LLC
Chambersburg PA
CBHW022051160426
43198CB00008B/186
* 9 7 8 9 3 5 5 4 3 6 8 9 4 *